Workplace Learning:

A Critical Introduction

Workplace Learning:
A Critical Introduction

John Bratton
Jean Helms Mills
Timothy Pyrch
Peter Sawchuk

Foreword by D'Arcy Martin

Originally published by Garamond Press 2004

National Library of Canada Cataloguing in Publication

Workplace learning: a critical introduction / John Bratton ... [et al.].

Includes bibliographical references and index.
ISBN 978-1-44260-113-0
(Previous ISBN 1-55193-047-1)

1. Employees—Training of.   2. Experiential learning.
3. Adult education.   I. Bratton, John

HF5549.5.T7W667 2004   331.25'92   C2003-905381-4

We welcome comments and suggestions regarding any aspect of our publications—please feel free to contact us at the addresses below or at news@utphighereducation.com / www.utphighereducation.com.

North America
5201 Dufferin Street, North York
Ontario, Canada, M3H 5T8

2250 Military Road, Tonawanda
New York, USA, 14150
Tel: (416)978-2239; Fax: (416)978-4738

customerservice@utphighereducation.com

UK, Ireland and continental Europe
NBN International
Estover Road, Plymouth, UK, PL6 7PY
Tel: 44 (0) 1752 202300
Fax: 44 (0) 1752 202330
enquiries@nbninternational.com

RECYCLED
Paper made from
recycled material
FSC
www.fsc.org   FSC® C103567

Higher Education University of Toronto Press acknowledges the financial support of the Government of Canada through the Book Publishing Industry Development Program (BDIDP) for our publishing activities.

Cover photograph courtesy of Peter Sawchuk.

Printed in Canada

Contents

About the Authors

John Bratton, Ph. D. is Associate Professor in the Faculty of Education at the University of Calgary, and Associate Professor of Sociology at the University College of the Cariboo, Kamloops. He was the first Director of the University of Calgary's Workplace Learning Research Unit. His doctoral work focused on the impact of new technology and management strategies in the mechanical engineering industry. He is author of *Japanization of Work: Managerial Strategies for the 1990s*, *Human Resource Management: Theory and Practice 3rd edition* (with Jeffrey Gold), and *Organizational Leadership* (with Keith Grint and Debra Nelson).

Jean Helms Mills, Ph.D. is Assistant Professor of Organizational Behaviour at St. Mary's University in Halifax, Nova Scotia. Seventeen years with the airline industry have instilled in her the need to make sense of culture and the process of change in organizations. She received her M.A. and Ph.D. from Lancaster University's Management School, Department of Behaviour in Organizations. She is currently involved in a long-term study of culture and discriminatory practices in the airline industry.

Timothy Pyrch, Ed.D. is a Professor in the Faculty of Continuing Education at the University of Calgary and an advocate for liberatory adult education. His background includes several years as a community development practitioner and as an historian of the community development movement. His main focus is participatory action research as a means to democratizing knowledge making.

Peter H. Sawchuk, Ph.D. is an Assistant Professor at the Ontario Institute for Studies in Education, University of Toronto. He has worked as an adult educator, press operator, trade union activist, educator and researcher. Forthcoming publications include, *Hidden Knowledge: Organized Labour in the Information Age*, (with D.W. Livingstone) and *Adult Learning and Technology in Working-Class Life*.

Acknowledgements

This book was originally inspired by our teaching and research at the University of Calgary and by the *First International Conference on Researching Work and Learning* held at the University of Leeds, England. The content, however, reflects more than our academic work, it reflects our active involvement, for two of the authors for over twenty-five years, in the adult education and trade union movement. Each of us has been encouraged, supported and mentored by many people. Each of us would like to take this opportunity to acknowledge some of the people who have shaped our journey in very many ways in writing this book.

John Bratton – I have had the privilege to know and work with many people in the liberation and trade union movement. In particular, Tim Enright, Jim Mowatt, Edna Hoad, Keith Edmondson, George Muirhead, Alistair Graham and in Canada, Bernard Igwe, Stacey Whiting, and Gary Worth. I am particularly indebted to Colin Jenkinson who gave me what the British education system failed to do: the self-confidence to pursue post-secondary education. Finally, Carolyn Forshaw, my best friend and partner for 31 years, who made the journey worthwhile.

Jean Helms Mills – I would like to thank my parents, Philip and Sue Helms for instilling in me early on the desire for learning, and my husband Albert Mills for keeping that quest for knowledge alive.

Tim Pyrch – I wish to acknowledge Jeannette who taught me to love uncritically and for Coolie Verner who insisted that adult educators think critically and act accordingly.

Peter Sawchuk – I would like to thank my co-authors for the wonderful diversity of debate over the course of the production of this text. More generally, I must acknowledge the debt owed to David Livingstone, D'Arcy Martin and Bruce Spencer who continue to model that mix of commitment, outrage and intellect that defines the best tradition of the Canadian left. And finally, I'd like to thank my wife Jill. Her perseverance and encouragement makes my work possible.

John Bratton • Jean Helms Mills • Tim Pyrch • Peter Sawchuk

July 2003

Foreword

Here is a map through contested and largely uncharted terrain.

A map is drawn by someone, about something, for some purpose. In this case, it is drawn by four academics in order to introduce students to a range of theories and experiences about the workplace as a site of learning. If you are exploring ways to support learning in the many waking hours that adults commit to their workplaces, this is a valuable reference guide.

This critical text is directed to students. Some will go into management, some into policy academic jobs, some into "non-standard form of employment, and some into the world of social or union activism, all of which are addressed comprehensively here. Precisely because this book is not prescriptive about where people might invest their energies and insights, it suggests multiple possibilities for doing something professional, political and practical to enhance the developmental and humanizing possibilities of work.

The text skillfully draws on both managerial and critical discourses. At some points it adopts a Human Resource Management (HRM) perspective, familiar to students in business and administration programs in which the primary objective is to mobilize human capital towards organizational goals of productivity. At other times, it adopts a worker-centred perspective, familiar to students in labour studies and adult education programs in which the primary objective is to identify the emancipatory potential to be realized on the job. In both traditions, international literatures on adult learning are referenced. A developmental, humanist stance underlies the writing, which keeps the book from being a recurring clash of disembodied ideologies.

These two perspectives are uncomfortable sleeping between the covers of a single book. In Chapter 1, the authors suggest, "modern adult education and training therefore seeks to fulfill the twin objectives of preparing men and women for their work roles on the one hand, and promoting independent and critical thinking for their social role on the other." As any union shop steward or front-line manager can tell you, these goals are difficult to reconcile "on the ground." The energy of this book comes from the tension between these two basic perspectives, a dialectic that plays out in the academy as well as the workplace. In its best moments, it allows us to hold competing ideas in our heads at the same time, to see simultaneously from above and from below the drama of learning and work. In the end, it equips us to assess the moments and conditions that move adults towards insight, skill and action that will reproduce or transform their work environments.

In Chapter 2, business academics will be alternately comforted and challenged, as the basic tents of productivity theory are laid out and then situated in a wider context of debate. Here, human resources are considered like natural resources, as elements to be channeled in the interests of the organization. In this view from above, the pressures of global competitiveness, technological innovation and lean production are taken as givens, as the starting point for discussion. Within this frame, "hawks" and "doves" engage in debate as to which camp can better "deliver the goods," but the nature of the "goods" is not in question. Rather, the issue is whether or not democracy is productive, a re-work of the classic Theory X and Theory Y styles of management articulated by Douglas McGregor a generation ago. To the degree that high-commitment systems can provide a "high road" of good working conditions, good wages and good quality production, the voices of conflict in the workplace can be muted, and the consciences of both employer and worker advocates soothed. To the degree that savage capitalism reigns in a sector and a region, the drive for improving quarter-over-quarter results pushes aside such considerations.

In Chapters 3 and 4 fully develop upon key concepts alive in many workplaces today: group learning and organizational learning. Here the concepts are particularly clearly laid out, and the link of developmental learning to good job design firmly established. Here we find a departure from much of the labour process writing based on Harry Braverman's study of the neo-Taylorist separation of head and hand. As "McJobs" swell, and "non-standard" employment becomes a majority experience among North American workers, the very basis of communities of adult learning provided by stable workplaces has been shrinking. The hawks have been in the ascendant, and work has been degraded.

In Chapter 5, there is a full elaboration of a workers' standpoint on workplace learning. A key lesson from this material is that workers and their organizations can and do influence work and learning in myriad ways: before work begins in terms of vocational education and apprenticeship policy, in the workplace through union education and bargaining, beyond the workplace in terms of national and even international trade frameworks, and (particularly interesting), even through engagement of workers imagination through culture and the arts.

In Chapter 6, the starting point is adult learning, and the perspective piques in a critique of the "job place." Here the generation of official knowledge, expert knowledge and people's knowledge is considered, with a more fully developed sense of what an emancipatory learning would be. The literature referenced is from English-speaking, industrial countries, with little from the rich experience of the South, but the articulation of critical trends are broad and provocative.

By the concluding chapter, we've seen discussions of perhaps the broadest range of literatures to be collected in one place on the field of workplace learning, and students and scholars alike will benefit from the reflexive analysis offered. In sum, this book is helpful in reminding us that this has not always been so, is not so everywhere even now, and may not always be so. It keeps alive and vivid the models available when the balance of power shifts. No single map is sufficient for a long or complex journey, but this book will certainly help part of the way towards constructive intervention in workplace learning. This critical introduction is directed at students. Some will go into management, some into policy and academic jobs, some into "non-standard" forms of employment, and some into the world of social or union activism, all of which are addressed comprehensively in this book. Precisely because this book is not prescriptive about where people might invest their energies and insights, it suggests multiple possibilities for doing something professional, political and practical to enhance the developmental and humanizing possibilities of work.

D'Arcy Martin

Labour Educator and Coordinator
Centre for the Study of Education and Work
University of Toronto

April 2003

CHAPTER 1

Introduction

Adult education presumes, then, to serve as one of the means by which the mind may be kept fresh for the assimilation of that knowledge which is synonymous with power. (Lindeman, 1926, p. 25)

What meanings are considered the most important, what experiences are deemed the most legitimate, and what forms of writing and reading matter are largely determined by those groups who control the economic and cultural apparatuses of a given society. (Giroux, 1994, p. 64)

Welcome to *Workplace Learning: A Critical Introduction*. It is no coincidence that the recent years have seen growing interest in workplace learning theory and practice. In response to such economic and political developments as globalization, privatization, and deregulation, both managers and workers realize they must continually focus on learning in the workplace. For employers and management theorists alike, work-based learning has come to represent a key "lever" that can act as the engine for sustainable competitive advantage. Beer *et al.*, (1984, p.85) muse, "employee development is a key strategy for organizational survival and growth." Others have argued that work-based learning and investment in work-based educational programs has become a "litmus test" of whether or not employers have adopted the so-called "progressive" human resource management (HRM) model (Keep, 1989). In the 1990s, academics and corporate leaders were attracted to the concept of the "learning organization" (Cohen and Sproull, eds. 1996), "management learning" (Burgoyne and Reynolds, eds. 1997) or the more encompassing term, "workplace learning" (Spikes, ed., 1995). Indeed, both adult educators and union educators are expressing broad and re-invigorated concern for the role this learning can play in the workplace and wider society. As an area of research, scholarship, and practice, workplace learning encompasses a range of modes of inquiry and theoretical framework (Munby, 2003).

The term workplace learning has become an established metaphor for capturing formal, nonformal, self-directed collective and even tacit informal learning activities. Workplace learning is also constructing contemporary management discourses (Solomon, 1999). It is an interdisciplinary body of knowledge and theoretical inquiry that draws upon adult learning, management theory, industrial relations and sociological theory, to name only a few. Ever more sophisticated conceptualizations of workplace learning suggest multiple approaches for understanding the phenomenon. Central to the advance of workplace learning as a field of inquiry is an openness to expand our understanding of both work and learning (Bratton and Sawchuk, 2001). In terms of expanding the notion of work, we feel it is important that readers understand that "work" expands beyond the boundaries of "paid work" in formal organizations. Building on the foundational arguments of Livingstone, (2001), Spencer, (1998), Waring (1999) and others, we feel that an understanding of the connections between work and learning requires consideration of unpaid work beyond the worksite, in the home, and the community.

Our understanding of how "learning" in the workplace is accomplished expands beyond notions of individual cognition and "self-direction" to incorporate awareness of situated, communities of practice, mentoring, and the role of social participation. We argue that an analysis of workplace learning is incomplete without taking into account the milieu of asymmetrical power relationships which exist in the workplace and the social structures in which people are embedded. A more inclusive understanding of learning in the workplace needs to acknowledge the general nature of capitalist employment relations, the way management control systems generate and express internal contradictions, the tensions between managerial control and work-based learning, and the effects of complex interconnecting levels of domination stemming from class, gender, and race relations in society (Andersen and Collins, 2004; Argyris and Schön, 1978; Coopey, 1996; Thompson and McHugh, 2002).

As a field of study workplace learning can be explored and interpreted from different perspectives. To guide you through our analysis and discussion, we differentiate between managerial and critical perspectives. We define a *managerial perspective* as one that is concerned with issues of organizational efficiency and profitability. In contrast, a *critical perspective* is predicated on a concern to examine how organizational economic imperatives and disparities of power affect working people and society in terms of equity, environmental degradation and democracy. From a managerial perspective, it is suggested that an organization's investment in workplace learning acts as a powerful signal of its intentions to develop its "human assets"; this can help develop commitment to the organization rather than simply compliance. Observers discuss the pursuit of worker flexibility through reflexive learning extensively as a lever to sustainable competitive advantage: the ability to learn "faster" than competitors (Dixon, 1992). Most advocates of Japanese or "lean" production systems emphasize the importance of investing in human capital and the processes of workplace learning (e.g. Schonberger, 1982; Womack, et al., 1991). Kochan and Dyer advise those firms adopting a "mutual commitment" strategy to gain competitive advantage to make the necessary investment in their workforce and adopt the concept of *lifelong learning* (our emphasis, 1995, p. 336). The leading American sociologist C. Wright Mills (1916-1962) suggested we can only produce a full understanding of human experience when we look beyond the personal experiences and locate those experiences within the larger economic, political, and social context that structures the experience. The "sociological imagination," Mills wrote, allows us to "grasp the interplay of man and society, of biography and history, of self and world." (Mills, 1959 [2000], p. 4). So too with learning in the workplace; it has to be placed in a larger context. This belief in the efficacy of continuous reflexive learning is linked to a broader discourse on human resource management (HRM) practices that attempt to enhance work-based learning for individuals, groups and teams in order to encourage and facilitate change (Bratton and Gold, 2003). The "progressive" HRM paradigm is thus linked by analogy to the "master" discourse of market economics: globalization, deregulation, privatization, and sustainable innovation (Garrick, 1998).

There is a growing body of work that has taken a critical approach to workplace learning, recognizing that class and gender relations, politics, and conflicts of interest shape learning in the workplace. Within this school, for example, writers, emphasize how "cultural control" can be reinforced through workplace learning (Legge, 1995) and how the training of "competencies" can render work more "visible" in order to be more manageable (Townley, 1994). John Coopey (1996) challenges the "academic entrepreneurs" such as Peter Senge, *The Fifth Discipline* (1990) asserting that workplace learning theory assumes a unitary perspective in which the goals of managers and workers are shared, conflict stemming from inherent tensions in the employment relationship are largely ignored, power is omnipresent in work organizations, and that political activity within the workplace impedes learning. He argues that the likely effect of new learning regimes is to strengthen the power of senior management. Neglecting the wider socio-economic dynamics and contested nature of learning might unwittingly make the "brave new world of pedagogics in relation to work and learning" a managerial tool for work intensification and control in the workplace (Forrester, 1999). As Bruce Spencer warns, the rhetoric and enthusiasm for workplace learning, both from adult educators and some corporate leaders, can form part of a social technology that masks "new forms of oppression and control in the workplace that should be acknowledged in workplace learning research" (2001, p. 33).

Despite the feminization of the paid workforce in most OECD economies, another notable feature of the workplace learning discourse is the tendency for academic research to be class, gender, and race-blind. Recently, some writers have focused critically on gender issues in workplace learning (Bierema, 2001; Probert, 1999). Belinda Probert, for example, adds depth to our understanding as to how sexuality and gender relations in the paid workplace can shape learning. Theoretically, one of the most important consequences of a gendered analysis of "work" and "learning" is its power to question research findings and analysis that segregates studies of learning in work from those of sex-segregated labour markets (Dex, 1988), patriarchal power (Witz, 1986), issues of workplace inequality (Dickens, 1998; Philips and Philips, 1993) and "dual-role" work-family issues (Knights and Willmott, 1986). As Probert points out, the recent explosion of workplace learning practices still privilege men and "it is worth recognizing the continuities in women's unequal access to and benefit from workplace learning" (1999, p. 112).

At the level of rhetoric, notions of "high quality," "flexible specialization," "functional flexibility" and "knowledge work" are underpinned by the assumption of the need for a well-educated and trained workforce

(Legge, 1995; Livingstone, 1999; Reich, 1991). However, empirical data show that in most Anglo-North American companies there is a growing trend in "non-standard" forms of employment (e.g. part-time and short-term contracts). Studies reveal that for the majority of workers the notion of lifelong learning remains a dream (see, for example, Lowe, 2000; Ritzer, 2000; Wharton, 2002). If we accept the plausible insight that "peripheral" or part-time workers tend to receive the lowest level of training (Ashton and Felstead, 2001) and the data showing that relatively few organizations in Canada or Britain have invested in training and education (Ashton and Felstead, 2001; Conference Board of Canada, 2002), there is an enormous gap between the rhetoric of "strategic HRM" and "strategic learning" and reality in the workplace. David Livingstone (1999; 2001) and Livingstone and Sawchuk (2000; 2003) have argued that while we might live in a "knowledge society," we are a long way from having a "knowledge economy" as immense amounts of skill and knowledge currently go unused. And, as already intimated, an effect of taking class, race, and gender relations into account (see Andersen and Collins, 2004) would be to challenge optimistic assertions that we are living in a "knowledge economy."

For traditional adult educators, the dynamics of organizational change and work-based learning are far more wide-ranging than an analysis of the relationship between learning and economic performance. The rationale for adult education goes back to the eighteenth century when men and women, caught up in the chaos of early industrial capitalism, tried to understand the reasons for their unemployment, dislocation, deprivation, and poverty. Leaders of a Mechanics Institute in the north of England (asked at a trial in 1790 to explain the purpose of their gatherings) responded:

> To enlighten the people, to show the people the reason, the ground of all their complaints and sufferings; when a man works hard for thirteen and fourteen hours a day, the week through, and is not able to maintain his family; that is what I understand of it; to show the people the ground of this; why they are not able. (Quoted in Simon (ed.) 1990, p. 9)

In the twenty-first century, this empowering role of adult education is expressed by Lindeman's (1926) inspirational statement that adult education is a "social movement"; its purpose is "to put meaning into the whole of life" (p. 5). This rationale that adult education is bound up with struggle of men, women and subordinated groups was further endorsed by the International Federation of Workers' Educational Associations' 1980 Charter, which declared:

> Education is of great importance to people in their struggle to overcome deprivation, exploitation and oppression. In leading to a better understanding of human problems, and assisting the search for possible solutions, education can be a liberating force. (Quoted in Simon (ed.) 1990, p. 313)

Industrialized capitalism and adult education have therefore developed hand in hand.

Contemporary adult education is an activity that is largely undertaken for instrumental ends. From a trade union and workers' perspective, adult education and training have long been viewed as a means of improving the experience of paid work and job security by developing job-related skills, both formal and tacit. D'Arcy Martin (1998) has observed that education and training should be portable, developmental, and equitable. Some Canadian and European unions have encouraged their members to engage (informally or formally through negotiated "social partnership" agreements) in workplace learning in order to potentially promote "mutual gains" (see, for example, Munro and Rainbird, 2000). In effect, the quality of work and employability objective of adult education and training is made a reality by turning the workplace learning rhetoric back on management (see Bratton, 1999; Spencer, 1998).

The rationale for adult education is perhaps best captured in an era of globalization by Bob Fryer's demand that adult education should continue "to help pose and sharpen the questions, to foster the self-confidence and technical skills needed to tackle the problems and to encourage the critical creativeness necessary to work out the range of individual and collective initiatives required to meet the challenges to working class life" (1990, p. 313). Within the labour movement there are unions that seek to fulfil the "social" object. In this regard, "adult learning is of a high value both for remedying injustices in the distribution of educational capital and for building a social movement for struggle" (Martin, 1998, p. 162). Adult education and training therefore seeks to fulfill the twin objects of preparing men and women for their work roles on the one hand, and promoting independent and critical thinking for their social role on the other. Adult educators cannot afford to neglect adult education's twin aims. Part of the debate concerns the extent workplace learning, as currently defined, contributes to furthering these two aims. In terms of improving the quality of paid work and employment skills there is much potential for improvement, particularly for part-time workers. With regards to whether the premise of the elusive "learning organization" can fulfill the "social" function of adult education, the best one can say is that "the jury is still out." Optimists could argue that the learning that takes place in the "learning organization" might extend to questioning the social relations of production, the realization of Lindeman's "revolution of the mind," thus beginning a search for alternative empowering and co-operative work organizations. For example, through co-operatives, which can better serve the interests of workers and their communities (see Spencer, 1998; Welton, 2001).

STUDY TIP

An important object of *Workplace Learning: A Critical Introduction* is to help you develop critical thinking skills when reading other texts in adult education, management and workplace learning and related fields. To do this effectively you need to be aware that all academic writing should be considered not only as a source of information and meaning as defined by the author, but also as a text revealing the author's standpoint on organizational life and power relations in society. Knowledge should be viewed in the context of power and consequently the relationship between writers, readers, and texts (including this one) has to be understood as sites at which different meanings, interpretations, and perspectives take place. Reinharz (1988) posits that most academic writing reflects a dominant perspective that is capitalist, racist, and androcentric in orientation. Read Reinharz's article and then look through recent workplace learning journals or adult education and management journals. Identify the dominant assumptions that underlie the article. Does the author make any assumption about organizational effectiveness and efficiency? Does the author ignore certain issues, such as gender, race and class conflict in the workplace? From what standpoint does the writer speak?

Whether viewed from a managerialist or critical perspective (and we vehemently argue it is important to be familiar with both) the workplace learning discourse has come to represent one of the most controversial elements of adult education. The idea and stimulus for this book stems directly from the success of the first two international conferences, *Researching Work and Learning*, held at the University of Leeds, U.K. in 1999, and at the University of Calgary, Canada in 2001. Workplace learning is, as stated, an interdisciplinary field and the authors – two from the field of adult education and two from a professional interest in critical management – represent the two main domains.

We believe *Workplace Learning: A Critical Introduction* offers an alternative to mainstream approaches that tend to be detached from the lived experiences of working people, and uncritical of human resource development (HRD) views of learning in the workplace. We view management neither as homogeneous nor omnipotent, and we contend that work-based learning is not always promoted solely to increase profitability or management hegemony. We share a concern to illuminate the power relations, contradictions of the paid workplace and learning therein, taking the view that learning is not value-free or politically neutral. Class, race and gender divisions shape everyday social relations, identities, work forms, and learning in the workplace. We believe that the development of workplace learning is dependent upon a better understanding that learning takes place in an arena where work designs and lived experiences are the outcome of interrelated power-relationships, resistance, negotiation, and co-operation. In other words, learning in the workplace cannot be studied independently of the political economy of work.

Importantly, we hope *Workplace Learning: A Critical Introduction* stimulates such questions as: How is learning in the workplace accomplished? How do new forms of work and employment relationships impact on learning? Is the HRM or strategic learning paradigm potentially a force for widening access to education and work-based learning? What role do trade unions play in facilitating workplace learning? Is work-based learning potentially a force for empowering workers? Do people of colour and women have equal access to workplace learning? What are the experiences of people of colour and women of learning in the workplace? Does the development of work-based learning imply further erosion of the traditional, liberatory adult education project? We hope this book will make a timely and useful contribution to the discussion of the nature and role of workplace learning in the labour process.

Overall, the chapters contribute to a developing, critical perspective on learning at paid work in advanced capitalist economies and attempt to uncover the roots, underlying assumptions, and paradoxes that make up the field of workplace learning. We hope they will stimulate interest in further research in this emergent field of adult education and management. In the second chapter we critically examine the connection between management strategies and workplace learning. In Chapter 3, developments in organizational design, with particular reference to work groups/teams, and the concomitant application of learning theories are critically explored. Chapter four critically examines the learning organization and organizational learning paradigms. Chapter five introduces the debates on the role of the union movement in workplace learning. Chapter six critically examines the liberatory tradition of adult education and its application in both paid work and the community. The final chapter brings together key themes and issues and discusses five conceptual themes or "tools" that are designed to help the reader to evaluation critically workplace learning literature across multiple traditions and perspectives.

CHAPTER 2

Management Strategies and Workplace Learning

> More of the effect [improved performance] undoubtedly comes from individuals "working smarter" – in part by being able to actually implement their wisdom and knowledge in the actual work process and in part because of the training and job rotation practices that enhance the opportunity to learn. (Pfeffer, 1998, p. 60)

> A company that gets an early start in accumulating knowledge, and then continues to learn faster than its rivals, can build an almost insurmountable lead. (Hamel, 2000, p. 101)

The above quotations provide an insight into how the field of workplace learning is currently viewed by some business academics: learning is part of a management strategy to achieve sustainable competitive advantage. Conventional management wisdom argues that market imperatives require organizations to change their control systems and the way paid work is performed in order to create a culture that promotes innovation and efficiencies through reflexive learning. The insight that competitive advantage relies upon managers using employees' tacit knowledge and skills is not new. The notion is embodied in the economic theory of human capital (Schultz, 1981) and the resource-based view of the firm (Barney, 1991). What is new is that, in the past decade or so, the learning – competitiveness link has become incorporated into mainstream management thinking. This chapter explores the connection between developments in management theory, the capitalist labour process and workplace learning. The analysis focuses upon the development of management thought that has direct implications for employees' experience of paid work, including skill levels, degree of autonomy, decision-making, and concomitant learning in the workplace. In the first section we locate management theory within a historical context before discussing the "progressive" human resource management (HRM) model, and exploring some paradoxes associated with the HRM model. A number of essential questions are addressed, concerning how modern organizations operate and the nature and significance of workplace learning within a broader management strategy. There is a common theme throughout this chapter; much of the academic work points out that, in addition to continuities in the capitalist labour process, there are economic, political, social and structural constraints that complicate the implementation of the learning organization ideal. Extracting adult education theory and practice from its familiar social milieu into the workplace presents both ideological, pedagogical, and analytical challenges for the radical adult educator, operating from a peoples'-centered agenda that puts social change before efficiency and profits.

CHAPTER OBJECTIVES

After reading this chapter, you should be able to:

1. Understand the connections between developments in management theory and practice, nature of work and concomitant interest in learning in the workplace;

2. Explain the role of human resource management in work organizations and the concepts underpinning the resource-based human resource model;

3. Critically evaluate the theoretical debate surrounding the "progressive" HRM model and adult learning in the workplace.

In the early twentieth century, traditional artisan working practices controlled the form and pace of production. The artisan culture and the artisan's power began to be challenged by employers intent on improving labour productivity. Throughout the last century, therefore, management innovations played a central role in shaping organization and work designs, and by extension, workers' experience of paid work, including learning opportunities. Responding to the various pressures of market competition and technological change, employers or their agents have attempted to maximise efficiency by transforming the labour process, either by investing in new technology, reorganizing the way work is performed, or by a combination of both. On the other hand, employers and managers have simultaneously faced motivation problems and various forms of worker resistance. Managers have responded to these employer-employee dynamics by developing new management strategies, including "scientific management" (1910s) to job enrichment "human relations" models (1960s), to the "progressive" human resource management (HRM) and "re-engineering" models of the 1990s. During both World Wars, American, British and Canadian manufacturers had to produce vast quantities of standardized military products. To increase productivity, what then went for "common sense" dictated that owners of capital invested in machinery, designed assembly lines to give workers narrow job specifications, and used time and motion study to monitor workers' effort levels, and minimize their involvement in any decisions affecting the labour process, (techniques originally developed by Frederick Taylor and Henry Ford). This manufacturing strategy was dominant until the 1970s. The Taylorism and Fordism movement in work design should be interpreted as a shift in the locus of production knowledge from shop-floor workers to management (Gospel and Littler, 1983). The aim of Taylorist and Fordist work regimes – epitomized by the auto-assembly-line – was to extract the tacit knowledge hidden in the routine of the work performed by skilled workers and convert it into codified knowledge owned and controlled by management (Braverman, 1974).

By the 1980s, the limitations of Taylorist and Fordist methods were increasingly apparent to corporate leaders. In the context of affluent consumers in the western economies and Japanese competition, the traditional way of doing things could not meet the demands for high quality and customized products and services – so-called "niche" marketing. Competitive survival depended upon greater labour flexibility and the enlistment of workers' creative agency. Thus, the enlargement of job specifications and worker "empowerment" to enable shop-floor workers to engage in problem-solving and quality decision making (the opposite of Taylorist [scientific management] principles) became the "common-sense" of contemporary management. This new manufacturing paradigm required three aspects of managerial control to change: organisational and work design, organisational culture, and human resource policies and techniques. Thus, "post-bureaucratic" organizations claim to increase the reflexivity of the labour process through "flat" hierarchical structures; an enlargement of job tasks and job autonomy, ideally centred on work "teams," and the careful management of organizational culture and knowledge.

STUDY TIP

There are many articles on the changing nature of work caused by new management strategies. A useful selection of readings is G. Lowe and H. Krahn, eds. (1993), *Work in Canada: Readings in the Sociology of Work and Industry* (Nelson Canada). Read James Rinehart's Chapter 8.1 "Improving the Quality of Working Life through Job Redesign: Work Humanization or Work Rationalization?" From Rinehart's perspective, what kinds of job design reforms would create a more humanizing and educative workplace?

Throughout the last ten years or so, support for this new management strategy came from mainstream academic commentators who insisted that the traditional approaches to managing workers were inappropriate because they could "no longer deliver the goods" (see, for example, Abernathy *et al.* 1983; Betcherman, *et al.,* 1994; Osterman, 1991). It was argued that, "Building a truly competitive organization also requires active enlistment of the best efforts of workers, especially line workers. Their skills, commitment, and enthusiasm are the means by which strategic goals get translated into practice" (Abernathy *et al.*, 1983, p 23). In the early 21st century, the belief that sustainable competitive advantage depends upon the effective utilization of workers' tactic knowledge, skills and innovating capacities has been reinforced by predictions about capitalism moving to a higher stage of development, in which the creative application of higher-level knowledge has become the main engine of growth in the "New Economy."

In this "globalized" scenario, the effective management of the employment relationship takes on new meaning. The term "employment relationship" appears self-explanatory; it describes dynamic interlocking economic, legal, social and psychological relations that exist between individuals and their employer. But, at its most basic, the employment relationship embraces an economic relationship: the exchange of pay for physical and/or mental work. It involves a legal relationship: a network of legal rights and obligations affecting both parties to the contract. It also involves a social relationship: managers and non-managers are not isolated individuals but members of social groups, responding to "social norms" that influence their actions in the workplace. The employment relationship typically involves an uneven balance of social power between the two parties, and the social dimension of the employment relationship thus relates to the issue of power. In recent years, more focus has been on the "psychological" component of the employment contract. The "psychological contract" is a metaphor that captures a wide variety of largely unwritten expectations and understandings of the two parties about their mutual obligations (Rousseau, 1995). An important reason for the increased focus on the more cognitive-driven aspects of the employment relationship is the debate surrounding knowledge management. When competitive advantage appears to depend upon effectively leveraging "knowledge workers'" intellectual assets, and when those same assets can "walk out of the door" and work for a competitor, the notion of employee commitment emphasizes the importance of managing the economic and the psychological aspect of the employment contract (Bratton and Gold, 2003).

In the *New Economy* managing the complexities of the employment relationship effectively means not only changing organizations structures, but also changing the way managers manage the employment relationship. Out go traditional "command and control" management, in comes "high trust and high commitment" management based on managing ideas (Thompson and Warhurst, 1998). Most critically, however, the key to realizing the potential for sustainable innovation and improved performance does not only lie in investing in the latest information technology and training. Rather, it depends on creating "a healthy informal organization" from which "individual creativity springs" and fostering a "culture of learning" in which learning is transformed from a one-off training activity into a continuous process within and beyond the workplace (Ashton and Felstead, 2001; Tushman and Nadler, 1996). Additionally, it will also depend on how well managers convert the tacit knowledge of workers and diffuse product and process innovations across much wider constituencies in the organization. As McKinlay's critical study of knowledge management (KM) contends, "The audacity of KM is breathtaking. To appropriate and codify not just the specificities of individual experience but also the reflexive meditation of workgroups on their collective activities and perceptions" (2002, p. 77). It is this dimension of competitive strategy, harnessing and codifying work-related learning, which is associated with the shift from orthodox personnel management to the "progressive" human resource management (HRM) paradigm. To make sense of HRM and to understand why old certainties about "how" to manage people have been upset by developments in capitalism, and why work-based learning is increasingly seen as the answer by contemporary management, it is necessary to examine the historical roots of management theory and practice.

DEVELOPMENT OF MANAGEMENT THEORY AND PRACTICE

The origins of a number of modern concepts and practices of management can be traced back to ancient times. Documents found in the Sumerian civilization of 5000 years ago provide evidence of managerial control practices (George, 1972). Management as a field of inquiry, however, is relatively recent and is rooted in the study of early industrialization. The significance of management for an understanding of the dynamics of organizational life has been long recognized in the foundational works of sociology: Marx, Durkheim, and Weber. Karl Marx argued in *Capital, Volume One,* about the way capitalist factory production caused *alienation*, thus preventing individuals from realizing their full human and social potential. Emile Durkheim's work on *The Division of Labour in Society* and his discussion of *"anomie"* was a critique of the unbridled free markets which undertook to demonstrate that the management practice of increasingly dividing work into discrete parts resulted in a lack of social cohesion, in which individuals felt unable to relate to others and the broader society. Max Weber's classical analysis of bureaucracy, *The Theory of Social and Economic Organization,* emphasized management's "rational" characteristic because it operated on the principles of expert knowledge and a calculable body of rules to control the conduct of work. Examining the historical context of management theory not only places developments in management theory and practice in chronological order, it also helps to understand the economic and political forces shaping organizations and the practice of management.

As in any field of social inquiry, there are different approaches to the study of management. Two broad categories can be identified: "managerialist" and "critical" (Mills and Simmons, 1998). The managerialist approach to the study of management is primarily concerned with issues of labour productivity and profitability. Thus, researchers adopting this approach have tended to develop theoretical frameworks and generate empirical data aimed at understanding organizational structures, work arrangements, and social processes that can improve an organization's effectiveness or can help solve people related "problems" in the workplace. The seminal work at the Western Electric Company Hawthorne plant in Chicago popularized by Elton Mayo, which became the foundation of the "Human Relations School" of management theory and practice, is an obvious example. Within this perspective, the study of management has also been augmented by texts that have focused primarily on the role of the manager and his or her concerns related to organizational goals and leadership. Henry Fayol's *Industrial and General Administration* (1930), and Peter Drucker's *The Practice of Management* (1954) are classics of this genre.

The critical approach to the study of management has been traditionally concerned with issues of exploitation and the alienating effects of work. Researchers adopting this approach tend to conceptualize organizational structures and management behaviour as control mechanisms that function to fulfill economic imperatives. The dominant economic imperative for managers is the need to achieve sufficient control over the work process necessary to appropriate surplus value in the labour process, in order to meet goals of efficiency and levels of profitability. Harry Braverman's in *Labor and Monopoly Capital,* (1974) argued that "Scientific Management" innovations and new technology enhanced managers' control over the work process, "deskilled" workers, intensify work in order to cheapen the cost of labour. Although Braverman's analysis has been severely criticized, his book is a classic work and during the 1980s was a point of reference for researchers investigating organizations and management from a critical perspective.

These broad categories of managerialist and critical approaches can be further sub-divided to reflect a particular focus of research. Within the managerial perspective three major approaches to management have evolved since the early 20th century: the *"technical" approach*, the *"human relations"* approach, and the *"management science"* approach. Within the critical perspective, three approaches have shaped research and debate: the *"labour process" approach*, the *"feminist" approach*, and the *"postmodernist" approach*. The underlying premise of these critical approaches to the study of organizations and management is that organizations are structures of inequality, sexuality is used as a form of control, and new technologies of "self empowerment" aim to make workers' behaviour more manageable (Littler and Salaman, 1984; Hearn *et. al*, 1989; McKinlay and Starkey, 1998).

The "technical" approach to managing the workplace is most closely associated with the work of Fredrick Winslow Taylor (1865-1915). Taylor, an engineer at an American steel mill, experimented with work arrangements and in a paper titled "Shop Management" he emphasized the need to formulate principles and standard work processes to improve labour productivity. Taylor's work configuration rests upon the principle of the technical and social division of mental and manual labour. Though often grouped toether, technical and social divisions of labour can be easily distinguished. Technical division of labour generally refers to how a complex task is broken down into component parts. Adam Smith's (1776 [1997]) classic observation of "pin manufacturing" gives us one of the first renderings of this in relation to the labour process and potential increases in labour productivity. Social division of labour refers to issues of whom, how, why, and for how long individuals and work groups occupy specific positions in the technical division of labour. *Quality of Working Life* (QWL) programmes, such as GM's, that deal with job enlargement and job enrichment, and Co-operative enterprises, in which workers share decision-making responsibilities, are examples of this. In addition, Taylorism (as it became known) involved maximum job fragmentation, the divorce of "direct" and "indirect" labour, the minimization of skill requirements and job-learning time, and the drastic reduction of material handling. These five job design principles gave to management "the collective concept of control" (George, 1972, p. 97.). Observers of Taylor's management practices used the term "scientific management" to describe these techniques. In terms of workplace learning, it should be noted that the fourth principle, minimizing skill requirements to perform a task, not only reduces labour's control over the way work is performed but also minimizes the need for work-based learning. As Littler correctly argues, Taylor's approach to job design embodies "a dynamic of deskilling" and offers to organizations "new structures of control" (1982, p. 52).

Other important management theorists were: Henry Gantt (1856-1915), a protégé of Taylor, who designed the Gantt Chart, a straight-line chart to display and measure planned and completed work as time elapsed; Frank Gilbreth (1868-1924) who helped to increase the intensification of work by improving labour productivity through pioneering use of time and motion techniques; Henry Ford, who applied the major principles of "scientific management" and Gilbreth's time and motion techniques to perfect the flow-line principle of assembly work. This management approach to job design is called not surprisingly, *Fordism*. The classical assembly line principle should be examined as a technology of control over employees and, as job fragmentation and short task-cycle times are accelerated, as a work regime that minimized investment in formal learning for manual workers. Henry Ford's key managing principle was said to be simple: "The idea is that man ... must have every second necessary but not a single unnecessary second" (Ford, 1922, quoted in Huw Beynon, *Working for Ford*, 1984, p. 33).

Until well past the second half of the 20th century, Taylorism and Fordism represented a "commonsense" management strategy concerned primarily with maximizing volume, minimizing unit costs and product tolerances in North America and Western Europe. Scant attention was paid to the long-term effects on employment relations. Scientific management and Fordist principles fostered adversarial employment relations, neglected human potential, and raised supervisory and coordinating costs. The principles espoused by Taylor and Ford reveal a basic paradox "that the tighter the control of labour power, the more control is needed" (Littler and Salaman, 1984, pp. 36-7). Contemporary disenchantment with the "technical" approach led to the development of the "human relations" approach to management.

The *Human Relations School* focus is on the social context of work: employee motivation, group dynamics and group relations. Data gathered at the Hawthorne plant of the Western Electric Companies – subsequently known as the Hawthorn studies – suggested a positive association between labour productivity and management styles. The research team "stumbled" upon their discovery that social and emotional needs, not physical, were the most significant variables determining output. The phenomenon can be explained as follows: "The determinants of working behaviour are sought in the structure and culture of the group, which is spontaneously formed by the interaction of individuals working together" (Mouzelis, 1967, p. 99 and quoted by Clegg and Dunkerley, 1980, p. 128). Elton Mayo is most closely associated with the Hawthorne studies. Another pioneering management theorist, Mary Parker Follet, is associated with the early Human Relations management movement. Drawing on her background in social work and philosophy, she contended that traditional authority as an act of subordination was offensive to an individual's emotion and therefore could not serve as a good foundation for cooperative relations in the workplace. Instead, Follet proposed an authority function whereby the individual has authority over her or his own job area (George, 1972).

The Hawthorne studies have been criticized at both technical and political levels. Technically, it has been contended that the researchers used a "rudimentary" research design and their analysis of the data was faulty. At a political level, charges of managerial bias, insularity from wider socio-economic factors, neglect of workers' organization (trade unions), and organizational conflict were effectively leveled against the researchers, and later followers of, human relations theory. The critique included the charge that human relations theorists conceptualized the "normal" state of the work organization in "romantic" and harmonious term. These familiar charges are presented by organizational theorists taking a critical perspective (see Clegg and Dunkerley 1980; Thompson, 1989). Clegg and Dunkerley, for example, argue that human relations theorists "emphasized harmony and neglected conflict, because of their pro-capitalist managerial bias" (1980, p. 134). Despite the criticisms, the Hawthorne studies provided the impetus for a new "commonsense" management strategy that focused on a paternalistic style of management emphasizing workers' social needs as the key to harmonious relations and better performance, albeit narrowly conceived,.

Maslow (1954) and McGregor, (1960) contributed to human relations theory after World War II. Abraham Maslow (1908-1970) suggested a hierarchy of employee needs starting with physiological needs and progressing to "self-actualization." Douglas McGregor (1906 – 1964), another important contributor, distinguished two major management styles, which he referred to as Theory X and Theory Y. The underlying assumptions of Theory X approach to managing people is that the average worker dislikes work and avoids responsibility, hence most employees must be coerced and controlled to maximize their effort level. McGregor believed that the "technical" approach was based on Theory X assumption about workers. The Theory Y approach is predicated on the assumption that the average worker does not inherently dislike work and under proper conditions they seek responsibility. Moreover, Theory Y assumed that the intellectual potential of the average worker is under-utilized. These contributions to management thought, and the Quality of Working Life (QWL) Movement, promoted five principles of "good" job design: *closure*, whereby the scope of the job includes all the tasks to complete a product or process; *task variety,* whereby the worker learns a wider range of skills to increase job flexibility; *self-regulation,* allowing workers to assume responsibility for scheduling the work and quality control; *social interaction* to allow cooperation and reflectivity; and continuous *work-based learning*.

The "management science" approach is distinguished by its application of quantitative techniques – statistics, mathematics, data processing – to management decision-making and problem solving (Daft, 2001). This approach emerged after World War II to meet the demands of mass production techniques to move large quantities of materials and components efficiently. Forecasting, inventory modeling, queuing theory, and break-even analysis are some of the commonly used methods. A study by John Bratton (1992) illustrates how the adoption of work teams is contingent upon such management techniques. The prerequisite for self-managed teams is a *management information system (MIS)*, providing relevant information to managers in a timely and cost-effective way.

Each of the three major approaches has become embedded in the "mainstream" thinking on work design. During the 1950s and 60s (the "golden age" of Fordism) market conditions and a more even balance of power between capital and labour, dictated "common-sense" management strategies that minimized workers' skills, autonomy and learning in order to satisfy low cost mass production goals. By the mid-1970s, the Fordist system was undermining profitability. During the 1980s and 90s "common-sense" dictated a management strategy that gave limited autonomy to workers and encouraged work-based learning. However, we should not make the mistake of conceptualizing scientific management, human relations, management science, and so on, as schools of "management thought," coming and going with the passing of time. Taylorism is not a failed ideology. According to Craig Littler (1982) it is important to recognize that all managerial ideologies affect organizational structures – how work is designed, who reports to whom, and the formal control mechanisms – but some have a greater impact than others do. Scientific management affected all aspects of an organization's structure, whereas the structural implications of human relations are more limited. Drawing upon the theoretical work of Harry Braverman (1974), writers, such as Tony Watson (1986) and Boje and Winsor (1993), contend that Taylorism is being "resurrected" and "re-packaged" in so-called high-tech companies under the total quality management label. It is therefore not a question of actually "resurrecting Taylorism" because Taylorism has never died (Littler, 1982). Paul Thompson (1989) has charged that new forms of work can be interpreted as "flexible Taylorism" and that "no qualitative break has been made in the organization of the capitalist labour process" (1989, p. 229). In the developed and developing economies elements of Taylorism, Fordism, and craft-control work structures still exist in labour processes. In other words, new management strategies ride on the back of the old. Further, each major stream of manufacturing strategy has been accompanied by changes in what constitutes rational "common-sense" management styles and practices.

Historical forces influence management thought, and change perceptions of what constitutes "common-sense" management, influencing organizational culture and practices. Current theorizing of workplaces as learning cultures have paralleled historical changes to organizations from Tayloristic managed organizations to knowledge-based postmodern "learning organizations" and, echoing Littler (1982), John Garrick correctly observes that these work configurations are not necessarily mutually exclusive but emphasizes the important connection between work design and the opportunity for informal learning (1998, p. 56-7).

Case studies of organizations that have undergone *business process re-engineering (BPR)* show that the social design of work continues to be influenced by principles of Taylorism and management strategies for controlling workers. The BPR movement declares that organizational structures has to be "radically" reconfigured so that the re-engineered organization can become flexible and orientated to continuous change and renewal. According to the re-engineering "guru," James Champy (1996), BPR is "about changing our managerial work, the way we think about, organize, inspire, deploy, enable, measure, and reward the value-adding operational work. It is about changing management itself" (p. 3).

An organization's structure, under PBR, is typically "de-layered" with decision-making being pushed down to the "front line" to meet the contemporary demand of quality, flexibility, low cost, and entrepreneurial autonomy (Hammer and Champy, 1993). The *re-engineered organization* has allegedly a number of common characteristics (see Figure 1). Central to these organizational forms, argues Hugh Willmott (1995), is the "reconceptualization of core employees" from being considered a variable cost to a valuable asset, capable of serving the customer without the need for "command and control" leadership style. Unlike earlier movements and tendencies in work design, such as the *Quality of Working Life Movement (QWL)*, re-engineering is *market driven*. It focuses on the relationship between buyer and seller of services or goods, rather than the relationship between employer and employee. Hammer and Champy emphasize that the "three C's " – customers, competition, and change – have created the need for re-engineering business processes. For Champy (1996), using language from political movements of the "radical Left" and the "new Right," contends that change is brought about by markets not management: "a dictatorship of the customariat or … a market democracy … is the cause of a total revolution within the traditional, machine-like corporation" (p. 19).

A number of academics are critical of "re-engineered" formulations (see Reed, 1993; Thompson, 1993; Craig and Yetton, 1993; Oliver, 1993; Willmott, 1995; and Grint and Willcocks, 1995). Paul Thompson, for example, accuses postmodern organizational theorists of having fallen victim to technological determinism and of mistaking the surface of work organizations for their substance. He argues that the "leaner" organization actually gives more power to a few: "Removing some of the middle layers of organizations is not the same as altering the basic power structure … By cutting out intermediary levels [of management] … the power resources of those at the top can be increased" (1993, p.192). Grint and Willcocks (1995) offer a scathing review of BPR, arguing that BPR is not novel and point out that it is "essentially political in its rhetorical and practical manifestations. Hugh Willmott (1995) is similarly critical about BPR, emphasizing that re-engineering is "heavily top-down" and pointing out that the re-engineered organization, using information technology, while creating less hierarchical structures produces "a fist-full of dynamic processes … notably, the primacy of hierarchical control and the continuing treatment of employees as cogs in the machine" (1995, p.91). When examined in the context of employment relations, BPR can be interpreted "as the latest wave in a series of initiatives … to increase the cooperation/productivity/adaptability of staff" (Willmott, 1995, p.96).

The notion that work-based learning embodies social purposes has been absent from much of the current theorizations of learning in the workplace. Critical theorists emphasize how learning is part of a battery of HR techniques designed to gain worker compliance. The focus is on mobilizing workers' reflective practices, problem-solving skills and instrumental knowledge: learning that improves productivity and helps workers become compliant "team players," rather than learning that encourages critical dialogue (Boje, 1994; Fenwick, 1998; Garrick, 1998; Townley, 1994). "Contemporary work-based learning strategies rarely deal in self-criticism, paradox, irony or doubt, yet it is precisely these qualities that give substance to learning," as John Garrick (1994, p.79) put it. Foucault's (1983) notions on the exercise of power *over* through the use of "soft" technologies of compliance and control is well illustrated by Boje's observation on the implications of new work designs for informal learning:

A seamless web of instructional apparatus where we are taught to be "politically correct" bureaucrats. The learning occurs in the minute-by-minute interactions and the spaces along the hallways, lunchrooms and e-mail networks. The iron cage of the bureaucratic teaching machine is so ubiquitous and [seemly] benign that the prisoners of modern learning no longer see the bars, the gears, or question the learning agenda. (Boje, 1994, p. 447 and quoted in Garrick, 1998, p. 79)

Figure 1: The Re-engineered Organization

Characteristic	Traditional Model	Re-engineered Model
Market	Domestic	Global
Competitive advantage	Cost	Speed and quality
Resources	Capital	Information
Quality	What is affordable	No compromise
Focal point	Profit	Customer
Structural design	Hierarchical	Flattened
Control	Centralized	De-centralized
Leadership	Autocratic	Shared
Labour	Homogeneous	Culturally diverse
Organization of work	Specialized and individual	Flexible and in teams
Communications	Vertical	Horizontal

Source: Bratton and Gold, 2003.

The Foucauldian model of organizational power draws attention to a nexus of seemly apolitical human resource practices (including workplace learning) that refine the nature of work and self-regulation, thereby making workers' behaviour and performance more predictable and measurable (Townley, 1994).

If current management literature is correct, the most significant changes now affecting management are free trade, deregulation and unprecedented global competition. It is these economic forces that explain the major paradigm shift that has occurred in corporate boardrooms in terms of competitive strategies and the soft technology of flexibility (Schenk and Anderson, 1999; see also Felstead and Jewson, 1999; Lowe, 2000 and Thompson and Warhurst, 1998). Those companies adopting a competitive strategy that focuses on high quality and customizing their products or services to a "niche" market require an organizational design that is fluid and flexible, with strong horizontal communications and coordination. Workers must continually experiment, innovate, and learn. At the heart of this competitive strategy is a management strategy which typically includes "just-in-time," multi-skilling, work teams, and continuous work-based learning. The soft technology of flexibility in the new "reengineered" organization is lubricated by a leadership style and human resources practices that encourages workers to be innovative, to make decisions, and to engage in self-regulation and discipline. The socially constructed organizational culture encourages workers to engage their hearts and minds in "relevant" learning. The basic philosophy remains unchanged; it is to maximize profits by minimizing costs. This goal is achieved by reducing or eliminating "non-value added" operations, such as material handling, quality inspections, maintenance and "down time" material handling, as well as break time. Of course, this new *lean production paradigm* relies ultimately on the worker's willingness to co-operate. And, as Littler and Salaman correctly argue: "Short of removing the worker from the production process completely … [through the use of new technology] … the employer sooner or later is forced to seek to recover workers' willingness by harnessing their participation" (1984, p. 37). Thompson (1989) has similarly observed, "co-operation and the generation of consent are systematically built into the capitalist labour process" (p. 244).

Management itself is a complex and multifaceted social phenomenon with differentiated groups and agendas, values and expectations, and power relationships. Consequently, the *type* of strategies adopted will depend upon economic forces, stakeholder pressures, and the values of senior decision-makers in the organization. Further, the way strategies are actually implemented *within* an organization might be different over time and also different *between* workplaces owned and controlled by the same management. Decision making interests may therefore vary both horizontally and vertically within large complex organizations (Kochan, McKersie and Cappelli, 1984). In this context, strategies might offer insights into an "ideal-type" towards which organizations can move. But circumstances and personnel change, strategies and practices might become obsolete or abandoned. Historically, depending upon economic and political imperatives, management have experimented with a plethora of strategies oscillating from the hegemony of a "hard" Taylorism-Fordism strategy to the hegemony of a "soft" human relations-QWL strategy, and back again to a "hard" neo-Taylorism/reengineering strategy. Consequently, any discussion of typologies of management strategies is bound to simplify a more complex social reality.

THE BIRTH OF HUMAN RESOURCE MANAGEMENT

Management practices dealing with the recruitment and selection of people, performance appraisal, discipline, rewards, and training and development, were generally referred to as "personnel management." The term "human resource management" (HRM) emerged in the late 1980s and has since been extensively debated. As the British academic John Storey (1989; 1995; 2001) notes, the concept of HRM is shrouded in managerial hype and its underlying philosophy and character is highly controversial because it lacks precise formulation and agreement as to its significance. The debate centres on two fundamental questions. The first is conceptual: What is meant by the term, human resource management? Other related questions included: How should this HRM model be viewed? How does it differ from the traditional personnel model? What is the significance of the HRM model for workplace learning? Is the model potentially a force for widening access to work-related learning? Clearly, the meaning of the term is elastic and the different versions of HRM will impact differently work-based learning. The second area of the debate focuses on the empirical data: What is the extent of the change in personnel practices, which give expression to the core concepts of HRM?

For some, the HRM model denotes a more strategic approach and a new theoretical sophistication in the area of people management. For others, however, HRM is simply personnel management renamed, or "old wine in a new bottle." A number of HRM scholars developed theoretical models that seek to demonstrate the difference, if any, between conventional personnel management and HRM (Beer et al., 1984; Fombrun, Tichy and Devanna, 1984; Guest, 1990; Hendry and Pettigrew, 1990 and Storey, 1992). It is outside the scope of this chapter to analyze the various models, but we offer the following definition to capture the salient features of HRM: Human Resource Management is a strategic approach to managing employment relations, one that emphasizes leveraging people's capabilities as critical to achieving sustainable competitive advantage. This is achieved through a distinctive set of integrated employment policies, programs and practices. HRM, as we portray it, underlines a belief that people really do make the difference; only *people* among other resources have the capacity to generate value. It follows from this premise that human knowledge and skills are a *strategic* resource that needs to be adroitly managed. Another distinguishing feature of HRM relates to the notion of *integration*. A set of employment policies, programs and practices need to be coherent and integrated with organizational strategy. It follows that if workers are so critical for organizational success, then the responsibility for HRM activities rests with all *line managers* and should not be left to HR specialists (Bratton and Gold, 2003).

REFLECTIVE QUESTION

Read Chapter 1, "Human Resource Management Phenomenon" in John Bratton and Jeffrey Gold's (2003) text *Human Resource Management: Theory and Practice*, London: Palgrave-Macmillan. To what extent is the "progressive" HRM model different from conventional personnel management or is it simply "old wine in a new bottle"?

The early literature identified a "Jekyll and Hyde" quality about HRM, so-called "soft" and "hard" versions (Sisson and Storey, 2000). The "soft" version focuses attention on the term "human" and emphasizes investment in training to leverage knowledge and skills, employee commitment and a "people-centred" leadership style. The "soft" version traces its roots to the human-relations school. By contrast, the "hard" version emphasizes the calculative and business-strategic aspects of managing people. It views people as a "resource" which should be managed in as "rational" a way as any other economic factor, as a cost that must be controlled (Storey, 1989). For some, the HRM model represented a distinctive approach to the organisation of work and the management of the employment relationship to fit the *new economic order*. The rise of radical conservative governments in Britain, Canada and the U.S., under Thatcher, Mulroney and Reagan, provided the political and economic backdrop to the shift in managerial thought and practice. Whereas old-style personnel management based its legitimacy within the organization on its ability to deal with the uncertainties stemming from relatively full employment and powerful trade unions, HRM focuses more attention on internal sources of competitive advantage with trade unions in retreat.

By the late 1990s, a "second wave" of academic debate emerged with four distinct themes: the significance of the economic and social context in shaping and reshaping the HRM arena; the links between HRM and organizational performance; the new organizational forms and social relationships; and the importance of work-based learning and "knowledge management." Indeed, in the context of the debate around "best" HR practices which allegedly give rise to "High Performance Work Systems (HPWS) the rhetoric of HRM has been replaced by the rhetoric *of human resource development (HRD)*. In the knowledge-based, high commitment workplace, continuous learning "is seen as one if not *the main source* of competitive advantage of the company" (Ashton and Felstead, 2001, p. 166).

The second area of the debate focuses on the number of organizations allegedly adopting the new HRM model. What is the nature and extent of change in HR practices, which give expression to the core concepts of HRM? How many organizations have adopted a learning model? One early study provided *prima facie* evidence of "a remarkable take-up" of HRM-type practices by large British businesses (Storey, 1992). For our purposes it is sufficient to note the two kinds of data available. The first relates to evidence about the diffusion of core HR practices. The other relates to evidence about the effects of these HR practices on organizational performance. In the UK, studies confirm that there is fairly extensive use of the individual elements of HR practices. However, the extent to which these practices are integrated into a coherent strategy is more contentious

(Cully, *et al.* 1999; Storey, 2001). It is reported that only a minority of "leading edge" UK companies are committed to investing in continuous learning as part of their competitive strategy (Ashton and Felstead, 2001). In Canada, an empirical study reported limited use of HR practices (Betcherman, 1994) and, similarly, fairly limited use of these practices was found in U.S. companies (Pfeffer, 1998).

FROM HRM TO STRATEGIC HRM

During the 1990s, it became "commonsense" to suggest that senior management need to adopt a more "strategic" approach to the management of people. Academics and practitioners began to attach the prefix "strategy" to the term human resource management and the notion of *"strategic integration"* became prominent in the literature. The concept of strategic integration embraced three management practices: the integration or "cohesion" of employment policies and practices (e.g. selection, rewards, training, communications and empowerment) in order to complement each other and to help achieve strategic goals; the internalization of the importance of employment practices on the part of line managers and, third, the recognition that people are the key to achieving competitive advantage and therefore needed to be integrated more fully to foster commitment or an "identity of interest" with their organization. The basic proposition developed here is that if these forms of integration are implemented, workers will be more cooperative, flexible and willing to accept change, and the organization's strategic plans are therefore likely to be more successfully implemented.

An influential view underscoring the premise that people are a strategic resource is the resource-based model. Put simply, this approach to strategic HRM draws attention to the strategic value of knowledge and skills, and by extension learning in the workplace, as a means to achieve sustainable competitive advantage: "it is a firm's ability to learn faster and apply its learning more effectively than its rivals, that gives it competitive advantage" (Hamel and Prahalad, 1993, cited by Boxall, 1996, p.65). Its origins can be traced back to macroeconomic theories of growth and development and in the microeconomic theory of human capital (Bouchard, 1998; Livingstone, 1999; Schultz, 1981; Spencer, 1998). Economists have traditionally viewed investment in education and training as an important factor explaining differences in international growth rates (see, for example, Denison, 1967).

STUDY TIP

Compare the perspectives of Marsick and Watkins (1990), Hart (1992), and Livingstone (1999) on the matter of the Human Capital model. Each author offers a different perspective on the model. What are the different perspectives each author operates from and which do you find more convincing and why?

In Canada, policy-makers recognized the links between education and economic growth as early as the mid 18th century. In 1848, Egerton Ryerson, the Chief Superintendent of Education for English Canada, addressed the question: "The Importance of Education to a Manufacturing and a Free People." Starting from the premise that education was a prerequisite to a competitive manufacturing sector, he declared: "educated labour is more productive than uneducated labour" (quoted by Graff, 1976, p. 58). A century later, this was a hypothesis figured strongly in the Royal Commission on Canada's Economic Prospects reports in the 1950s. Slow economic growth and raising unemployment among the least educated, some observers maintained, were caused by insufficient investment in public education, particularly at higher levels (Francis *et al.,* 1988). Schultz (1961, 1981) was strong advocate of the hypothesis that investment in "human capital" promoted economic growth. He contended, "investment in population quality and in knowledge in large part determines the future prospects of mankind" (Schultz, 1981, p. 31). The hypothesis was restated by Smith's (1991) inquiry on Canadian university education: "No advanced society can be competitive without a large proportion of its citizenry educated to participate in a global, knowledge-intensive economy" (Smith, 1991, p. 13). More recently, the "New" Labour government in the UK reaffirmed the importance of learning: "Investment in human capital will be the foundation of success in the knowledge-based global economy of the twenty-first century" (DfEE, 1998, p.7). Underpinning this approach is the assumption that an individual's level of education and training is linked to their employability in the labour market and to long-term economic growth. This optimistic belief, that investment in education and training leads to employability and economic growth, has influenced politicians and policy makers, and in turn, the providers of adult education. It compelled institutions "to justify their educational activity in economic terms, as opposed to liberal educational ones" (Spencer, 1998, ɔ). The current debate on the "value" of higher education in Canada ⸱ɔntinues to be shadowed by the human capital theory. The utilitarian purpose of education and training, rather than its intrinsic value, is central to the resource-based view. By way of example, in 2000 the University of Toronto proclaimed the benefits of a university education in terms of "mind training" for the job market by advertising "You have an English degree. Now what?"

REFLECTIVE QUESTION

Perhaps not surprisingly, the argument that education should *serve* business and the economy has been fiercely debated (see also Spencer, 1998 and Foley, 1995). What are your views on this?

The resource-based model (henceforth, RBM) contends that sustainable competitive advantage are conferred to a business organization by resources (human and non-human) which are *scarce* relative to their demand and difficult to *imitate*. In an era of global competition when new technology can be purchased on the "open" market, it is argued that it is the idiosyncratic nature of organizational-specific knowledge assets that creates sustainable competitive advantage. Jeffrey Pfeffer (1998) puts it like this, "What provides long-term advantage are those things that are core to the firm and not readily duplicated by competitors – and purchases on the open market cannot be sources of unique or distinct capabilities" (p. xviii). Thus, the overall objective that informs the RBM is to establish a link between the dynamics of competitive advantages to the characteristics of form-specific resources (Foss, 1997).

The genesis of the RBM can be traced back to Selznick (1957) who contended that work organizations each possess "distinctive competence" that enables them to out perform their competitors, and to Penrose (1959) who conceptualized the firm as a "collection of productive resources." She distinguished between "physical" and "human resources," and drew attention to issues of learning, including knowledge and experience of the management team. Moreover, Penrose emphasized what many organizational theorists take for granted, that organizations are "heterogeneous" (Penrose, 1959, cited in Boxall, 1996, pp.64-65). More recently, Barney (1991) has posited that *"sustained* competitive advantage" [our emphasis] is not achieved through an analysis of its external market position but through a careful analysis of the firm's skills and capabilities –characteristics that competitors find themselves unable to imitate. Barney describe. four characteristics of resources and capabilities important to sustaining competitive advantage: value, rarity, inimitability and non-substitutability. From this perspective, the collective learning in the workplace by managers and non-managers, especially coordinating workers' knowledge and agency and integrating information technology, is a strategic asset that rivals find difficult to replicate.

One dimension of an organization's strategic resources is *"core competencies"* (see Hamel, 2000; Prahalad and Hamel, 1990) which refers to "the collective learning of the organization, especially how to coordinate diverse production skills and integrate multiple streams of technology" (quoted in Foss, 1997, p.8). Amit and Shoemaker (1993) make a similar point to Barney and Prahalad and Hamel when they emphasize the strategic importance for managers to identify, *ex ante,* and marshal "a set of complementary and specialized resources and capabilities which are scarce, durable, not easily traded, and difficult to imitate" to enable the company to earn "economic rent" [profits]. A more rhetorical version of this strategy espouses that training and learning in the workplace is a vital part of the necessary "retooling" for "the age of revolution" (Hamel, 2000). The strategic role for HRM, argues John Purcell (1995), is to develop "horizontal" long-term strategies which places a "premium" on the organization's people and which "emphasize intangible, learning, and skill transfer and the reduction in transaction cost" (Purcell, 1995, p.84). The RBM focus is on "relevant learning" because, according to its advocates, learning tasks are performed better and quicker through the process and new opportunities are identified (Teece, *et al.,* 1997). If this current conventional wisdom is correct, then the message for corporate executives is clear; they have to create work structures and a culture conducive to continuous work-based learning if they are to achieve "above average" economic performance.

REFLECTIVE QUESTION

What is meant by a "resource-based" SHRM model of competitive advantage? What are the implications for adult learning of this competitive strategy?

The resource-based model has been extensively critiqued, but pressed for space we can only mention a few issues of concern. One problem is that the term "resource-based" appears to mean different things to different authors. Definitions range from narrow specific interpretations to very broad descriptions and are "sometimes tautological; resources are defined as firm strengths, and firm strengths are then defined as strategic resources; capability is defined in terms of competence, and competence is then defined in terms of capability" (Nanda, 1996, p.100). Taken from a critical perspective, another problem with the resource-based approach stems from its implicit acceptance of a unitary perspective of the post-industrial workplace in which goals are shared and levels of trust are high. Advocates omit the dynamics of capitalist employment relations, workplace trade unionism and conflicting interests in the strategic equation. The RBM or learning paradigm is increasingly understood by some trade unions to be a managerial strategy that ultimately serves the interests of capital. It is viewed as a means to mobilize knowledge and learning in order to achieve flexibility and capital accumulation, rather than as an opportunity for improving the quality of work and the security of workers (Bratton, 2001).

DOES STRATEGIC HRM MAKE A DIFFERENCE?

Human resource professionals have become increasingly concerned in recent years with demonstrating the financial contribution – the "value-added" or the "return on investment" (ROI) – HR practices make to the organization's performance. The early debate about HRM and strategic HRM was conducted in the absence of limited empirical evidence on the HRM-performance link. Advocates often simply assumed that an alignment between business strategy and HR strategy would improve organizational performance and competitiveness. The resource-based view assumed a simple causal chain of "soft" HR policies of empowerment, team working and workplace learning employee commitment synergy improved organizational performance. In the late 1990s, demonstrating that there is indeed a positive link between HRM and performance became "*the* dominant research issue" in the HRM field (Guest, 1997). Researchers began asking: Do "commitment-learning" type HRM systems produce above-average results when compared to "control-low learning" type systems? Do learning organizations have superior performance?[1]

Longitudinal case studies, intra-industry investigations – steel making, automobile assembly, apparel manufacture and metalworking – and cross-industry analyses appear to reveal that different work configurations and worker empowerment arrangements associated with the progressive HRM model have superior output and quality performances. For example, Gordon Betcherman's *et al.*, (1994) analysis, using data Canadian generated from Canadian companies found a statistically significant association between the new HRM approach and unit costs. The evidence also suggested that new HRM practices operate best in certain organizational "environments." The more intangible corporate "ideology" variables – "progressive decision-making," "social responsibility" and "supportive work environment" – tend to have a more significant impact on performance outcomes than team-based programs or incentive-pay plans. This view is consistent with Casey Ichniowski's *et al.*, main conclusion that "There are no one or two "magic bullets" that are *the* work practices that will stimulate worker and business performance. Work teams or quality circles alone are not enough. Rather, *whole systems* [our emphasis] need to be changed" (1996, p.322).

The methodology used to gather the data and the magnitude of the impact is, however, contentious. The actual variables used to measure the value-added of HR strategy and individual HR practices, such as investment in work-based learning, is not consistent. Moreover, the notion of what constitutes "superior performance" takes on a new meaning given the accounting and scandals reported in the summer of 2002 (Byrne, 2002, p. 69-78). Notwithstanding the tough methodological challenges (Betcherman *et al.*, 1994), there is now a substantive body of empirical data that demonstrates that "bundles" of HR policies and practices can and do make a positive impact on a variety of organizational outcomes (Bratton and Gold, 2003). The upshot is that organizations implementing a package of internally consistent and mutually reinforcing HR practices, closely associated with work-based learning, experience significant improvements in performance. In general, the studies seem to demonstrate "impressive evidence of robust impacts and outcomes" writes John Storey (2001, p. 13).

REFLECTIVE QUESTION

Some researchers have emphasized the difficulty of quantifying the benefits of "soft" HRM learning model for organizational performance. See Bratton and Gold (2003), Chapter 13 for an extensive discussion on this). What do you think about this debate? How important is this debate for the advancement of workplace learning?

DETRACTORS, PARADOXES AND CONTRADICTIONS

The HRM model has its detractors. A number of scholars consider it a manipulative form of management control representing a renaissance of a unitary (non-union) style of management, causing work intensification (Wells, 1993); as a cultural construct concerned with moulding employees to corporate values (Keenoy and Anthony, 1992) and as a new form of power/knowledge designed to control the workforce, what Michel Foucault termed new "technologies of self" (McKinlay and Starkey, 1998; Townley, 1994).

Typically, the debate on the various HRM models tends to be gender-blind. Recently, though, there has been interest in the gender implications of HRM models (Dickens, 1998). Dickens has suggested that the HRM model "might be at odds with the promotion of equal opportunities" and that the gender equality assumption in the HRM model, which emphasises the value of diversity and individual learning and development, is rhetoric rather than reality. Theoretically, one of the most important consequences of a gendered analysis of the workplace is its power to question research findings and analysis that segregates studies of management and work-based learning from those of gender divisions in the labour market (Dex, 1988), patriarchal power (Witz, 1986), issues of inequality (Philips and Philips, 1993), "dual-role" work-family issues (Knights and Willmott, 1986; Platt, 1997), and the gendering of both work and learning opportunities (Probert, 1999).

Paradox involves ambiguity and inconsistency, two or more positions that each sound reasonable yet conflict or even contradict each other. Paradox results when, in pursuit of specific organizational goal(s), managers call for or perform actions that are in opposition to the very goals the organization is attempting. Detractors have drawn upon the Weberian notion (Weber, 1968) of "paradox of consequences" arising from HR practices. For example, new organizational forms (e.g. contracting out services or department work) have been introduced to improve productivity. On the other hand, productivity benefits impact negatively on the "psychological contract," undermining espoused goals such as trust, loyalty and commitment. A common paradox of HR policies and practices is that it espouses "team values," "collaboration," and the importance of being a "team-player" yet the firm's payment system rewards individual performance rather than collective or team effort. More broadly, there is ambiguity with regard to whether the main role of the human resource professional is a "caring" or a "controlling" one (Watson, 1986). Barbara Townley (1994), for example, applying the work of Michel Foucault to HRM, argues that HR practices are designed to make employees more "governable" and to bring order and stability to organizational life, but HR practices can also develop into sources of disorder or instability. And Karen Legge's (1995) incisive critique of HRM identifies further paradoxes. The rhetoric that asserts "we are all managers now" due to "empowerment" conceals the legitimate question as to whether a social group holding privileges and receiving inflated salaries should hold on to corporate power: "Paradoxically, then, a rhetoric adopted to enhance managerial legitimacy might prove the thin edge of the wedge for at least some of the advocates" (1995, p. 56). By illustrating the inevitable paradoxes contained in the employment relationship, readers will be encouraged to scrutinize assumptions underpinning HRM and the new discourse on human resource development (HRD).

The critical literature also exposes familiar contradictions inherent in the phenomenon of management. John Godard (1991), the Canadian professor of industrial relations, identifies a number of contradictions underlying the new HRM paradigm due to the nature of the capitalist employment relationship. When people enter the workplace, they enter a contractual exchange whereby their behaviour is directed by controllers towards the achievement of specific tasks. As Godard (1991) argues, legally, workers "alienate" themselves from the right to control the labour process and, consequently, workers have "little objective reason to develop more than an instrumental orientation to their work" (p. 381). The wage-effort employment contract places an obligation both on the employer and the worker; in exchange for a wage, paid by the employer; the worker is obligated to perform an amount of physical or intellectual labour. The essence of the labour market is that workers *sell* their labour and seek to *maximise* their wage. To the employer, wages and benefits are a *cost* that negatively impact on profit and therefore need to be *minimised*. Thus, the wage-effort contract is inherently conflict prone as the logic makes a reward to one group a cost to the other (Hyman, 1975).

STUDY TIP

You should be aware that Harry Braverman's (1974) book, *Labor and Monopoly Capital,* is a classic study of the transformation of work caused by conscious management strategies. Read Chapter 4 "Scientific Management" and Chapter 5 "The primary effects of scientific management." Do the principles of scientific management still influence the design of the modern workplace? What effect, if any, does scientific management have on the quality of work-based learning?

The "effort" side of the contract also generates conflict because it is inherently imprecise and indeterminate. The contract permits the employer to buy a *potential* level of physical or intellectual labour. The function of management therefore is to transform this potential into *actual value-added* labour. This is, in effect, the *raison d'être* of management. HRM is about narrowing the gap between workers' potential and actual performance or, as Barbara Townley explains, "personnel practices measure both the physical and subjective dimensions of labour, and offer a technology which aims to render individuals and their behaviour predictable and calculable ... to bridge the gap between promise and performance, between labour power and labour, and organises labour into a productive force or power" (1994, p.14). Furthermore, workers have the ability to evaluate, to question, and to resist management's actions; they also have the capacity to form organisations in order to defend or further their economic interests. In sum, these apparent contradictions have the potential to impact negatively on workplace learning. Exposing the tensions and contradictions here should make readers sceptical of the evangelical teachings of management consultants offering "quick fix" interventions to solve complex workplace issues.

Finally, we should note another apparent contradiction in the HRM "strategic learning" discourse. If the pursuit of "best" HR practices leads to improved organizational performance, from the perspective of "economic rationality," one would expect such practices to be widely used. To date, however, empirical studies have lagged behind this model of strategic HRM. Nanda (1996) makes a pertinent observation: "While the analysis has been sophisticated at macro-theoretic level, it stands relatively unsupported by micro-theoretic foundations on the one side and empirical verifications on the other" (Nanda, 1996, p.97). In Canada and Britain, the general record of investment in work-based training and education is "dismal." In Canada, Gordon Betcherman and his colleagues reported that "the large majority of firms do not take a systematic, forward-looking approach to training; roughly 20 per cent appear to have a training budget and about 15 per cent have a formal training plan" (1994, p.36). In 2002, the Conference Board of Canada reported that only about 30 per cent of adults of labour force age engage in training and education (Munby, 2003, p. 93). In Britain, researchers have expressed concern for attention to work-based learning. Ashton and Felstead (2001), for example, report that only a minority of "leading-edge" companies uses a learning strategy to achieve competitive advantage, and there has been no wide-scale transformation from one-off work-based training to lifelong learning. Moreover, a significant majority of senior British and North American managers have placed more emphasis on reducing labour costs by "downsizing', non-standard employment contracts, and de-emphasizing, explicitly or implicitly, employment security. Such employment practices suggest a limited acceptance of the resource-based and learning strategy as it applies to "progressive" HRM (Boxall, 1996).

When faced with the various exigencies of global price competition, the majority of Anglo-North American companies have opted for a low cost strategy and a market-driven HR strategy and minimized their investment in people. The consequences of such a low-cost strategy in "free" market global economy leads to second-round effects on the workforce. Line managers, clerical and manual workers realize that their jobs are more insecure, and that their employers are compelled to be increasingly aggressive on employment relationship matters; that, in turn, affects workers commitment to the organization and the value they place in upgrading their skills. Thus, a market-driven "hard" HR strategy can perpetuate a low-skill, low-wage economy. Despite all protestations, it appears that much of the "progressive" learning-oriented HR strategy has been put back on the shelf. This may be a result of the long-term investment costs associated with the resource-based approach to strategic HRM, and the pressure on individual managers to achieve short-term financial results to satisfy the stock market.

SUMMARY

This chapter provides an overview of the development of management and organizational theory, and explores the implications for learning in the workplace. We have discussed some of the major contributions of management theory, placing the workplace learning discourse in context. Although most of the theories embodied in the HRM model can be found in either organizational behaviour or management textbooks of two decade ago, the so-called "progressive" or "soft" HRM model offers a new way to managing the workplace, emphasizing that people, empowered and continuously learning, are central to organizational economic performance. The ideology of workplace learning can therefore be seen as serving the economic needs of business organizations and strengthening managerial hegemony.

Challenges to the new "commonsense" view of managing the employment relationship come not only from within its own theoretical ambiguity. As John Storey wrote, "the HRM model is ... a symbolic label, behind which lurk multifarious practices, many of which are not mutually dependent upon each other" (Storey, 1995, p. 14), but also from persistent economic turmoil and the propensity of the management class to seek new tools to solve old economic and motivational problems. As such, "management" and "learning" are concepts inextricably linked to economic imperatives (Garrick, 1999).

We also discussed how management could choose from a variety of employment strategies to meet their organizational goals. The empirical evidence suggests that the great majority of work organizations have not adopted the "soft" HRM or the Learning Organization model, others have adopted only elements of the model, and others have emphasized different features of the model to build a "high performance" workplace. For example, some firms emphasize investment in workplace learning as a building block to high commitment/performance, while others have chosen a sophisticated reward system and job security (Guest, 1997). Furthermore, within the *same company*, management may adopt different strategies for different categories of workers. For highly skilled or professional workers, a work-based learning model may be adopted; while unskilled workers, relatively easy to recruit, experience a "low trust" "low learning" management regime. Conditions in the external labour market are therefore another factor determining management style, policies, and learning opportunities and experiences in the workplace. What is important to understand is that there are a number of possible configurations of management policies and practices, which account for variations in management strategy and style.

The current HRM-learning discourse places considerable emphasis on the apparent transformation of paid work and the need for work-based lifelong learning. Indicators of this are the repeated references to high-tech "knowledge economies" and "knowledge worker." David Boud and John Garrick (1999) begin an engaging review of workplace learning by asserting "the nature of work is changing with "knowledge" being regarded increasingly as *the* primary resource, thus giving rise to unprecedented demands for learning ... " (p.3). An increasing number of professional workers are undoubtedly selling their intellectual assets, but adult educators should be cautious of joining a long line of academics infatuated with information technology, adopting what Paul Thompson (1993) calls "a technical determinist vision" of the modern workplace. The popular management rhetoric around e-commerce and "knowledge work" should be tempered by a recognition that in all economies there is still an army of low-skilled, low-paid workers – the "McWorld." The empirical evidence indicates that work for millions of men and women remains vastly differentiated, heterogeneous, and diverse. Moreover, in a large proportion of work sites, work is systematically non-educative in the sense that there is little opportunity for formal or informal learning (Bratton, 1999).

The notion that knowledge and learning are key economic commodities has been historically located in the ideology of "investment in human capital." In the 1990s, the resurrection of Shultz's (1977) treatise served to perform a function of reification and legitimization for the "soft" learning-based HRM strategy and to fuel a powerful discourse on learning at work (Garrick, 1999). Finally, our critical evaluation is not intended to dismiss the potential of new work organizations and HRM practices for adult learning, but to help clarify the HRM – workplace-learning discourse. By examining the theoretical issues behind these various strategic options, we have had the opportunity to discover how contesting perspectives complement and negate each other, and we have also provided an antidote to the evangelical rhetoric of "success through learning" of many self-interested HRD practitioners.

Notes

1. The notable studies include Arthur (1994), Huselid (1995), McDuffie (1995) Ichniowski (1996), Pfeffer, (1998) in the U.S. and Betcherman *et al.* (1994) in Canada. In Britain, notable studies have been undertaken by Guest (1997), Addison *et al.* (2000) and Buyens and De Vos (2001).

CHAPTER 3

Groups, Work Teams and Learning

Knowing-behavior, which is intelligence, is social in two directions: it takes others into account and it calls forth more intelligent responses from others. If then learning adults wish to live in a social environment in which their intellectual alertness will count for something ... they will be as eager to improve collective enterprises, their groups, as they are to improve themselves. (Lindeman, 1926, p. 104)

There has never been a greater need for mastering team learning in organizations than there is today ... if teams learn, they become a microcosm for learning throughout the organization. (Senge, 1990, p.236)

Workgroups have been part of human social development for centuries; management consultants did not invent them. For thousands of years, humankind has lived in small hunting and gathering groups or in small farming or fishing groups. With the advent of industrial capitalism and the development of the factory system, small work groups became the exception rather than the rule. Prior to the factory system in Europe, in most households an adequate subsistence depended on a complex of various forms of work processes and wage-labour: regular, full-time paid employment was not the norm (Malcolmson, 1988). Most work centered on the home – the cottage – with household members using their own tools, organizing their own work, and relying upon the cooperation of neighbours to get things done. Social interaction, cooperation and coordinated action in workgroups was ubiquitous, with little of the radical social division of labour and machine technology we are familiar with today. Pre-industrial group working arrangements gave group members control over their hours, effort, and quality of paid work, as well allowed the group to control their own skill and knowledge. From a contemporary socio-cultural learning perspective, the dominant apprenticeship model found in the traditional trades and professions (e.g. blacksmith, carpenter, tinsmith, lawyer and physician) provided an "authentic" context in which "guided learning" at work was situationally located, tool dependent and socially interactive (Brown *et al.* 1989; Englesтröm, 2001; Lave and Wenger, 1991; Schõn, 1987; Vygotsky, 1978).

Artisan production, the putting-out system, and cooperatives were too inefficient to meet the needs of an emergent capitalist market economy. The solution to the problem was the factory. Orthodox historical theory asserts that the factory system, with its specialized machines and specialized human labour, developed largely because of technical reasons. Large-scale production, driven by water, and later by steam, power required a central site. A number of writers, notably Stephen Marglin (1974), offer an alternative interpretation. He argues that the primary reason for locating workers under one roof was a managerial, rather than a technical revolution. The factory provided the social infrastructure to subvert craft control through the minute division of workers and close supervision of the labour process, thereby offering a more efficient means of managing a recalcitrant workforce in order to increase productivity and profitability (see Thompson and McHugh, 2002).

STUDY TIP

The term "globalization" is used extensively for justifying the importance of workplace innovation and learning. Globalization is mistakenly used to describe any human activity that spans national borders. Globalization should be defined more precisely to describe unimpeded shifts in traditional patterns of international investment, manufacturing, and trade.

The popular discourse is that these interrelated changes need well-trained and highly skilled workers. But there is more to these economic and technological trends. Downsizing and new technologies have led to higher levels of unemployment and, for those still working, higher levels of work-related stress. Obtain a copy of *Work in Canada* (1993) edited by G. Lowe and H. Krahn, and read Part 3

"Canadian Workers and the New Global Economy" pp. 100-134. How do these readings differ? Is Canada capable of being competitive in the global economy? What are the implications of changes in the Canadian labour market for learning at work?

It is worth noting that, in recent decades, hierarchy and division of labour have become a "problem" to be solved by management. As we explained in our review of management theory in Chapter 2, specialization and the principles of "scientific management" undermine innovation, flexibility, and threaten to destroy work organizations. Paid work designed around teams, with workers engaged in "group" or "team" learning," is intended to resolve or transcend alleged problems of inflexibility, poor quality, low employee commitment and motivation. As Procter and Mueller (2000) suggest, work teams as a management concept have a history and the current interest in work teams is linked to "strategic" goals. Work teams and team learning should be understood in the context of the management debate over globalization and whether the workplace can be transformation into a more flexible system of working using teams in order to facilitate capital accumulation. However, it is important to pose several conceptual questions. What is a work group and how does it differ from a work team? How are we to interpret the current interest in work teams: as the latest in a succession of "management fads," or as a social technology to increase management control over labour? What theories underpin the idea of the work team? How is individual learning different from group or team learning? This chapter introduces the complex phenomenon of work groups and group learning. It focuses on how job design characteristics, such as autonomy, task and skill variety, interconnect with work groups and learning. The argument for "group learning" is placed within the context of contemporary management analysis of identifiable problems of traditional organizational designs and work processes.

CHAPTER OBJECTIVES

After reading this chapter, you should be able to:

1. Outline some basic concepts associated with groups and teams;

2. Explain the current popularity of teams in work organizations;

3. Describe the dynamics of team development and team members' interaction;

4. Critically analyze and understand the theories of "group learning;"

5. Articulate the connections between work groups, community groups and adult learning.

DEFINITIONS AND CONCEPTS

Trying to understand group learning is both intriguing and frustrating: intriguing because of the complexity of the phenomenon, frustrating because this same complexity seems to defy simple description. The words "group" and "team" are themselves elastic and interchangeable. It is important to distinguish between a cluster of people and what social psychologists call a *"psychological group."* The term psychological group is used in a descriptive sense to refer to the visible interactions of a cluster of individuals and the non-observable perceptions of members. A commonly used definition of a group is that offered by Johnson and Johnson (2000):

> A small group is two or more individuals in face-to-face interaction, each aware of positive interdependence as they strive to achieve mutual goals, each aware of his or her membership in the group, and each aware of the others who belong to the group. (2000, p.20)

In management parlance the word "team" is often applied in a normative sense to a special type of group with positive traits (Hertog and Tolner, 1997). It has connotations of collaboration, mutual support and shared skill, and decision-making (Buchanan, 2000, pp, 33-34) like a hockey or soccer team. The observation and implied criticism that "S/he is not a team player" or "This group is not a team" expresses the difference in meaning between "group" and "team" in management lexicon. Theorists argue that a team is not just a number of employees working together. A team, argue Johnson and Johnson, is "a set of interpersonal interactions structured to achieve established goals" (Ibidem 1997, p. 507). Similarly, Katzenbach and Smith, define a team as "a small number of people with complementary skills who are *committed* [our emphasis] to a common purpose, performance goals, and approach for which they hold themselves mutually accountable" (1994, p.45).

Another variant of "teams" has recently found its way in the management literature: the words "self-managed work team" (SMWT). The self-managed work team, insist Yeatts and Hyten (1998), are not the same as "work groups" as defined by Johnson and Johnson (2000). A self-managed work team (SMWT) is "a group of employees who are responsible for managing and performing technical tasks that result in a product or service being delivered to an internal or external customer" (Yeatts and Hyten, 1998, p.xiii). The difference between work groups and SMWT is explained in terms of degree of interdependency and accountability. The interdependence among SMWT members is typically high, and the accountability for the work focuses primarily on the team as a whole rather than the individual group member. Another distinguishing feature of SMWT is their longevity: SMWT are typically an integral part of a redesigned organizational structure brought together for long-term performance goals.

Formal definitions of *work teams* are not so different from that of a formal *work group*, which explains why both terms are used interchangeably in the organizational behaviour literature. However, use of the word "team" is not a question of simple semantics. Mainstream management rhetoric is awash with what Bendix (1956) called "a vocabulary of motivation." In this instance, management communication emphasizes the "team" (e.g. we must all pull together) metaphor to cover power disparities and conflicting interests between management and workers. Labour process theorist Michael Burawoy (1979) refers to this as the strategy of "secure and obscure": secure surplus labour and obscure the power relations that make this process possible. The effectiveness of the work configuration is the outcome of a complex set of group processes, including learning, whether employees are organized into a "work group" or a "work team."

REFLECTIVE QUESTION

How important is it to distinguish between a work group and a work team? Is the term "team" simply a masculine metaphor to cultivate cooperative relations and support management goals? What do you think of this argument?

THEORIZING WORK TEAMS

The theoretical interest in work teams draws upon classical human relations, socio-technical, and Japanese perspectives on organizational design (Benders and van Hootegem, 1999; Procter and Mueller, 2000; Yeatts and

Hyten, 1998). Contrary to the HRM rhetoric, many of the concepts inherent in the works of classical organizational theorists, for instance, Frederick Taylor, have influenced the design of work teams. Scientific management theory provides a "control-oriented" approach to work teams (Lawler, 1992). When managers have reconfigured work processes around the team concept, elaborate computer information systems have been developed alongside teams to support a control-oriented philosophy (Heatts and Hyten, 1998). One study found that while team members had increased autonomy in performing the work and additional responsibilities, management had increased control through a computerized production system. Management control-oriented approach can be conceptualized by the term "computer-controlled autonomy" (Bratton, 1992). In another study, Baldry *et al.* (1998) offer a scathing account of team working in white-collar work, arguing that evidence from their case studies demonstrates "that workers experience forms of team organization as being no less coercive than classically understood Taylorism" (1998, p.168-9). The authors use the term "Team Taylorism" to bridge this dichotomy between classical Taylorism and allegedly new "empowering" team working designs.

The pioneering work on human relations by Roethlisberger and Dickson, (1939), Maslow (1954), McGregor (1960) draw manager's attention to the importance of social relations within work groups. In the late 1970s, advocates of the human relations school also emphasized the need for worker participation in decision making related to their work to enable workers to satisfy "higher order" needs to improve productivity (Antony, 1978; Hackman, 1980). Thus the neo-human relations approach to job design, which refers to managerial styles that emphasize the ways in which workers' alleged "social needs" are or are not met through job design, emphasized the fulfillment of social needs by recomposing fragmented jobs.

Much of the early research on work teams in Europe was conducted within the framework of socio-technical systems theory. This theory developed from work on autonomous work teams in the British coal mining industry under the supervision of Trist and Bamforth (1951). These researchers proposed "responsible autonomy" be extended to primary work groups and that group members should learn more than one role, so that interchangeability of tasks would be possible within the group; this flexibility would permit the completion of significant parts or whole units. Trist and Bamforth's study showed that the labour process in mining could be better understood in terms of two systems: the technical system, including machinery and equipment, and the social system, including the social relations and interactions among the miners. Advocates of the socio-technical systems approach to organizational design later opined that work teams provide a work regime for achieving the "best match" between technical and social considerations or "systems." The term "best match" is used to describe the relationship between the social and technological aspects of the organization, where each responds to the demands of the other system (Yeatts and Hyten, 1998).

Attempts to implement the socio-technical systems approach have included work redesign to "enrich" jobs. The concept of *"job enrichment"* refers to a number of different processes of rotating, enlarging, and aggregating tasks. It increases the range of tasks, skills and control workers have over work, either individually or in teams. Job enrichment theory, also known as job characteristics theory, was made prominent by the work of Turner and Lawrence (1965) and Hackman and Oldham (1980). Building upon the work of Turner and Lawrence, Hackman and Oldham's (1980) model of job enrichment has been influential in the design of teams. It suggests a causal relationship between five core job characteristics, the worker's psychological state, and positive outcomes. The five core job characteristics are defined as:

· Skill variety: the degree to which the job requires a variety of different activities in carrying out the work, requiring the use of a number of the worker's skills and talents.

· Task identity: the degree to which the job requires completion of a "whole" and identifiable piece of work.

· Task significance: the degree to which the job has a substantial impact on the lives or work of other people.

· Autonomy: the degree to which the job provides substantial freedom, independence, and discretion to the worker in scheduling the work and in determining the procedures to be used in carrying it out.

· Feedback: the degree to which the worker possesses information of the actual results of her or his performance.

The model suggests the more a job possesses these five core job characteristics, the greater the motivating potential of the job. The existence of "moderators" – knowledge and skills, growth need strength, context satisfactions – explains why jobs, although high in motivating potential, in theory will not automatically generate high levels of motivation and satisfaction for all workers. Workers with a low growth need, it's posited, are less likely to experience a positive outcome when their job is enriched (see Figure 1).

Figure 1: The Job Characteristics Model

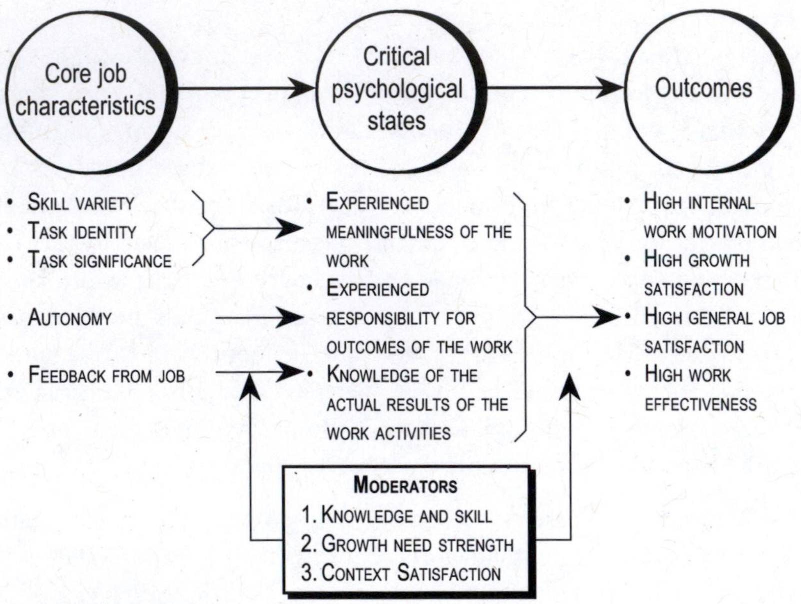

Source: Adapted from Hackman & Oldham (1980, p. 90)

This model recognizes the importance of individual cognition to individual achievement motivation and development goals. Individual learning is implicitly linked to the existence of "moderators" integral to the model. This means that an employee with a low "growth need" is less likely to experience a positive outcome when her or his work is "enriched." Hackman and Oldham (1980) extended their work on job design to encompass the redesign of work teams. These American researchers suggested that, under certain circumstances, self-managed teams could provide an alternative to individual job enrichment. Though there are some obvious connections between the job characteristic model and simplistic notions of "transformational" and individual cognition, research has not clarified the worker characteristics that should be considered prior to determining how to design work (Yeatts and Hyten, 1998) or how expanded notions of workplace learning – such as situative perspectives of learning with its focus on how learning is rooted in the culturally designed context of everyday life (Lave and Wenger, 1991; Rogoff, 1990) – impact on outcomes.

Self-managed teams incorporate five principles of "good" job design we discussed in Chapter 2. First, there is the principle of wholeness, whereby the scope of the job includes all tasks necessary to complete a product or process, thus satisfying the social need of achievement. Second, there is task variety whereby the worker acquires a range of different skills so that job flexibility is possible. Third, there is the incorporation of self-regulation, whereby the individual or group assumes responsibility for problem solving and quality control. Fourth, there is self-regulation of the speed of work. Fifth, there is a job structure that permits some social interaction, a degree of cooperation among workers and reflexivity. Figure 2 shows three important dimensions to team work: technical, governance and socio-cultural. The technical dimension refers to the level of knowledge, skills, integration and range of tasks assigned to the team. The governance dimension covers the extent of autonomy of the labour process. The socio-cultural dimension of team working relates to relationships, team dynamics and communities of practice.

Figure 2: Three Dimensions of Team Working: Technical, Governance and Socio-cultural

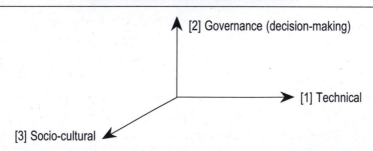

Drawing upon the work of Klein (1994), key work design principles can be used to compare alternative forms of work organization: Tayloristic (Type A) and Group (Type B) as shown in Figure 3.

Figure 3: A Comparison of Tayloristic, and Self-Managed Group Work

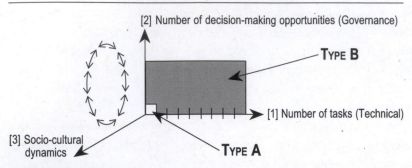

The horizontal axis represents the functional tasks that are required to produce the product or service (technical). The vertical axis represents decision-making activities and the degree of autonomy undertaken by individual workers or work groups (governance). This would include scheduling work activities and budgeting. Here the diagonal axis and the arrowed arc lines depict team dynamics. These three dimensions help us to graphically compare two alternative models of job design: Tayloristic and Self-managed Team Work (SMTW).

Type A job design model, the traditional Tayloristic/Fordist form of work structure, shown in this example involves one task with a minimal degree of autonomy. In terms of work-based learning it's an "impoverished learning regime" (Bratton, 1999). The goal is to reduce task-cycle time. The essence of this approach to job design is captured by the words of Henry Ford: "The idea is that man [*sic*] … must have every second necessary but not a single unnecessary second (Ford, 1922, and quoted in Beynon, 1984, p.33). Such a management philosophy does not place systematic training and learning at the centre of the business strategy. Despite all the rhetoric in the popular management press, the majority of workplaces in advanced capitalist countries have this type of environment, which means, if true, in most establishments noneducative work is systemic. The "McDonaldization of work" is the symbolic term often used by critics to capture the realities of work for many in the 21st century (Ritzer, 2000).

In this example, type B job design model, the self-managed team, numerous interlocking tasks with some control over the functional tasks, quality control and work scheduling. According to some writers, team working represents an ideal-type intrinsic learning regime: one that facilitates non-formal and informal learning at work *for* organizational goals. In this arrangement, work is designed to give workers a range of horizontal tasks – "functional flexibility" – and a high degree of autonomy: "members are expected to learn all functional tasks assigned to their team" (Klein, 1994, p.154). It is also associated with a participative leadership style designed to encourage informal learning in order to coax the best performance from workers. When an organization chooses this strategy, "enlightened" leadership is that which inspires informal learning and encourages workers to perform beyond their contract. Leadership agency is equated with adult learning facilitation principles, such as collaboration, reflection and self-directiveness. The intrinsic learning regime, it is argued, encourages workers to develop a questioning frame of mind and to place knowledge and skill acquisition in a broader context: in other words, it encourages workers continuously to learn, albeit within clear boundaries that respect private ownership and managerial prerogative.

Some types of small work teams may be compared to the traditional "craft" job design model, where defined skill sets are transmitted through formal training, either on-site or off-site, requiring workers to assimilate these skills or competencies in a manner prescribed by the trainer. This "instrumental learning regime" is typical of many organizations employing skilled craft workers, technicians or professionals, all of whom have relatively high degree of autonomy and skill (Bratton, 1999). The "craft" model is an early example of situated learning and mentoring or "guided learning," which forms the foundation for studies in situated cognition (Billett, 2001; 2003; Wilson, 1993). Figure 3 underscores that organizational controllers make strategic choices between breadth and depth of skills and degree of worker empowerment. While Tayloristic job design principles aims to minimize labour costs through minimal investment in training, the team working model emphasize investment in training and informal learning, albeit less than the traditional craft model.

WORK TEAMS: THE HALLMARK OF POSTMODERN ORGANIZATION

Management interest in work teams is a recent phenomenon. From early experiments in socio-technical job design techniques in the 1970s, teams have become the hallmark of postmodern work organizations in the 1990s. In theory a postmodern structure, the management structure is functionally decentralized, eclectic and participative. A strong culture and information networks binds together the organization's fluid diversity (Thompson, 1993).

REFLECTIVE QUESTION

What is postmodernism? To what extent does postmodernism represent a "yearning for alternatives" or a "distraction" from critical analysis of current trends in organizations. Read John Hassard's chapter, "Postmodernism and Organizational Analysis: an Overview," in J. Hassard and M. Parker (eds), *Postmodernism and Organizations* (1993). What do you think of the modernity-post-modernity discourse? Have the basic principles that define capitalist work organizations fundamentally changed, i.e. tendency to minimize costs, antagonistic employment relations over pay versus individual effort? How does your own experience of work organizations align with popular management rhetoric?

In the 1970s, there were limited experiments in designing post-bureaucratic structures. Automobile manufacturers in Germany, Sweden and the U.S reconfigured assembly lines so that machinery became organized into clusters or groups – referred to as "group technology" (Littler and Salaman, 1982). The most celebrated example of group technology and work teams was introduced in Sweden at a new Volvo car plant in 1987. The new assembly line avoided the traditional problems associated with short work cycles of only one or two minutes by enrichment. Teams improved productivity and quality, but the increase was not sufficient. The closure of Volvo's plant at Uddevalla in 1992 suggests that Taylorist and neo-Taylorist solutions still dominate management thinking in the automobile industry (Cressey, 1993). In the UK, autonomous work groups and teams expanded with the introduction of cellular manufacturing (Bratton, 1992). This system involves arranging machinery in a "cell" or a "U-shaped" configuration to enable the workers to complete a whole component, similar to the group technology principle. The job design underpinning a cellular work structure is the opposite of "Taylorism." A generalized, skilled machinist with flexible job boundaries substitutes for the specialized machinist operating one machine in a particular workstation. In the U.S. almost half of the largest corporations reported using self-managed teams for at least some of their workers (Cohen *et al*, 1996; Katzenbac and Smith, 1993; Womack, et al, 1990; Yeatts and Hyten,

1998). A Canadian study reported that over 20 per cent of electrical companies surveyed had implemented work teams (Betcherman, *et al.*, 1994).

STUDY TIP

Go to the following web sites: the Centre for the Study of Work Teams, www.workteams.unt.edu; DaimlerChrysler AG, www.daimlerchrysler.com; and Canadian Autoworkers Union, www.caw.ca. Why have organizations introduced teams? Do teams always improve organizational performance? Why are some trade unions skeptical of team-based working?

Although socio-technical theory had a strong influence on early experiments in group technology in the 1970s, it was the competitive success of Japanese manufacturing that captured the interests of European and North American managers and saw the widespread adoption of work teams in the last two decades of the 20th century. Peter Turnbull's (1986) account of new production methods at Lucas Electrical (UK) led to a spate of research and publications in self-managed work teams (SMWT). The Japanese model of work teams has three elements: flexibility, quality control, and minimum waste. First, flexibility is attained using multi-skilled work teams. Second, the philosophy of *Total Quality Control (TQC)* builds quality standards into the manufacturing process by making quality every worker's responsibility. Third, waste is eliminated or at least minimized by *just-in-time (JIT) production*, by producing the necessary components, in the necessary quantities at the necessary time. JIT production also attempts to modify worker behaviour and maximize commitment to managerial goals (Schonberger, 1982). Empirical research strongly suggests that the Japanese production model is more than a "passing fad" (see Jones, 1997). In the past two decades, for *avant-garde* management consultants and managers, on both sides of the Atlantic, Japanese management techniques have come to represent the state-of-the-art in team-based work design.

STUDY TIP

For an appreciation of how team-based work has been interpreted differently by observers, read Chapter 2 "The Day-to-Day Team Experience by Henry Sims and Charles Manz, in *Business Without Bosses* (1993), New York:Wiley and "Listening to Workers: The

Reorganization of Work in the Canadian Motor Vehicle Industry, by Wayne Lewchuck and David Robertson, in *Reshaping Work 2*, (ed.) C. Schenk and J. Anderson, Aurora, ON: Garamond Press. How do the two accounts of team-based work agree and how do they differ? Are there situations in which team-based production produce a "win-win" situation, that is, one in which management and workers equally benefit?

Job design techniques are introduced by managers in different forms, in different manufacturing sectors, and at different times (Procter and Mueller, 2000). In addition, the nature of work teams varies considerably between organizations, depending on whether they are engaged in small- or large-batch production, or provide a service. Nonetheless, managers have focused on teams and the potential value of workplace learning to help improve organizational performance motivated by the prospect of connecting the synergy of teams with corporate goals. This strategy has received a strong endorsement from academics (see, for example, Cunha and Louro, 2000; Edmondson, 2002; Foley, 2001; Kasl, Marsick and Dechant, 1997; Senge, 1990). Thus, the perceived connections between job design, learning, and organizational performance needs to be appreciated to understand the current wave of corporate interest in teams and team learning.

PARADOX IN WORK TEAM DESIGN

Paradox is evident in work team design. As already discussed, self-managed work teams can empower workers to make decisions over their work and simultaneously increase management's control over work activities. This is achieved using both "hard" technology (e.g. computers) and "social" technology (e.g. group norms). There are competing perspectives offered by academics on organizational change such as new technology and teams. One, the "labour process" theory, draws on Marxist perspectives and seeks to explain organizational change in terms of capitalist imperatives to control labour and maximize profit (Braverman, 1974). Critical analyses of "new" management strategies to engage workers in the labour process through "job enrichment" provided an important corrective to the popular view that such work structures enhanced learning and the quality of the work experience. In what is a classic case study of the period, Theo Nichols and Huw Beynon (1977) provide an engaging study into the effects of job enrichment on the everyday experience of chemical workers. One worker at "Chemco" explained his workday like this: "You move from one boring, dirty, monotonous job to another boring, dirty, monotonous job. And then to another boring, dirty, monotonous job. And somehow you're supposed to come out of it all 'enriched.' But I never feel 'enriched' – I just feel knackered." (1977, p. 16) More recently, contributors to Wardell *et al.* (1999) have argued that the same dynamics identified by Nichols and Beynon remain today.

> ### REFLECTIVE QUESTION
>
> Which perspective on organizational change seems more realistic to you? Who are the prime beneficiaries of new technology and team-based working? Read Chapter 12, "The Modern Corporation" in H. Braverman's (1974) text, *Labor and Monopoly Capital* (1974). Is Braverman correct when he asserts that the overall purpose of all administrative controls is the elimination of uncertainty? What implications does Braverman's analysis have for workplace learning?

An alternative view, within the labour process perspective, acknowledges the indeterminate nature of the outcomes and that numerous variables and forces mediate the relationship between the capitalist imperative of accumulation and the control of work (Knights and Willmott, 1986). This thesis is supported by John Bratton's (1992) study. He found that although workers were empowered, managers had more control because peer-group pressure created a compliant work culture. This is how one team member explained peer-group pressure to adopt effort norms:

> I think it's a matter of conscience. A person who under the old system might go away for an hour, now he will think twice: Are they [co-workers] going to think they are carrying me because I've been away? … Because you are a close-knit community in the cell system. You get niggly remarks: "Where have you been all morning?" That sort of thing, and it gradually works its way in psychologically. (Team member, quoted in Bratton, 1992: 186)

Similarly, Don Wells (1993) notes how the workers' discipline was more punitive than the managers:

There was tension by workers against workers who were not pulling their weight. Peer pressure in the groups was very important. [Team members] are tougher on [fellow workers] than management. (Wells, 1993: 75)

Self-managed teams create a work culture that reproduces the conditions of workers' own subordination, because team members perceive a moral obligation to work hard, to "put a full day in," because of peer-group pressure or clan control, thereby unwittingly creating a "coercive culture system." (Burawoy, 1979)

In their account of team learning processes, Kasl *et al* (1997) unwittingly provide further evidence of the control culture generated by work teams. When one particular work team "failed" some team members left the company, others worked on "disheartened."

The team became the laughingstock of the whole company and the people who weren't involved in it at all, the people who worked on a different floor, would walk right in and say, "How's logistics, ha ha ha?" They heard about it, it was like this big disaster. (Kasl, Marsick and Dechant, 1997, p.238)

Some researchers have discussed paradox in another way. They have challenged the popular logic that self-managed work teams lead to a more skilled workforce. The debate has centered upon the ambiguity involving alternative scenarios of "upskilling" and "deskilling" of workers. On the one hand, Piore and Sabel (1984) argue that *self-managed work teams (SMWT)* exemplify "the re-emergence of the craft paradigm." On the other hand, detractors argue that SMWTs give limited empowerment do not reverse the general "deskilling" trend but have a tendency to increase the range of tasks and the intensity of work (Clarke, 1997; Malloch, 1997; Sayer, 1986; Tomaney, 1990; Turnbull, 1986). Paul Thompson (1989), for example, argues that many team and job enrichment schemes "offer little or nothing that is new, and are often disguised forms of intensified [managerial] control" (1989, p. 141). Using Foucault's "panopticon" metaphor Barbara Townley (1994) explains that job enrichment work practices function to "reconstitute the individual as a productive subject" in order to enhance managerial control. Others offer more optimistic analyses, in which the outcomes of team working are less pre-determined. Whether work teams results in "upskilling," "deskilling," or work satisfaction or intensification depends on many factors, including batch-size, managerial choice power relationships, and negotiation (Bratton, 1992 ;Lowe, 2000).

GROUP DYNAMICS

Redesigning the labour process around teams does not necessarily lead to improved performance. Managers and workers alike must learn to work in team-based structures. This is the lesson from the socio-technical approach to organizational design, which recognizes the dialectic relationship between the technical and social aspects of the system. Group or team members not only learn new skills and knowledge resulting from an enlargement of tasks, they must, equally important, learn to work together in a team.

Team dynamics is the study of human behaviour in groups. According to Johnson and Johnson (2000), this field studies the nature of groups, group development, and the interrelations between individuals and groups. Group dynamics or processes emphasize changes in the pattern of activities and the subjective perceptions of individual group members and their active involvement in group life. Studies in group dynamics by mainstream researchers draw attention to two sets of processes that underlie group dynamics: task-orientated activities and maintenance-oriented activities. Task-orientated activities undertaken by the group are aimed at accomplishing goals or "getting the job done." Maintenance-oriented activities, on the other hand, point to the subjective perceptions of group members and their active involvement in keeping acceptable standards of behaviour and a general state of well-being within the group. Conventional wisdom argues that the two processes constantly seek to co-exist, and over-emphasis of one realm at the expense of the other causes discontent and withdrawal. An effective group or team is one that creates a reasonable compromise between both realms (see Crawley, 1978; Hertog and Tolner, 1998).

Mainstream research on group dynamics emphasizes the importance of developmental stages a group must pass through – groups are formed, they consolidate, and they disperse. Typically, it is argued a group must reach the mature stage before it achieves maximum performance. Of course, it is also acknowledged that not all groups pass through all the stages, and some groups can become fixed in the middle and remain ineffective and inefficient. A good example of the life cycle metaphor is Tuckman and

Jensen's (1977) five-stage cycle of growth model: forming, storming, norming, performing, and adjourning. Tuckman and Jensen's model is predicated on the premise that a group must pass through each stage before being able to move on to the next stage, and every transition holds the potential risk of regression to an earlier stage. Organizational behaviour theorists with a managerial perspective tend to relate the five-stage model to levels of performance, group productivity being higher after the group has passed the second – norming – stage. What makes a work group effective is more complex than this model acknowledges, however.

Tuckman and Jensen's (1977) five-stage model has become entrenched in management training, but it has been strongly criticized by other researchers of group dynamics. Theresa Kline (1999), for example, asserts that the model has been shown "to be of little or no assistance in getting teams to perform better" (p. 34). Gersick (1988) offered an earlier critique of Tuckman and Jensen's model. In her work on project teams, Gersick found what she calls "punctuated equilibrium" to explain group development. In essence, the "punctuated equilibrium" model characterizes work groups as exhibiting long periods of inertia interspersed with shorter busts of activity initiated primarily by their member's awareness of the impending completion time. Gersick's findings suggest that not all groups develop in a universal linear fashion. Kline (1999) is critical of laboratory-based research on group development. She points out that Tuckman and Jensen's model was developed from work with therapy, laboratory or training groups, not "real teams in real contexts." She argues that the "contextual variable" is an essential tool for understanding group dynamics and group performance.

Although alternative research suggests that not every group goes through all development stages, Tuckman and Jensen's model can be a useful heuristic for understanding group dynamics and why some groups fail to perform. A group might be ineffective and inefficient because its goals have not been agreed on, and individuals are pulling in different directions. Alternatively, individuals might have the tendency to dismiss other's ideas and feelings, which leads to low trust among the group. For all these reasons, effective group functioning and learning might be hindered. The main conclusion drawn from the models briefly reviewed here is that an understanding of team learning at work has to take into account group dynamics. Moreover, the efficacy of a team is dependent on the learning process of individual member's experience through successive developmental stages. This reinforces Peter Senge's (1990) argument that team learning is critical because teams, not individual employees, are the fundamental learning unit in the workplace.

LEARNING IN TEAMS

Redesigning work around multitask teams has significant implications for learning in the workplace. Management must invest in work-based learning and workers must expand their knowledge and skill-sets in order to perform a new repertoire of tasks. But *how* do team members learn, what are the key processes of learning? A theory of team learning must provide answers to six important questions: [1] What do team members learn?; [2] How do they learn, what reflexive group processes facilitate learning?; [3] What is the relationship between individual cognition and situated cognition?; [4] What is the effect of the inherent tensions in the capitalist employment relationship on the key processes of learning?; [5] How are team learning processes shaped by class, gender and race?; and [6] Do team learning processes offer new forms of oppression and control in the workplace?

The theory of expansive learning (Engeström (1987; 2001) provides a helpful theoretical framework for exploring team learning. However, as we explained in Chapter 2, the empirical evidence on the six questions we have identified as important is rudimentary at the very least. Given that academic research, in contrast to "research" conducted by management consultants, into work-based learning provides a case where the "gate keepers" to the research, that is management, are typically more powerful than the researchers themselves (Easterby-Smith et al. 1991), it should not be a surprise to readers that critical studies of team learning is an under-developed area of inquiry. With this caveat, the following section examines two models of team learning.

Yrjö Engeström's (1987, 2001) model expands Vygotsky's (1978) famous triangular model that envisions learning as a social process: individual and team agency occurring through interlocking human activity systems that includes the object (e.g. problem(s), the perspectives of the individuals (subjects), and mediating artifacts (social language, tools, and technologies), shaped by rules and social norms, power, a community of practice, and division of labour or job design (Figure 4).

Figure 4: A Structure of Team Agency

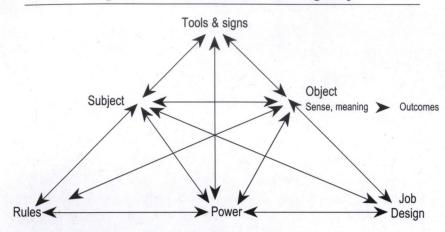

Source: Adapted from Engeström, 1987, p.78)

The "third generation" of activity theory incorporates five central principles: [1] a collective, artifact-mediated and object-oriented human activity system; [2] a community of practice of multiple voices, traditions and interests; [3] historicity, that is, learning is shaped and becomes transformed over periods of time; [4] contradictions in the capitalist labour process drive change and development; and [5] expansive transformations in an activity system are accomplished through contradictions when "the object and motive of the activity are re-conceptualized to embrace a radically wider horizon of possibilities than in the previous mode of activity" (Engeström, 2001, p.137). Learning in self-managed work teams using this theoretical framework can be understood as the sum of the social interactions of team members, line-managers and users (subject/producers/customers), mediated by interlocking levels of power.

In their analysis of team learning Kasl, Marsick, and Dechant (1997) conceptualize team learning as a social process through which "a group creates knowledge for its members, for itself as a system, and for others" (p.229) in the organization. The team learning model developed by Elizabeth Kasl and her colleagues is derived empirically from data from two U.S. case studies. It attempts to address one key question, *how* teams learn in the workplace. The authors posit that team members evolve through stages of maturity in their learning capacity, moving from "fragmented to pooled to synergistic" modes of learning. Using elements of grounded theory and content analysis, the researchers coded employee transcripts for learning processes and conditions that helped or hindered learning in work teams. Team learning is described as a "dynamic process" in which learning processes, as well as the conditions that support them, change qualitatively as the team potentially journey through three stages or modes of team learning: fragmented, pooled, and synergistic. This perspective recognizes that the context – the historical, material and cultural milieu – is an integral aspect of learning (Rogoff, 1984). Comparisons can also be made here with Tuckman and Jensen's (1977) well- known theory of team development. Figure 5 summarizes the interconnectedness of the process: team-learning conditions, team-learning processes, team-learning modes and outcomes.

Figure 5: Team-learning Conditions and Processes, Team-learning Modes, and Team-learning Outcomes

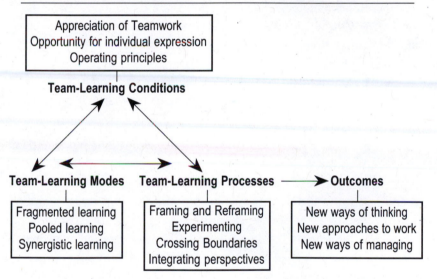

Source: Adapted from Kasl, Marsick and Dechant (1997)

Based upon their interpretation of interview transcripts, Kasl *et al.,* explain that in the fragmented mode, the team focuses on meeting the needs and enhancing the value of the individual contributor. In the pooled mode, the team continually balances individual needs against the team's needs. In the third mode, synergistic, members acquire a deep understanding of the creative potential in teams. Learning in the synergistic mode is associated with collective "insight" when the group experiences learning that is holistic and collective. However, Kasl et al.'s research is inclined to be preoccupied with maximizing team members' performance for formal organizational ends, as does most of the mainstream literature. In other words, it is a managerialist perspective on team learning. This description of synergistic team learning illustrates the point:

> All team members reported in their interviews that an unanticipated crisis in March was the force that helped them coalesce as a *real* [our emphasis] team ... The crisis was a production deadline ... Everyone "chipped in ... did what it took" ... The team was proud that it was able to complete the project deadline. Nonetheless, Amy and Peter found Leroy's behavior erratic during the crisis ... Leroy missed deadlines and was tardy or absent from work without adequate notice ... For his part, Leroy thought that the organization was not sufficiently respectful of family values. The culture of the organization demanded that people work late if needed ... After the crisis ... With help from an HR-sponsored training program that taught team members how to give each other feedback, the ... team focused on Leroy's issues ... [As a supervisor observed] "they discussed a very delicate performance issue openly, honestly, and it was very obvious that it was hard for them to do, that they were not doing it to pick on this person." (1997, p. 235)

The team in this example functioned in the synergistic mode and employed the learning processes outlined in the Kasl *et al*. model. That is, experimentation was "frequent and bold, leading to new frames," "taken-for-granted" HR practices were challenged, and "boundary crossing" occurred as the team gathered information from outside sources (HR department). Taken from a critical perspective, we can conclude from these informal learning activities that a "real" team is one that meets organizational performance goals and adopts self-regulatory practices on its members. We can also suggest the everyday experience – "lived reality" – of team-based work provides a dynamic milieu, a type of informal "pedagogy," that enables workers to cope with, and shape management strategies.

Although not directly related to adult learning theory, the labour process discourse sheds light on the relationship between changing job designs, skills, and informal learning. Rainbird (1988), for example, noted: "The process of learning the skills required for a new job occurs informally, through one person training another ... new skills are being acquired without the legitimization of a formal training period (Rainbird, 1988, p. 171, quoted by Garrick, 1998, p.8). John Bratton's (1992) critical study of self-managed work teams described how the new work regimes affected workers' skill sets:

> Before the cell system was introduced, I was on small turning for three months. Whereas now, I can be anywhere in the day. Yesterday, I was on the big planer-miller, then on the milling machine, then back on the planer-miller. I might be on the grinder this afternoon. You never know what's going to crop up. Team member (age 43) (Bratton, 1992, pp. 166-8)

The qualitative data suggests that a high-involvement, self-management team strategy requires a high-involvement learning regime. This link between work-based learning and workplace governance has been a theme in radical politics for many years. For example, 19th – century social critics, William Morris and Antonio Gramsci, were advocates for both the reorganization of work and workers' control of production.

Academic researchers, especially in North America, have been occupied in recent years with investigating the relationship between work teams and a number of measures of organizational performance (see, for example, Betcherman, et al., 1994; Ichniowski et al., 1996; Ramsey et al., 2000). Prominent in this discussion is the concept of high-performance work teams and "bundles" of innovative HR practices attaining synergistic performance benefits. Ramsey's et al. (2000) study questions the prevailing view that positive performance comes from synergistic team working via positive employee learning. However, more conclusive research needs to be done in this area.

A team's belief system affects learning. The team's belief system – its understanding of its task and of itself as a team – it's argued "structures its capacity for learning" (Slepian, 1993, p.18). As mentioned earlier, a related body of literature on "situated cognition," "situated learning," and "expansive learning," with its focus on communities of practice, has emerged on learning in the workplace, which contends that it is only possible to really comprehend adult learning from the perspective of the fully contextualized, participatory social relations. Thus, Arthur Wilson (1993) argues, "to understand the central place of context in thinking and learning, we have to recognize that cognition is a social activity that incorporates the mind, the body, the activity, and the ingredients of the setting in a complex interactive and recursive setting"(p. 72). Similarly, Järvinen and Poikela (2001) emphasize that context and social relations are central to adult learning, " [i]ndividual learning ... is always context-bound. Group learning cannot be described without the individual, just as organizational learning cannot be explained without individuals and groups" (p. 286).

Team learning is typically presented as a complex phenomenon but all too often it is assumed to be essentially unproblematic, essentially offering "a wonderful opportunity for individuals and groups to mobilize their (sometimes hidden) capacities" (Harris, 1996, p. 169). Others have emphasized that the team's learning is circumscribed by market imperatives and employer/employee conflicts, and that learning can be used to create effective, more invisible power/knowledge regimes to control workers' behaviour. Drawing on the critical reading of situated learning as well as cultural historical activity theory, Sawchuk (1999a; 1999b; 2003; see also Livingstone and Sawchuk, 2000) has argued that everyday learning is conflictual, sometimes ratifying forms of class conflict, as well as gender and racial divisions. Writers using Foucault's theory of knowledge-power have also argued that self-management and concomitant informal learning can be used to strengthen management control over the labour process (Garrick, 1998; Sewell, 1998; Townley, 1994). The dominant, legitimized culture perpetuated around self-managed teams extols workers to work beyond contract for the "common" good and to engage in self-regulatory norms. At one level, work teams and team learning management strategies appear to empower and develop workers. However, at another level, the work team model shifts the focus away from the hierarchical nature of organizations, hierarchical control processes, inherent conflicts of interest between managers and workers, and dominant power relationships, and mechanisms of self-control (e.g. Alvesson and Billing, 1992). The combined effect of this restructuring is a shift towards the individualization of the employment relationship.

Management theory which is concerned with looking down from the "top" of the organization – giving most attention to those who manage and control – focuses on how work teams are best able to enhance learning and improve productivity. A contrasting perspective is one concerned with looking at the "bottom" of the hierarchy – focusing on those who are controlled – tending to emphasize that learning in the workplace is by no means a neutral process; it takes place within a contested arena. Moreover, individual and team learning is shaped and determined by social choice and negotiation and a complex configuration of opportunities and constraints, *inter alia*, market imperatives, the nature of the product or service, management strategies, workers' level of skills and development, and power relations. Thus, for example, when an firm's survival and profitability is contingent upon producing high value-added products using highly skilled workers, management is much more likely to choose an employment strategy that encourages broadly based participatory and learning processes in the workplace.

GROUP LEARNING UNDER CAPITALISM

"By God, this strike has been a bloody education."[1]

This quote provides a segue to help us shift our focus from those who control work arrangements and the basic "curriculum" of workplace learning to those who are controlled. Although some writers, (see, for example, Billet, 2001) have discussed the way traditional work arrangements and coercive authority regimes help to encourage intentional and unintentional learning, most theorists have ignored how workers learn through union-led activities. Workers learn *at* work, for example, that improvement in their terms and conditions of employment can be better accomplished by combining into trade unions. In turn, workers, through the direct experience of strikes and other forms of industrial action, learn collectivist values as opposed to the more individualist values current in society. In addition, in a few cases workers have challenged the priorities and purposes of capitalist production by developing worker-owned and controlled cooperatives.

The worksite is a rich arena for learning. Within the socio-cultural constructivist framework (see Fenwick, 2001), we contend that understanding the social dynamics derived from antagonistic capitalist employment relations is essential to developing a more inclusive theory of work-based learning that crosses institutional boundaries of the paid workplace, the home, and the community. Direct action in the workplace (e.g. strikes, occupations, and union campaigns to defend public services) offer everyday experiences for workers and groups to learn *in* and *beyond* the workplace. Workers' agency give quite a new meaning to David Beckett's "hot action at work" (2001) but in principle and in practice illustrate how learning is structured by the dispute activities and goals of the collective voice. For example, a strike over the pay-effort bargain – captured by the union axiom "a fair day's pay for a fair day's work" – may offer a learning experience on the nature of labour markets, whereas a dispute to prevent the closure of a hospital or a factory or the opening of a for-profit health facility may potentially offer experiences to learn about global capitalism's self-cannibalizing tendencies, "vested interests," NAFTA, and the role of financial institutions and governments in the global economy. Not surprisingly, this form of workplace and community learning does not enjoy "legitimization" either through formal certification or informal management recognition, but drawing upon Billet's (1999) analysis these everyday learning experiences and outcomes cannot be considered *ad hoc* or incidental. They are a potent instrument for ongoing authentic opportunities to reinforce and extend individuals', trade unions', and communities' knowledge. Hence, collective and union-led strike activity represents another type of informal pedagogy.

This situated framework for adult learning dates back to the 18th century European industrial revolution. Early socialists debated the political significance of learning under capitalism. Karl Marx and Frederick Engels argued that the development of industrial capitalism, as an agency of revolutionary change, forces together workers whose common experience of exploitation leads them to form trade unions. In their early writings Marx and Engels suggested that trade unions provide a training ground for working class activities and that union organization would ultimately challenge the organization of the capitalists:

> These strikes … are the strongest proof that the decisive battle between bourgeoisie and proletariat is approaching. They are the military school of the working men in which they prepare themselves for the great struggle which cannot be avoided … And, as schools of war, the unions are unexcelled. (F. Engels, *The Conditions of the Working Class in England,* Moscow: Progress Publishers, 1975, p. 261)

Subsequent writings of Marx and Engels, and later radical writers, however questioned the ability of trade unions to act as a social change agent (see Spencer, 1989 for a discussion on this).

Unions as radical change agents in society might have their limitations, but radical adult educators have shown how everyday life experiences of workers and their union experiences have the capacity to create the conditions of a rich learning process. Bruce Spencer (1989) argues that strikes, factory occupations, and the development of workers' alternative business plans provides an experience that can challenge managerial hegemony. Moreover, unions "Provide an experience outside the dominant ideology, an experience that emphasizes collectivism as a method of progress for groups of workers – in opposition to individualistic competitive emphasis of capital (Spencer, 1989, p.16). Workers engaged in industrial action learn about the politics of conducting a strike, how to write letters to the press, organize a strike fund, to communicate to wider audiences, as well as how to negotiate with managers. In other words, they learn about the social relations of work or "what it means to be a worker and take orders from supervisors (Spencer, 2001, p. 33). Further, this informal learning is an essential means of maintaining the solidarity among the strikers and their supporters in the community.

Canadian social histories of the working-class and the labour movement illustrate the importance of union activities and working-class community activities as a rich source of informal learning (see, for example, Bowen, 1982). Those scholars who align themselves with the liberatory tradition in adult education, as we do, have continued to document informal learning in working class communities. In Nova Scotia, the Antigonish Movement, through co-operative stores, lobster factories and local credit unions, enabled "common people" to learn about "some of the reasons for their economic exploitation and political dependency and exercise some control over their life-situations" (Welton, 2001, p. 255). Peter Sawchuk (2000) captures the informal learning arising from the everyday cultural life of union members like this:

> How we actually learn things … I'll give you a quick example. Four people in this room learned about health and safety the hard way. They learned about workers' compensation the hard way. Only through their experience. They never went to any union course – they learnt it when the employer fucked them … That's the best … experience a worker can get because it cuts through all the nonsense because it hits you directly, it gives you time to think and to read and to ask questions and start understanding what it's all about. (Chemical worker quoted by Sawchuk, 2000, p. 1)

Learning under capitalism is certainly not limited to the workplace. Social activism, such as engagement in community food banks, low-cost housing groups, anti-poverty groups, anti-globalization groups, and environmental campaign groups, provide a distinctive learning process whereby people learn, not only to challenge the *status quo*, but begin to articulate a progressive agenda for their communities, one grounded in local democracy and control and principles of sustainable development. The burgeoning field of workplace learning scholarship tends to ignore the fact that much profound informal learning is a result of workplace unionism, collective struggles, and community activism: groups of men and women challenging power structures which control workplace or community decision making. In this context Lindeman's (1926) declaration that the purpose of adult education is "to put meaning into the whole of life" puts these everyday educative experiences in union locals and the community front and centre of liberatory adult education (see Chapter 6 for more discussion of this theme).

REFLECTIVE QUESTION

Drawing on your own work experience and your reading to date, do you think it is useful to consider collective and union-led strike activity a type of informal pedagogy?

SUMMARY

We began this chapter by reviewing the key job design principles of small work teams and noted some general tendencies. We gave details of how learning and workers' control is built into team structures, although we also discussed how some theorists have critiqued mainstream assumptions on this tendency. We discussed how design choices are guided by managerial philosophies, which are centred on meeting the exigencies imposed by market forces. We have argued that one dimension of workplace learning is inextricably linked to management's job design strategies and leadership styles in the workplace. Despite all the attention given to the need for "employee development" and lifelong learning in the literature, we explained that in the majority of contemporary workplaces in North America, Europe, and other advanced capitalist economies (e.g. Australia) non-educative paid work is systemic and, indeed, most work structures discourage learning, let alone lifelong learning (see also Hager, 2003). Critical observers of capitalism have identified increasingly polarized work opportunities, the growth of non-standard forms of employment, and social inequality. Non-standard employment contracts not only facilitate a "looser contractual relationship" between the workplace and the worker, they raise the controversial argument whether women have equal opportunities for workplace learning, either formal or informal (Boud and Garrick, 1999).

Scholars have emphasized that a firm's "competitive advantage "can be achieved equally well using two management strategies: a cost-cutting numerical flexibility strategy (extensive use of part-time and low-skilled workers) or a developmental job flexibility (use of full-time and high-skilled workers) strategy requiring, amongst other things, extensive workplace learning. From the second management strategy has emerged the notion of the "high-performance work system" which entails managements ceding a degree of control to workers and introducing more "humanizing" or "progressive" HRM policies. These include measures to enlarge tasks based around team working and improve the knowledge, skills and learning opportunities for workers discussed in this chapter. Some types of work arrangements, in particular self-managed work teams, represent a type of informal "pedagogy."

The second general tendency we emphasized is that the workplace learning discourse is related to the broader discourse on "high-performance work system," "soft" strategic HRM practices, and market economics. The essence of the argument goes like this. Management reaps positive performance outcomes by actively fostering, or at least allowing, space for the co-operative and learning potential of workers. On the other hand, workers have a stake in maintaining the existence of the organization in which they are employed and develop their own intellectual abilities.

We contend that the redesign of work within the context of global capitalism does not automatically lead to widespread benefits – echoes here of the technology debate in the late 70s on how the computer "chip" would create the "leisure society" (see Bratton and Waddington, 1981) – including an "educative workplace." In market-driven organizations the *raison d'être* of work teams is higher productivity and profit. But we have acknowledged that workers are not necessarily passive recipients of management's strategies: workers have the capacity to resist, or at least modify, management plans, including a workplace learning strategy. Furthermore, we have noted in this chapter, an issue developed more fully in Chapter 5, that workers and their collective organizations – trade unions – play an important role in shaping the workplace and workers' learning experiences.

We examined two theoretical frameworks for analyzing the complex interconnections between work arrangements, group dynamics, and workplace learning. Team learning, as we conceive it, is best understood as collective agency – a matrix of trail and error, boundary crossing, framing and reframing, experimentation, reflexivity, and communities of practice – shaped by group dynamics, mediating artifacts, and embedded in rules, interlocking levels of power, and division of labour that stem from societal social structures.

We went on to suggest that collective action in the workplace and the community (e.g. strikes, occupations and union campaigns) represents a type of informal "pedagogy." Given the nature of capitalist employment relations, union-led activities are a powerful instrument for ongoing authentic opportunities to reinforce and extend individuals, unions, and community knowledge.

All this suggests team-learning practices and workplace performance linkages are likely to be different depending on the choice made by key decision-makers, the political process associated with organizational design, acceptance or resistance by workers to change, and the development and motivation of individuals. A universal workplace learning thesis, associated with the learning organization paradigm, is therefore difficult to sustain long term because of complex countervailing technical and social determinants in capitalist production.

Notes

1. Striker quoted in T. Lane and K. Roberts, (1971). *Strike at Pilkington,* London: Collins/Fontana. P.201.

CHAPTER 4

Organizational Learning and the Learning Organization

I came to see that these very people who perform productive tasks were themselves creating the experience out of which education might emerge. (Lindeman, 1926, p. xi)

The metaphor of the Learning Organization could well [be] translated into an instrument for control so that the ambiguities of organizational life, potentially fruitful for learning and creativity, are suppressed in favour of a dominant and stable set of beliefs and interests. (Coopey, 1996, p. 365)

Learning Organization is a broad term that is used to describe any organization that employs various learning principles as a means of coping with current challenges. These challenges arise from increased competition and globalization, the result of both real and perceived changes in the economy, and a dissatisfaction with existing organizational development techniques. The focus of learning paradigms is on how people learn in the organization and what types of learning are considered important (Matthews 1999). The concept of organizational learning is far from new. Indeed, it is rooted in earlier organizational development (OD) techniques, including participatory management and self-managed work teams. By 1994, with the publication of Peter Senge's book, *"The Fifth Discipline"* (1990; 1994), the concepts of the learning organization (LO) and organizational learning (OL) were firmly elevated from academic theories to the cutting edge in the management of organizational change processes (Abrahamson, 1996; Jackson, 2001; Kieser, 1997). Once organizational learning and the learning organization became a management fad (Macdonald, cited in Case 1994) interest in it was assured.

This status was the result of two related factors; a combination of management consultants embracing the latest organizational development techniques and organizational change, which had become an imperative in organizations. Yet, Rylatt (1994) argues that workplace learning goes beyond change, to a level of commitment and opportunity. Thus, Peter Senge's five disciplines appealed to the discourse of the time, and the notion of the learning organization was embraced as the way to increase organizational effectiveness and productivity. Senge joined the ranks of management "gurus," and was duly credited with influencing organization reform.

This overwhelming acceptance of workplace learning and the creation of learning organizations as another method of change may seem surprising. But in recent years, a recurring theme of the change management discourse has been to adopt a coherent or programmatic approach to change. *Change for the sake of change* has become a mantra among academics and practitioners alike (Helms Mills 2003). Managers are being influenced by "gurus" promoting change as the key component of organizational success. This is reinforced by media promoting the idea that change can be dealt with through straightforward solutions, and consultants implementing the work of the gurus with simple and easy to execute techniques (Ibid.). The cyclical, faddish nature of change programmes contributes to a need to adopt the latest offering of the change gurus and organizations are strongly influenced by the desire to succeed where others have failed. Little attention is given to whether or not such programmes benefit the company, or are even necessary. The emphasis on change programmes has switched focus over time, from ways to improve employee satisfaction to the present day goal of customer-driven corporate effectiveness (Ibid.). As a management development technique becomes recognized, and once the financial value of promoting the concept of the learning organization is established, the principles of creating a learning organization become an "easy sell" to companies seeking readymade solutions for coping with continuously changing economic trends.

The learning organization literature is particularly appealing because it stresses the importance of continuous individual and team-based learning focusing on developing and refining work-related problem-solving skills. The notion of the organizational learning is associated with a range of practices, including an emphasis on self-management, matrix-type structures, dedicated training and learning support and flexibility in working practices (Sims *et al.,* 1993). Proponents offer a prescriptive approach emphasizing trust, empowerment, and sharing as the necessary ingredients for creating a learning organization. Consequently, one of the main reasons for the popularity of this type of organization has been its ability to undo the backlash of bad feeling created by previous de-humanizing programmes, (such as re-engineering, which reduced worker input to value-added versus non value-added). The learning organization emphasizes the importance of community and the creation of a more humanistic workplace, and has led to the creation of a new management paradigm now used as a framework to analyze organizational outcomes.

The learning organization literature is the focus of a number of different theorists, and confusion still surrounds the differences between the learning organization (LO) and organizational learning (OL). Some theorists suggest that there is little difference between the two, while others compare OL and LO to process versus structure. Generally the writings in both these areas can be distilled into a common set of principles, which stress the need for organizational re-invention in order to create continuous learning and innovation through empowerment, open dialogue, co-operation, shared learning, and the creation of a common vision (Fenwick 1998). In this way, a learning organization which is the result of organizational learning (OL) will be able to react effectively to environmental threats by employing practices that allow it to be in a continuous state of change. Matthews (1999) suggests that the development of a community of learners into a learning organization is the ultimate goal of workplace learning. The learning organization paradigm has its champions and detractors, and there are different underlying assumptions within these two perspectives.

CHAPTER OBJECTIVES

After reading this chapter, you should be able to

1. Understand the concepts relating to the learning organization paradigm, including the differences between organizational learning and the learning organization;

2. Understand how the organizational learning paradigm fits within the workplace learning literature;

3. Outline the different approaches to organizational learning;

4. Critically analyze the concepts of the learning organization paradigm;

5. Link the problems of organizational learning to functionalist/ managerialist and critical analysis perspectives

DEFINITIONS AND CONCEPTS

The concepts of organizational learning have been implicitly accepted as part of the management of change literature for a long time. However, in recent years, fuelled by interest in globalization and the new economy, the learning organization has become a metaphor for what organizations should *be* in order to remain competitive. This has led, in turn, to a paradigm shift in strategic management away from the "hard" HRM approaches used in re-engineering programmes towards the more humanistic "soft" HRM model. As we explained in Chapter 2, this is an attempt to enlist workers' intellectual assets and cooperation in the labour process and increase employee involvement.

A number of scholars recognize (Easterby-Smith, Burgoyne and Araujo 1999) that *organizational learning* and *the learning organization* are separate and distinct concepts, although in the past both terms were often used interchangeably. According to Garavan (1997, p. 25), a *learning organization* implies a relatively intangible concept that signals a specific organizational direction (e.g. a company that has a specific plan to achieve a specific goal, such as achieving effectiveness through the continuous adaptation of different change strategies). *Organizational learning* is most often described as an heuristic, or prescriptive device, used to explain quantifiable learning activities. In other words, specific organizational development strategies (i.e. a planned culture change, adaptations of Senge's principles) are employed as heuristics that are expected to result in changing behaviour. These tangible changes can then be viewed as representative that organizational learning has taken place. Therefore, as the interest in creating learning organizations grows, the learning organization (LO) has become a metaphor for a *type* of organization, and organizational learning (OL) a descriptor for the transformational *process* that occurs in that type of organization.

ORGANIZATIONAL LEARNING

Organizational learning is the general term used to describe the process of how organizations learn. Emphasis is placed on the "potential" individuals have to learn, and the means, through "empowerment" and changing leadership style they have to achieve these goals. These factors are only seen as desirable as long as the learning results in outcomes that are beneficial to the organization (Senge, 1990). Ultimately, organizational learning is synonymous for the activities that lead to successful outcomes.

Researchers are unable to reach a consensus on what activities constitute organizational learning and who gets to participate in the learning process. For example, Steven McShane (2004), defines organizational learning as a management process in which "organizations acquire, share, and use knowledge to succeed" (p. 23). With this approach, learning is centred round problem solving and primarily involves only those workers whose paid work is seen as adding knowledge to the organization. Specifically, workers whose jobs require certain skills that assist the organization in increasing its competitive advantage are the most likely to participate in continuous work-based learning initiatives. As McShane (2004) explains, *communities of practice*, which he defines as "informal groups bound together by shared expertise and passion for an activity or interest (p. 24)," enable organizations to share knowledge. But participation in these communities of practice is always limited to those employees who have something that contributes directly to the growth of the organization.

STUDY TIP

There are a number of articles on different perspectives of organizational learning. Levitt and March(1988) provide an excellent overview of the different approaches to organizational learning in Organization Learning, reprinted in Cohen and Sproull's Organization Learning (Sage, 1996), while George Hubert (1991) offers an evaluation of the different perspectives in a reprint of his article in the same book.

The increased interest in the concept of organizational learning from both academics and consultants has forced scholars from various disciplines to tailor their understanding to their own particular areas of interest. At the same time, management consultants, who have adopted OL as the latest organizational strategy, embracing it as a managerial tool to improve performance, have caused the field of organizational learning to become conceptually more fragmented. Academics and practioners, in trying to impose their model of organizational learning as the one correct one, are intensifying the shift towards collective learning, but still remain unclear about what constitutes the paradigm.

THE LEARNING ORGANIZATION

Proponents of organizational learning equate the learning organization with organizational success. Mike Pedler *et al* (1989, p. 2) defined a learning organization as one that "facilitates the learning of all its members and continually transforms itself." The focus in a learning organization is on creating an environment that fosters learning through strategies that promote a "growth-oriented workplace" (Fenwick 1998). However, the type of strategy used to create growth will be dependent on who is implementing them. For example, Easterby-Smith *et al.* (1999, p. 1) suggests that business strategists will look for strategies that will help outwit competitors. Economists, stressing a more pragmatic approach, will focus on experiential and explicit learning techniques (i.e. learning by doing, combined with formal learning techniques). Sociologists and psychologists, who take more of an interpretive approach, focus on an understanding of the connections between the process of learning, the relationship to organizational knowledge, and the dynamics of organizational politics in a learning organization. Regardless of the approach taken, the end result is still the same. A learning organization is normally understood as one that is "good" at learning because of the types of activities it employs.

Thus, the learning organization typically describes organizations that promote and develop activities which help address organizational problems arising from globalization and increased competition. Learning is driven by external demands, and a learning organization can be understood as the direction an organization takes to accomplish its goals (Garavan, 1997, p. 25). Learning organizations are understood as places where individuals "expand their capacity to create the results they truly desire," and where people "learn how to learn together" Senge (1990). Thus, the notion of a learning organization is more closely related to the concept of organizational culture, rather than something tangible.

STUDY TIP

For a review and evaluation of the learning organization literature, see Thomas Garavan's article, "The Learning Organization: A Review and Evaluation," in *The Learning Organization*, Vol. 4, number 1, 1997.

As mentioned, the idea of organizational learning is not new. What is new is how organizational learning concepts have been repackaged into a concept promoting the idea of a learning organization. This specifically uses established management principles to create successful high performance work systems and cutting edge organizations capable of meeting current economic demands. Despite earlier models of learning, organizational learning can basically be categorized into two types (Garavan, 1997). These are based on Argyris' (1987) single loop (adaptive) learning model, whereby learning is limited by environmental constraints, and Argyris and Schon's (1974, 1978) double loop (generative) learning model, where the focus is on developing new ways of problem-solving.

The Fundamentals of Organizational Learning

Since the mid 1960s, research has been carried out on the adaptive behaviour of organizations over time. For example, Cyert's (1963; 1959) work on standard operating procedures and organizational rules provided an early prototype of organizational learning. This linked the process of learning to a set of routinized responses that reflected the way to achieve organizational goals. Over time, this view of organizational learning as an individual process continued to be refined. Initially, the single loop learning model was introduced, which focused on basic detection and problem solving. By the late 1970s, Argyris and Schon's (Argyris and Schon 1978) groundbreaking research into double loop learning had moved forward and demonstrating how the concept of "theories in use" could be questioned in order to question underlying organizational assumptions and find new ways forward. The distinctions their double loop model made expanded the knowledge of organizational and experiential learning and it became representative of hierarchical and transformational organizational learning processes. Their double loop learning model became popular with managers, who found ways to link the learning loops directly to both incremental and radical organizational change, while recognizing the importance of individual learning as a mainstay of collective learning.

While Argyris and Schon's work was recognized as a significant contribution to the field of organizational learning, it still does not explain how organizational learning was transformed into the "superstar status" of a management paradigm. To understand this, we need to explore the management of change imperative discussed in the introduction to this chapter.

Towards the Learning Organization: Management Fads and Fashions

Once the concept of organizational learning became more refined, focusing on a more sophisticated processual approach, its value as a theoretical framework to explain individual and collective learning became more evident (Argyris and Schon, 1978). Likewise, the tangible concept of the learning organization began to take on importance as a descriptor of companies that were trying to increase "knowledge intensity" as a means of meeting increased competition (Prange 1999). Coupled with the rhetoric of organizational change, which had become a major phenomenon throughout North America, it was natural that the notion of creating a learning organization was embraced wholeheartedly. It became the latest management fad to capture the interest of organizations looking for "cutting edge" change.

Since the mid 1970s, particularly in the English speaking world, there has been a rapid growth in the number of books and scholarly journals on organizational change, and particularly, specific models of change. In practice, since the beginning of the 1980s a vast number of companies have adopted one or other of the major change programmes. For example, by the onset of the 1990s, eighty percent of Canadian companies were planning, or had implemented, TQM programs and seventy percent of the largest US corporations had undergone a process of re-engineering by 1994 (Helms Mills, 2000) .

Change has become a conventional management practice, developed and sustained through a powerful management discourse, whose "ongoing" character influences the decision-making of large and small companies (Weick 1995). Management decisions reflect a continuous process of acting and reacting to various crises and opportunities, rather than "managerial rationality." Thus, managers often choose a course of action based on what seems to make sense, rather than what is, in fact, a "perfect" decision for the organization (Cohen, March, and Olsen, 1971). Rather than characterizing management decision making as a rational act toward a common purpose, for example, maximizing profits, critics have likened the decision making process in formal organizations to a garbage can.

To understand processes within organizations we view a choice opportunity as a garbage can into which various kinds of problems and solutions are dumped by participants as they are generated. The mix of garbage in a single can depends upon the mix of cans available, on the labels attached to alternative cans, on what garbage is currently being produced and on the speed with which garbage is collected and removed from the situation (Cohen, March and Olsen, 1971, p. 2, and quoted by Godard, 1994, p. 179).

REFLECTIVE QUESTION

Have management gurus had any influence on "sensemaking" in your workplace? For a comprehensive explanation of Karl Weick's work, see his 1995 book *Sensemaking in Organizations* (Sage) and for an historical perspective on this model, see *The Social Psychology of Organizing* (Sage, 1979).

We can see why the successful adoption rate of programs such as TQM, re-engineering, and, in this case the learning organization paradigm is attributable to the marketing of these programs through a focus on "practical" solutions, rather than detailed theory and research findings. Once a manager is convinced that change is an inevitable process that needs to be managed, he or she is receptive to plausible claims of expertise from business writers or consultants. Every so often, a theory of change is promulgated that, for whatever reason, captures the imagination of a large number of practitioners. When sufficient numbers of companies have hired that "theorist" as a consultant, when sufficient "success" stories surface, and when large numbers of copies of his or her book have been sold (e.g, Senge 1994), the "theorist" often takes on the status of "guru." Czarniaska-Joerge (cited in Alvesson and Berg 1992) takes this one step further and refers to these gurus as "merchants of meaning" because of their ability to create a need for solutions in the eyes of managers.

Similarly, Abrahamson (1996) argues that the adoption of "theories of management fashion" are shaped not only by "organizational performance gaps opened by technical and economic environmental changes" but by "socio-psychological forces," including "aesthetic taste, childlike excitement, mass conformity, and even something akin to manias or episodes of mass hysteria." It is this type of sense-making that helps to explain how the concept of a learning organization was quickly accepted as a panacea for organizations seeking ways to manage the change and meet the challenges of increased competition and globalization. It is not so much about what the particular technique has to offer, because they each promise organizational success, but it essentially proves that timing is everything.

Macdonald (cited in Case 1994) divides the time span of a management fad into six distinct phases. By the early 1990s, OL and LO were so successful that they had reached what MacDonald refers to as the "universal elixir phase." The learning organization had become not only a management buzzword by 1993, but had led to the creation of a new management paradigm focussed solely on organizational learning as a way to understand and organize.

The interest in organizational learning is clearly attributable to changing management fads and fashions, and in this case interest was aroused by a perceived need for new ways to motivate employees. It can be argued, therefore, that OL and the LO, with its emphasis on community learning (cf. Brown and Duguid 1991), was accepted because it was able to move beyond other popular organizational development trends that were popular at the time, meeting the demands of more humanizing organizational development techniques. Whereas the principles of TQM and re-engineering stressed multi-skilled employees, accountability, team learning, and process, radically changing the nature of work, these techniques have been credited for paving the way for the introduction of the learning organization (Fenwick 1998) because organizations recognized the benefits for the organization of shifting away from effectiveness, efficiency and leanness (predominant in the late 1980s and early 1990s) towards an emphasis on collective, continuous and community learning and a focus on people. (Burgoyne, Pedlar and Boydell 1994) pointed out, the promise of a new survival strategy with a focus on people and community, has legitimated the management gurus' call for organizations to reinvent themselves (Senge 1990), at the same time promising to add a more humane approach to change.

The success of OL and LO was evident in the number of articles and books published. During the entire decade of the 80s there were more academic publications in the area of management learning than any other management area. The number of companies who have implemented and endorsed management learning concepts continues to grow. Over time, the concept of a learning organization has come to be viewed as a necessary element to humanizing the workplace. There are several journals dedicated to the topic (see *The Learning Organization Journal*).

PUTTING IT INTO PERSPECTIVE

Garavan (1997) differentiates organizational learning as a *descriptor* of organizational activities, whereas the learning organization is understood as the *direction* of the organization. The literature on organizational learning and the learning organization is quite distinct, targeting the audience for which it is written. For example, those writing from a learning organization perspective are most often academics, or consultants, working in a management consulting role (Easterby-Smith, Burgoyne and Araujo 1999). The focus of these "entrepreneurial" academics is on prescriptive formulas that can be used by other practitioners of this perspective. On the other hand, those whose research focuses on organizational learning are driven by a desire to understand how the *process* of learning occurs within an organizational setting, both at the individual, group and organizational level. They come mainly from the academic community, and their approach is more detached and objective. Writers whose work fits into this perspective are usually academic researchers, whose goal is to provide a theoretical framework to validate the learning organizations' activities, or, as we have explained, its relevance to the adult education movement.

Organizational learning is focused on learning *in* the organization (Argyris 1973; Cohen and Sproull 1996; Cyert and March 1963), the concept of a learning organization assumes a managerialist approach that centres on learning *for* the organization (cf. Pedler, Burgoyne and Boydell 1994; Senge 1994; Senge 1990). This latter approach offers prescriptions on how an organization should be constructed, and how organizational learning should be understood. Ultimately, these ideological standpoints have caused disagreement over the future of research and development into the learning organization. Specifically, Easterby-Smith et al. (1999) question whether the different viewpoints should be regarded as ontologically incompatible, and thus requiring distinct research, or, if they can be considered complementary, and, therefore, necessary to the holistic development of the discipline.

Despite ongoing popularity and a common set of principles, (i.e. empowerment, collective vision, and continuous and shared learning) the literature of organizational learning theorists continues to create controversy because of a lack of agreement on; a) what actually constitutes a learning organization; b) its narrow approach to learning, and; c) its managerialist approach (e.g. its emphasis on the goals of the organization at the expense of the worker).

These viewpoints became sharply divided between those who believed the organization is a variable to be manipulated, versus those who understood the learning organization as a cultural metaphor. Consequently, the organizational learning literature became further divided ontologically between those who view it as a *technical process* versus those who conceptualize it as a *social process* (Easterby-Smith et al, 1999). Similarly, the literature on the learning organization is also categorized into these two approaches. For those who understand OL from this latter perspective the LO becomes a metaphor for the type of hegomonic values which are admired in the organization. In the first instance, organizational learning becomes a vehicle for the learning organization, in the second, organizational learning creates the culture that metaphorically defines the organization.

ORGANIZATIONAL LEARNING AS A TECHNICAL PROCESS

Levitt's (1988) definition of organizations learning "as a process of encoding, storing and retrieving the lessons of history, despite the turnover of personnel and the passage of time, in order to maintain organizational continuity" is reminiscent of earlier theorists of OL, which assumed that organizations would remain relatively stable over time, and who focused their learning efforts on the continuous improvement of existing procedures. With this dominant paradigm (Matthews, 1999), the basic objective of those who view organizational learning as a technical process is to design a learning organization by manipulating specific variables, leading to increased performance. This is done by acquiring knowledge or skills necessary to accomplish the tasks at hand (Ibid, p.5).

For example, Argyris and Schon (1978), and Senge (1990, 1994) have fairly explicit and narrowly defined rules concerning what learning entails. In general, their commonly held understanding is that the isolation of certain traits that can be controlled for the betterment of workplace performance will, in turn, lead to the creation of successful learning organizations. Although this approach recognizes that learning cultures contribute to the development of learning organizations (Garavan, 1997), such an approach to understanding learning organizations as entities that can be manipulated tends to focus on learning as the processing of information, rather than a political process of social interaction.

This perspective and remains popular with most practitioners. Perhaps because of a increased emphasis on competition, and the instability of many organizations, the managerialist focus of the technical approach appeals to consultants who are concerned with seeking ways to make the organization more efficient. The manipulation of certain traits in order to influence employee behaviour is advantageous to organizations trying to gain the competitive advantage (Garavan, 1997). This approach has most often been associated with private enterprise [1], but more recently, as Tara Fenwick (1998, p.143) points out, there has been an increased demand by policy-makers for government agencies to start to utilize learning organization principles. Many Canadian Crown Corporations and a wide range of government organizations have begun adopting principles of continuous learning, a key element of the learning organization. Dixon (1992) describes how Canadian museums have implemented learning organization principles. Following a report from the Auditor General of Canada to parliament, stressing the need for continuous learning to meet the demands of a changing environment, the Canadian Consortium for Organizational Learning was established in 1995 (Fenwick, 1998). In the same year, Public Works Canada initiated a continuous learning programme.

Limitations of the Technical Process

A number of concerns with the technical approach to organizational learning have been raised concerning the emphasis of the technical approach on measurement and productivity. This narrowly focuses on the concept of learning itself, ignoring or understating the influence of politics and individual sense making on the realization of this productivity (e.g. behaviour that can get in the way of learning). While recognizing that politics does exist, Peter Senge (1994) suggests that it be treated as a variable that can be controlled or eliminated through open dialogue. Politics is downplayed on the assumption that a shared meaning of experiences exists, one which does not account for resistance to suggested plans of action. For example, employees share the experience of re-engineering, yet hold different interpretations of whether it was a success or a failure. In some cases employees may embrace the plans, in other cases they may respond with apathy or resistance to the re-engineering initiatives.

A classic example of social relations influencing learning and productivity also took place during the bank wiring experiments of the Hawthorne Studies. The researchers observed that workers who violated the production norms set by the group, were verbally and physically abused by their co-workers, and decreased their performance to fall in line with what their co-workers, not necessarily the management, wanted (cf. Roethlisberger and Dickson 1939).

Finally, managerialist approaches to organizational learning as a technical process have been criticized for minimizing both the role and voice of the worker (i.e. learning only what is necessary to help achieve organizational goals). The technical approach raises some interesting issues about the implementation of learning principles, and the rigidity and narrowness used to define, control and evaluate the learning process.

ORGANIZATIONAL LEARNING AS A SOCIAL PROCESS

The organizational learning paradigm has gained popularity with academics, each within their different theoretical frameworks, and a different perspective of the learning process has emerged. By the early 1990s, as the deficits of the technical approach began to emerge, organizational learning from a social perspective became dominant. For example, failure to recognize the complicated nature of organizational dynamics and the inevitable problems that occur when people do not behave in a predictable and rational way was a central concern (Easterby-Smith, Burgoyne and Araujo 1999). Thus, political behaviour was accepted as a reality. Researchers, (already focused on the influence of social interactions on workplace outcomes) began to use an interpretist approach as an alternative to the more technical managerialist approach. The work of Vygotsky (1978), which placed greater emphasis on the social construction of (jobplace) learning, took precedence.

Contributors to organizational learning as a social process stress the importance of understanding organizational learning as a series of interrelated actions of individuals towards the creation of a collective mind, where shared meaning drives the learning process. For example, researchers such as Brown (1996) and Weick (1996) believe that an understanding of the *process* of organizational learning is more important than seeking out a universal and prescriptive approach. Proponents of this approach recognize that learning is only validated by the meaning given to it by organizational actors, which often occurs through the informal exchange of information and cultural artifacts, such as stories and rituals. In fact, Karl Weick (1996, p.170) suggests that individual learning occurs when people give a different response to the same stimulus, but organizational learning occurs when groups of people give the same response to different stimuli. Thus, it is vital to have an understanding of the process of learning and the influences upon it.

Organizational Learning as a Cultural Metaphor

A major difference between the social approach and the technical approach is the acceptance of the learning organization as a cultural metaphor. The socio-cultural perspective takes the position that learning is an artifact of the ideology of a learning culture, which is created through the fostering of learning-related values. From this perspective, the creation of a learning culture takes into account elements of the existing culture, the socialization process, and the individual sense making that drives employees' understanding of organizational rules. In other words, learning organizations are understood as socially constructed entities that are less concerned with outcomes and more concerned with the processes that create a learning culture. Some researchers in this area (e.g. Weick 1995) focus on how people make sense of their paid work, and in so doing, uncover the influences of organizational culture on the learning process. Others, (i.e. Solomon, 2001) take a more critical point of view that learning is a cultural practice and a form of cultural control, while Agashae and Bratton (2001) argue that cultural norms stand in the way of workplace learning. In any event, organizational learning creates a culture that has become synonymous with the concept of a learning organization This accepts that politics has a natural place in the organizational process, that it can be managed, but never eradicated.

THE SOCIO-CULTURAL APPROACH TO UNDERSTANDING THE LEARNING ORGANIZATION

The conceptualization of the LO as a cultural metaphor mainly attracts academics who are interested in understanding the process that leads to the formation of the ideology and cultural artifacts of a learning organization. Research from this perspective focuses on the meaning that is assigned to actions in order to make sense of outcomes. In other words, instead of focusing on what skills and knowledge the organization needs to accomplish its goals and strategies, those who understand the learning organization as an expression of its culture are taking what Weick calls a *"sensemaking" approach* (Weick, 1995). This is based on the understanding of culture as a root metaphor (Smircich 1983), which represents something an organization "is," not something an organization "has." Thus, organizational variables cannot be manipulated. Instead, this approach maintains that learning organizations are studied and understood as organizations that possess cultures that contribute to and support the learning process. Matthews (1999) suggests that the key learning tool in this approach is learning from past experience.

Socialization is a good illustration of how these factors (i.e. culture, past experience, politics and control) impact on the learning environment. During socialization, new workers are often paired with "old" employees to learn the ropes and assimilate the organizational culture. Assimilation occurs when workers figure out the difference between "the way things are done" versus "the way they are supposed to be done." This enactment of organizational rules (Mills and Murgatroyd, (1991) reflects the culture of the organization. This may not be what the organization wants employees to learn (i.e. formal rules). Instead, learning is a result of socialization. For example, when one of the authors of this book first went to work for Air Canada in the early 1970s it did not take her long to learn that although the rules of the company allowed for two 15 minute coffee breaks each day, everyone else was taking 20 minutes, so she quickly adapted her behaviour, even though it contradicted what she knew the company wanted.

REFLECTIVE QUESTION
What is the difference between socialization and tacit learning?

Strengths and Weaknesses of the Socio-cultural Perspective

There are a number of strengths of the social perspective of organizational learning. Those who focus on learning as an interpretive process (Brown and Duguid 1991) recognize the socially constructed nature of learning and view this process as one that overcomes some of the limitations of the technical perspective by giving meaning to actions. Similarly, organizational learning as a social process does not discount the influence of politics and individual interpretations.

However, the social perspective of organizational learning also has its weaknesses. The dichotomy of organizational learning as a social process is that it can also be interpreted as fitting within the technical framework. For example, individual and group learning processes that emphasize humanistic principles (e.g. the creation of autonomous work groups, such as Saturn, Volvo, and VW) are seeking ways to improve productivity through improved work relationships, whereas those who see organizational learning as a technical process seek out measurable outcomes (e.g. re-engineering, which measures "value-added" versus "non value added" jobs) (Cressey, 1993; Murakami, 1995; Womack, Jones, and Roos, 1990). The only apparent difference between these two approaches is that the technical process debate centers on *quantifiable* issues of productivity, whereas the social approach assumes that productivity will be an outcome of job satisfaction and social interaction. It is assumed that learning occurs through social interaction. Workers, therefore, learn workplace behaviours, either informally by discussion or observing the behaviours of others, or formally through training and occasional individual/union-management negotiation.

The notion of the learning organization as a cultural metaphor raises some concerns. Although it is recognized that organizations with strong learning cultures possess certain core characteristics that make them more receptive to having a learning organization culture (Kanter 1989), this has not been proven. Instead, the LO is analyzed as a network of shared symbols, and meanings that contribute to shared learning. Shared learning does not always result in creating an integrative culture (Martin, 1991), or one that reflects the goals of learning. Instead, the strength of the LO is its focus as a cultural metaphor on understanding the process of social construction, and what makes some organizations more susceptible to learning than others.

While this approach makes sense of how the culture comes to be interpreted, the abstract nature of the socio-cultural perspective is perhaps what makes it less popular with those who are concerned with taking a more pragmatic approach. Yet the questions this approach raises about what constitutes a learning organization culture, and whether or not it is possible for organizations (versus individuals in the organization) to learn, also raises questions about the nature of work organizations. As Bate (1990) has asked, do organizations exist on their own, or are they are the sum of their members?

At the present time, the only commonalties between the technical and social approaches that are agreed upon by researchers are; a) the acceptance that learning occurs from experience; b) a concern to find ways to create better learning practices, and; c) a focus on outcomes. According to Easterby-Smith *et al*, (1999) organizational learning can only occur with the growth of the organizational community becoming an even more highly politicized process. Although the social process approach is gaining momentum in organizational learning research (cf. Easterby-Smith, Burgoyne and Araujo 1999; Weick and Westley 1996), it requires more empirical methodologies before it can be considered useful to those of the technical process persuasion, who see its use of discourse analysis as problematic (Easterby-Smith, et al 1999). Although these different points of view make it difficult to rate one approach better than the other, the importance of the discrepancies between these two viewpoints is in the implications these divergent models have on the interpretation of a learning organization.

STUDY TIP

Read Diane Watson's chapter, *Power, Conflict and Control at Work* (pp. 386-413) in John Allen *et al*. (eds.) (1992). What is the relationship between power, control, and conflict?

CREATING A LEARNING ORGANIZATION

Peter Senge, in his role as Director of the MIT Center for Organizational Learning, and with the publication of his book *The Fifth Discipline"* (1990, 1994), brought the learning organization concept into prominence. Senge the believed that creating a strong learning organization would lead to a positive performance for the organization. His pragmatic approach refined earlier models of organizational learning (i.e. organizational development (OD) techniques) into a pre-packaged transformational process that capitalized on an increased interest in workplace learning and dissatisfaction with "hard" management strategies, downplaying the role of the employee.

Senge's model isolated five interwoven "disciplines" (or variables), which he considered necessary ingredients for designing an organization that was flexible and knowledgeable enough to thrive in turbulent times. His prescriptive approach to learning centered on the building of these five disciplines: [1]Personal mastery, [2] Creating new mental models, [3] Team learning, [4] Shared vision and [5] Systems thinking. These variables, Senge maintained, are driven by critical self-reflection and open dialogue, in order to expose and challenge existing dysfunctional beliefs that can inhibit and prevent organizational learning. If these elements are in place and acted upon, they will, according to Senge, create an environment where continuous learning is nourished and cultivated, through the creation of a collective vision that overcomes the personal biases and beliefs that contribute to dysfunctional thinking.

While Senge's ideas are certainly not new, his ability to promote them in the right way and at the right time has been fortuitous and has made him the most widely read author in the field (Hawkins 1994). He was one of the most cited authors in business journals and seminars during the 1990s (Fenwick, 1998). His ability to provide new ways of perceiving organizations just as the old ways were becoming stagnant, and provide testimonies from company executives who had applied his techniques, contributed to his guru status.

Since the late 1990s, the organizational learning paradigm has moved towards what MacDonald (cited in Case, 1994) refers to as the "determined exploitation and benefits phase" of the lifecycle of an organizational fad. A growing number of learning theorists have started to question the validity of many of the principles in the popular paradigm. Despite these issues, the desire of companies to adapt a prescriptive approach and create learning organizations remains strong. This need continues to be met by consultants, who, seeing the financial benefits of developing and implementing the latest in management techniques, continue to promote the learning organization as a panacea for improving organizational performance.

CASE STUDIES: LEARNING ORGANIZATION IN ACTION

As examples of learning organizations two of the authors of this book have undertaken research at Nova Scotia Power, an eastern Canadian electrical utility, and Pan Canadian Petroleum. Nova Scotia Power is an example of a company that has adopted learning organization concepts, directly linked to a series of changes, including privatization in 1991. In order to meet the increased demands of competition it has undergone, in rapid succession, a culture change programme, followed by a re-engineering program, balanced scorecard initiatives, and various other strategic programmes focused on improving its competitive edge. By restructuring, with a focus on team-based learning, Nova Scotia Power has positioned itself as an organization that is continuously learning to adapt to organizational challenges, and as a company involved in serial change.

Between 1987-1991, N.S. Power implemented two major change programs; culture change and re-engineering, and subsequently, between 1991-2002, a Balanced Scorecard programme, under the direction of the new president. Significantly, each program was at the height of its popularity at the time of implementation, and was touted successfully in addressing the problems Nova Scotia Power was facing. In the first instance, the recently appointed CEO introduced culture change in order to overcome a perceived problem of low morale. Implementing four values that were to loosely define employee behaviour, the culture change met with varying degrees of acceptance throughout the province.

Approximately four years after the culture change was implemented, Nova Scotia Power was privatized and faced a new set of concerns. Competition suddenly became the key issue, and the company sought new ways to meet these demands. The introduction of a re-engineering program meant that the values, which had previously focused on the employee, the province, the environment, and the customer, were no longer a priority. Instead, the company formed "business process initiative" teams to look for ways to streamline existing workplace tasks. Involvement in these tasks was limited to those who possessed knowledge that could help design these new work processes. Only employees who had this knowledge were invited to serve on the teams.

The measurable result of re-engineering was a decrease in the workforce of approximately 700 employees, from 2,420 to 1,720 between 1993 and 1995. Nova Scotia Power's share values remained strong, and in 2001 they purchased an electrical company in Bangor, Maine. While Nova Scotia Power did not promote itself as a learning organization, *per se*, their *modus operandi*, including vision statement, rationale for change, and human resource management (HRM) techniques employed were similar to the principles associated with learning organizations. For example, a focus on shared vision, team work, continuous learning, open dialogue was used in each change process, and, in the culture change and re-engineering, participation was limited to those who had a particular knowledge or skill necessary to accomplish the goals of the organization.

PanCanadian Petroleum, based in Calgary, Alberta, is another company that has declared itself to be a learning organization. Using survey data gathered from 400 full-time workers, a recent study (Agashae & Bratton, 2001) examined Senge's proposition that leadership behaviour, conceptualized in terms of three roles: steward, designer and teacher, facilitated informal learning in the job place. The study revealed the presence of all three roles in the case study. Of the three, the "Designer" role was the weakest at 57 per cent agreement from respondents followed by 63 per cent for "Steward" and 67 per cent for "Teacher." Significant differences in the level of agreement were found within duration of employment and occupational group. The apparent success of Pan Canadian in re-engineering to incorporate "business units" and work teams and develop a "learning culture" has to be examined in the context of the economic buoyancy of the gas and oil industry and the absence of any challenges from trade unions.

STUDY QUESTION

How did Nova Scotia Power plan for culture change, re-engineering, and the balanced scorecard compare to the views of organizational learning and the learning organization as a technical versus a social process?

PARADOXES AND CONTRADICTIONS

The OL/LO approach has been accused of ignoring types of job design arrangements that generate little knowledge, and creating impoverished learning regimes (Bratton, 1999). Consequently, learning organization literature has been criticized for its failure to recognize the importance of other types of learning, how they affect the outcomes of the organization, and how opportunities for job place learning are influenced by work configurations (Bratton, 1999; Fenwick, 1998). From this perspective the learning organization is thought of as a managerial tool dedicated to "bottom-line" definitions of growth. Moreover, organizational learning, as defined by management, does little to democratize the job place. Hence, the theory/strategy/process not only subverts individual aspirations to organizational needs, but also obscures the inherent conflictual relations within the economic system.

There is a great deal of debate surrounding the validity and future of OL as a management technique, despite its being a relatively new management paradigm. At one level, as we have seen, there is little agreement on what constitutes a learning organization. At another level, despite an emphasis on collective action, the principles of the learning organization have done little to assist in the emancipation of the worker from managerial ownership. In fact, the "unilateral" principles of OL suggest a non-democratic form of social organization that worsens rather than overcomes the problem of control, and that so called "emancipatory processes" are, in fact, violations of workers' rights and privacy.

Drawing upon the work of Barbara Townley (1994), we have presented a view that HRM practices are designed to make workers more governable. The learning organization, as an HRM tool, is no exception. Moreover, despite claims to empower workers and involve them in the decision making process, the learning organization has been accused of being little more than a control mechanism used to benefit the goals of the organization at the expense of the worker. Those who take the viewpoint that organizations are socially constructed (Huysman 1999) argue that hidden assumptions that omit important facts, need to be uncovered. By setting the boundaries for how learning takes place, and by ignoring issues of race, class, and identity at the expense of the worker, the learning organization has been accused of exacerbating the inherent conflict associate with capitalist employment relations.

Who Contributes?

The first problem with the OL literature concerns the type of knowledge that is identified as central to the learning organization. Critical theorists would argue that, despite an emphasis on community learning, empowerment and open dialogue, the OL literature fails to take into account the input of non-managerial workers. A major cause of this criticism has been the uneven distribution of power that excludes the majority of employees, except those in management or knowledge reliant positions, from the decision making process. Despite an implicit assumption of team learning and collaboration, the LO literature provides a narrow definition of learning that limits the generation of knowledge to reflect only the interests of those whose goals are to be achieved. This exclusion effectively limits the participation and contribution to a select few employees, while ignoring types of learning that do not generate knowledge considered important to the evolution of the learning organization. The work of an employee who holds a low level position not directly involved in a learning initiative or the generation of knowledge, will be ignored. This is worsened by the structural and cultural characteristics of an organization, which can affect the actions of its members and disqualify many of them from actively participating in the learning process. In short, the OL literature is written for those who have the power to manage change. Paradoxically, this viewpoint contradicts the principle of OL, which considers learning an activity made up of individuals interacting to construct new behaviours that will increase workplace productivity.

What is Contributed?

Organizational learning has been accused of being too focused on a prescriptive approach that ignores the influences of prior experience, emotions and memories (Garavan 1997). By setting boundaries for what constitutes knowledge, and what constitutes learning, the OL literature is not so much excluding a number of employees from the process, but downplaying the worth of the knowledge of the majority of employees, and exploiting them for the benefit of organizational outcomes. In a study carried out on an organization that refitted ships for the Canadian navy (MacLeod 1994) it was discovered that "voluntary" participation in quality circles was based on selection by the CEO, and limited to those "who would contribute the most valuable information to the team for a particular project." Similarly, during Nova Scotia Power's re-engineering programme, employees were "selected" to take part in Business Process Improvement (BPI) teams based on the value they could add to the project. Participation was based on the type of knowledge employees could generate towards redesigning work units. This limited participation by other employees who might have wanted to be on the teams but were disqualified because their knowledge or skill was not seen as central to the accomplishment of organizational goals.. At one level, this interpretation of who can learn devalues the skills others bring to the workplace (i.e. skills that are not directly related to the problem-solving process, such as those found in support positions). At another level, it eliminates workers whose jobs are technology based, rather than knowledge-driven or problem-solving focussed. More importantly, it suggests that OL is a discriminatory and elitist practice. An emphasis on continuous improvement limits employees' ability to contribute meaningfully to the process of learning, while disregarding other types of knowledge generated by those workers. This is compounded by the fact that the majority of new jobs available today offer workers little chance for generating knowledge through creativity or innovation (Paquette, 1995).

Gender Race and Class

The learning organization literature generally assumes that learning is isolated within the confines of the paid workplace. While this perspective ignores such factors as individual beliefs and values, culture, and prior knowledge, which all influence the organizational learning process, it also contradicts the assumption that critical reflection and open dialogue expose and reshape dysfunctional assumptions and beliefs by suggesting that employees' existing values and beliefs are not good enough for the organization. The inference is that employees should be loyal to their organization, ignore external influences (e.g. influences of family, home, education on their value systems), and align their "mental models" to fit with the goals of the organization. Again, this raises issues about whose interests are being served.

It can also be argued that gender and diversity are ignored at the expense of narrowly defining a particular type of learning. This is because the LO literature ignores what constitutes different types of knowledge, by only looking for knowledge that relates directly to job competencies. Karl Weick (1995) argues that identity construction is one of the key components of sensemaking, and therefore, learning. So, individual differences that contribute to the construction of meaning are marginalized, and learning that does not fit the traditional model is downplayed in the OL literature. For example, MacKeracher and McFarland (cited in Fenwick, 1998) describe differences in learning styles between men and women. Women tend to engage in relational learning, which has an emphasis on the centrality of self, contradicting organizational assumptions. Yet, this is largely ignored in the OL literature.

Weick (1995) states that shared meaning of an experience is difficult to establish because of individual sensemaking. For example, some female employees at Nova Scotia Power considered re-engineering to be a particularly masculinist change programme because of the methodology and language it used (e.g. the words most commonly used to describe the consultants were gunslingers and undertakers). Some of the male employees discounted the culture change because of its humanistic implications. In both cases, because of different learned responses, these attitudes impacted on employees' behaviour.

In a similar vein, it has been suggested that workplace learning ignores current knowledge about adult learning (Garavan, 1997). Although adult learning has been discussed at length (Burgoyne, Pedlar and Boydell 1994; Senge 1990), the OL literature fails to recognize the importance of experiential learning, and instead stresses the importance of deconstructing existing belief systems in order for learning to take place. This is an important omission, because it supports the allegation of a unitary perspective of management learning, oversimplifies management learning and excludes critical issues such as politics (Burgoyne and Jackson 1997).

Empowerment, Emancipation and Privacy

While empowerment and emancipation are allegedly the central building blocks of the learning organization, Tara Fenwick (1998) suggests that these principles actually create paradoxes that impede the emancipation of workers and hinder, rather than help, learning. One of the specific criticisms of organizational learning centres around the issue of its dominance over workers, and charges that it is being used as a management tool to modify undesirable employee behaviour (i.e. that which is incompatible with organizational goals (Elkjaer 1999). Michel Foucault's conceptualization of the individual as both an object and a subject of power and knowledge, and the use of the "confession" for producing self-knowledge of the subject, posits that open dialogue is a calculative technology that aims to change, or reconstitute, individuals' behaviour in a way which is more productive to the organization (Townley, 1994). Furthermore, the practice of "confessional appraisal," used to identify training and learning needs, harnesses personal wishes and desires of the worker with the aim of creating an internalized "self-discipline based on evaluation." Moreover,

> To the extent that authoritive norms, calculative technologies and forms of evaluation can be translated into values, decisions and

judgements of citizens in their professional and personal capacities, they can function as part of the "self-steering" mechanism of individuals. Hence, "free" individuals and "private" spaces can be "ruled" without breaching their formal autonomy. (Miller & Rose, 1990, p. 19 and quoted in Townley, 1994, p. 118)

If that is the case, even limited empowerment is not an emancipatory process as it is only realistic when the worker's needs happen to coincide with organizational goals.

Organizational learning has also been accused of invading privately-held workers' beliefs and values under the guise of concern with their well-being and the advancement of workplace learning through open dialogue (Fenwick, 1998). The LO literature suggests that individual worker privacy is being violated at the expense of overall organizational well-being. In other words, as part of what Senge and others (Argyris 1993) call *critical self reflection*, workers are asked to share their innermost thoughts, in order to break down their existing negative beliefs which are holding them back from being more creative. Practices such as sensitivity training force employees to share intensely private information with others in the name of personal development. In reality, it is the organization's goals that are of primary concern. This not only reduces the autonomy of the individual worker to reflect the vision and agenda of those in control (Fenwick, 1998), but suggests that OL is nothing more than an attempt to control the culture of the workplace (Legge 1996). This exposure of one's innermost thoughts also leaves employees vulnerable to disciplinary action should they disagree with corporate ideology, represents a violation of individual rights, and strengthens the argument presented in Chapter 2 which questions the intent of mainstream HRM models. The rhetoric of organizational learning (payment for knowledge, flexible learning, and continuous learning,) and its associated technologies (open dialogue, self-appraisal, learning needs analysis) actually legitimizes structural changes (e.g. downsizing) that are detrimental to workers (Fenwick, 1998). Tara Fenwick (1998, p. 152) sums up the paradox of the LO paradigm as one that ultimately presents itself as a romantic ideal, appearing to encourage worker's personal growth, but continuing to dictate what type of growth is most valued. Weick and Westley (1996) sum up the debate by arguing that to organize in fact limits the number of learning opportunities, so that the idea of organizational learning becomes an oxymoron.

> **REFLECTIVE QUESTION**
>
> Does organize mean to limit, or are limits part of only certain ways to organize work?

THE FUTURE OF ORGANIZATIONAL LEARNING RESEARCH

It is easy to see how disparate views of what constitutes the LO and OL have contributed to significant growth and interest in the management learning paradigm. At the same time, these views have contributed to fragmentation within the paradigm and have led to confusion over a universally acceptable model of organizational learning. Prange (1999) has tried to debunk some of the major criticisms leveled against the OL literature. Some of this criticism centres around the suggestion that organizational learning lacks theoretical integration, and that its research is being carried out in a non-cumulative way, relying on either metaphorical or analogous sense making, This is not useful knowledge for practitioners. As Prange points out, it is the quest for a useful and prescriptive approach to meet managerial needs, focusing on measurable outcomes, which has impeded the progress of learning organization theory. At first glance, because of its metaphorical meaning, OL theory appears vague and ill defined, and its development has been held back by trying to build a theory that is useful and practical. Yet, according to Prange, this metaphorical meaning *is* useful because it provides a way of thinking that "has an enormous potential for scientific knowledge of organizational learning" (Ibid. p.37), because it forces people to re-examine the influence of experience and social interactions in the creation of reality. This means that many organizations, while borrowing from some of the elements of OL principles, fail to initiate change because they do not have a clear idea of how to proceed.

Researchers need to seek out new ways to make the organization truly empowering to all employees (Fenwick, 1998), and pay attention to the type of employee who is best suited to a learning organization (Garavan, 1997). Easterby-Smith et al (1999) suggest that one way of achieving this is by conducting more empirical studies, and in this way researchers might be open to new methods of evaluation. This approach does not address the fundamental problem of the learning organization paradigm being perceived as another form of managerial control.

This analysis of the different approaches and their limitations raises issues about whether or not the OL literature offers anything new. Is it nothing more than the repackaging of existing OD techniques, designed to rectify current organization problems? We think not, since one of the many myths of the organizational change story-line is that the solutions offered by management consultants and gurus to problems such as globalization are unique and radically different from existing techniques. Coupled with the idea that change is an imperative that has been inadequately dealt with in the past, the claims of uniqueness made by various approaches such as OL may apparently offer a "real" solution, and a strategy for putting management on the cutting edge. However, as Matthews (1999) points out, they are not that much different from what has existed since the beginning of formal and informal work patterns emerged. What is different is the increased focus on learning.

In particular, more than one researcher has raised the issue of whether or not it is possible to create a learning organization, while at a broader level of analysis, assumptions upon which management learning is based have been questioned. Specifically, the blueprints for the creation of the learning organization are supposedly premised on the notion that shared understanding is a part of the learning process (Senge, 1994). This has not always proven the case, when we look at some of the organizational outcomes that have resulted from different interpretations of the same experience. These opposing standpoints raise questions about whether or not a learning organization can be created, and if so, what is its purpose? For example, those using a critical perspective lens might assume that the primary function of a learning organization is to help workers find significance and identity in their paid work, whereas those who approach it from a managerialist perspective might focus on the benefits that stressing continuous learning opportunities can contribute to the organization's "bottom line."

STUDY TIP

For an in-depth analysis of shared experiences which have resulted in different interpretations, see Karl Weick's work on organizational disasters (i.e. "Drop Your Tools: An Allegory for Organizational Study," in ASQ, volume 41, or "The collapse of sensemaking in organizations: The Mann Gulch disaster," ASQ, volume 38). As well, his work with Karlene Roberts on aviation disasters can be found in Chapter 15 of *Organizational Learning* (Cohen and Sproull, eds.) Sage, 1996.

SUMMARY

This chapter has provided an overview of the learning organization debate, including the different approaches taken by the researchers of this paradigm, and critically analyzed the processes employed by proponents of organizational learning. In pointing out the paradoxes found in the LO literature, we show that, despite what the literature may say, the benefits of OL are mainly geared towards developing processes and techniques leading to desirable outcomes for the organization. Some workers may benefit from these initiatives, but many are disadvantaged by them. Yet, as Albert Mills (1998) suggests, we should not be deterred by mainstream approaches to organizing. Instead, we should learn from this unequal distribution of power, find new ways of organizing the labour process that can overcome the imbalance of power, and promote authentic and democratic workplaces.

Notes

1. Just a few of the most notable companies that have used LO principles include, Ford, Shell, and General Electric.

CHAPTER 5

Unions and Workplace Learning

The trade union of the future will be a creating, not merely a fighting, organization. (Lindeman, 1926, p. 27)

Learning isn't icing on the cake or an optional extra for trade unions. It's our business. It underpins our member's well-being and future prosperity ... — British Trades Union Congress President, John Monks (Quoted in Forrester, 2002)

The paid workplace is one of the most important spheres of learning in society today. The learning that goes on in this sphere can be understood from at least two perspectives: that of management and owners on the one hand, and that of workers and their organizations on the other. In fact, as we have explained in previous chapters, workplace learning represents a contested terrain of social, political and economic struggle. The purpose of trade unions is to represent the interests and worldview of the diversity of workers, and the goals of workplace learning can be seen as overlapping as well as opposing those of management. Unions represent these interests by providing organizational, and, in most liberal democracies, legal frameworks for workers to mobilize around issues they deem important. The labour movement, more generally, is comprised of the trade union movement, the co-operative movement and workers' political parties. Within this stream of movements, trade unions in particular have incredible capacity to shape the character and experience of learning at work through course provision, collective bargaining and other forms of intervention. Unions also play an important role in shaping training and vocational education policy at various sectoral, national and, more recently, international levels (in many cases with the help of established workers' political parties). Perhaps most pervasively, however, unions can and frequently do play an important role in shaping the everyday experiences of workers within the labour process through specific information and action campaigns, as well as through their effects on learning through mass media, literature, drama and art.

CHAPTER OJECTIVES

After reading this chapter, you should be able to:

1. Understand the full range of means through which unions affects skills and knowledge in the workplace;

2. Explain the alternative perspectives and purposes of unions, as opposed to management, in terms of workplace learning including the historical, contemporary and possible future issues over which these alternative standpoints play themselves out;

3. Critically evaluate an array of international research literatures that bear on issues of workplace learning from a worker/union standpoint.

Although frequently touted as dead or dying, the union movement remains, arguably, *the* most important form of working-class representation in the world today. In terms of education and training specifically, a variety of scholars (e.g. Hopkins, 1985; Kett, 1994; Linton, 1965; Schneider, 1941; Simon, 1990) generally date the emergence of an organized and explicit array of worker educational offerings in North America at the close of the 19th century. In the UK the start date can be placed about a hundred years earlier, rooted in the activities of philanthropists, Mechanics Institutes, Corresponding and Mutual Improvement Societies, Chartist Reading Rooms as well as early trade unions. In either example, forms of worker or labour education represent organized practice that far pre-dates comparative levels of organized human resource practice, including mass, compulsory schooling. Despite these origins, union-based education, training and learning has still barely registered in the minds of most trainers, researchers, and students when they think of workplace learning.

Conventional labour education literature is not new. It has a relatively rich heritage of treatment in historical as well as policy and practice documents issued by unions and related organizations. As a form of social science or humanity-based scholarship, however, it is composed of relatively small, insular sets of discussions, only recently entering into broader debates in the research field of workplace learning. In fact, we can say that union education and union-based workplace learning are more often the subjects of practical use and development than of academic writing. This is quite different from discussions dealing with, for example, the "learning organization" in which more is written about the concept than is actually put into practice. Nevertheless, when we read broadly across education and training literatures (as well as sociology, industrial relations, economic and social history, international development, economics, feminist studies, communications and cultural studies to name the ones we discuss below), we see a rich tapestry of theories, approaches, research and reports on existing practice that constitutes a broad view of union movement learning as it relates to and directly shapes the processes of work.

The discussion offered in this chapter is more focused than most workplace learning literature, and broader than most discussion of labour education. In terms of workplace learning literature, the discussion is more focused in the sense that while we address a range of influences, programs, policies and practices, we focus on the unique role of unions who represent the standpoint of workers at work. In terms of labour education, like the Spencer (2002) collection, as well as an earlier text by Hopkins (1985), this chapter is broad in that it takes an international approach. We focus primarily on the most recent writings, exploring examples from English-speaking and non-English speaking countries, with a bias toward the former for practical reasons. How do unions mediate workplace training? To what extent do unions provide this training themselves? Do issues like gender, race, region or nation affect the role of unions in workplace learning? What are the policies and politics of unions in regard to workplace learning? Answering these questions and others provides the basis for a more or less conventional discussion of unions and workplace learning. The chapter is also broad in terms of union education writing, however, because we look at the role of union movement throughout the full array of formal as well as informal and everyday learning effects and practices. We note, for example, that the vast majority of learning that workers do is *not* done in the context of formally organized courses. We therefore discuss labour's role in mediating the labour process and hence the informal learning process at work; labour's use of the arts, mass media and technology to affect member's learning, understanding and behaviour at work; and, the effects of strikes and campaigns on workers' learning.

For the purposes of this chapter, we define union-based workplace learning as whenever and wherever labour unions affect the skill and knowledge capacities of workers and this includes the important role that unions play in shaping the policies and practices of paid work. Formalized training and union programs are fair game, as are the myriad of individual and group informal and even tacit practices that make up everyday learning. This broad approach not only expands the notion of learning, but in fact calls for the expansion of our ideas of the purpose and meaning of "work" as well. For example, is the learning that goes into developing union activists, and effective representatives establishment, national or international levels to be understood as a form of workplace learning? We would say yes, particularly when the effects are aggregated, as this learning directly affects the way work is organized and carried out.

Closely linked with the notion of expanding our conception of work, we also recognize that labour's "agenda" is different from that of management's. While productivity, efficiency and quality top the list for managers, for workers and their organizations these are not only low on the list, but they take on a different (sometimes fundamentally different) meaning. "Productivity" and "efficiency," for example, may be understood from a working-class standpoint as productive, efficient *and* satisfying work, fairly compensated, over the entire life course. Likewise for management, "quality" may mean a consistent and predictable standard of product or service, but from a worker's standpoint it can also mean good health and safety, the opportunity for humane and creative work, and so on. Indeed, one of the foremost purposes of union-based workplace learning against which any notions of productivity, efficiency or quality may be measured, concerns building democratic workplaces. Similar to the liberatory tradition discussed in the previous chapter, union's want to contribute to meeting the material needs of society, in a way that contributes to greater equity for all participants, at work and beyond.

"Theories" of the union movement exist, and there are several systematic attempts to clarify its different forms, purposes and motives (Crouch, 1982; Hyman, 1973, 1997, 2001a; Lyman, 1995; Perlman, 1958) and see related work in Tilly and Tilly, 1981; Kok, 2002). Larson and Nissen (1987) comment it is appropriate to think of a theory of the labour movement in terms of "overall social roles." For them, the different aspects of the labour movement can be understood as follows: 1) an agent of revolution; 2) a business institution for economic protection of its members; 3) an agent for extending industrial democracy; 4) an instrument for achieving the psychological aims of groups of workers; 5) an agent for moral and spiritual reform; 6) an antisocial, destructive monopoly; and 7) a subordinate mechanism with "special interest" functions in a pluralist industrial society (p.4). Social class and/or occupational features are central to the theories of these and many other authors. In this chapter, we begin with the basic model explained by Bernard (1998). In particularly accessible form, she highlights the danger of the false dichotomies of "social and political" unionism (i.e. broad concerns over equity and democracy in society) versus so-called "bread and butter" unionism (i.e. focused on issues such as pay and conditions of work amongst members only). Clawson and Clawson (1999), Carter (2000), but in particular Richard Hyman (1997), offer more elaborated theoretical frameworks which point toward a typology of trade unionisms, but for our purposes we begin from three basic forms of unionism that each play out differently across the different policies, politics and practices of workplace learning: company unionism (workers' organizations that accommodate the prerogatives of management); service unionism (workers' organizations that seek to improve the "bread and butter" conditions of their members only); and social movement unionism (workers' organizations that seek to build equity throughout society (see related discussion in Cohen, 2000; Greene and Kirton, 2002; Grevatt, 2001; Heery, 1998; Munro, 2001; Wets, 2000). The following sections expand and clarify worker perspectives and action with this basic model as a backdrop testing it against the specifics of union interventions into the broad world of workplace learning.

UNION-BASED EDUCATION AND WORK

We should talk about the role played by labor unions in democratizing work relations by giving voice to the less powerful, within a critical evaluation of union activity ... The changing questions for workplace learning researchers are to be found in education for workplace democracy. How does educational opportunity benefit workers? Is the claim that workers are empowered real? To what extent are so-called empowered workers given meaningful influence in a corporation's affairs? (Spencer, 2002, p.38)

For their own part, unions provide (or partner with other organizations in providing) a great many educational services that affect the workplace and the experience of it by workers. It has become a convention in recent discussions of labour education to use a three-category model: "tools" courses, "issues" courses, and broad "labour studies" courses. There is considerable variation in terms of specific topics and curriculum and these programs may be provided by an individual union local (United Food and Commercial Workers Union Local 175), a union organization (e.g. the International Brotherhood of Electrical Workers), a union federation (e.g. the British Trades Union Congress), a specialized public institution created to serve union members (e.g. South Africa's Development Institute for Training, Support and Education of Labour), or these courses may even be delivered through union/school partnerships (e.g. the McMaster University/Canadian Autoworkers Labour Studies Program in Canada, or the Harvard Trade Union Program in the USA).

REFLECTIVE QUESTION

In a policy paper adopted by the Ontario Federation of Labour (Canada) there is included an addendum that lists the eight "myths" of training. Similar statements on training have been made by national labour movements around the world. This particular list is a good summary of the type of approach to training that emerges when one takes a "labour standpoint" on the matter. To test your ability to understand this standpoint in relation to training, review the following statements and think about how and why they can be considered "myths": 1) More training is necessary because we are moving to a high tech future; 2) Highly-trained high-technology jobs mean higher wages; 3) A more highly trained workforce will mean jobs in Canada; 4) A lack of training has hindered the development of the Canadian economy; 5) Good planning for specific skill shortages is a priority; 6) Training is not a controversial issue; 7) Training is a good thing; and 8) Multi-skilling will provide greater job security. Now compare your responses to the American Federation of Labor – Congress of Industrial Organization's perspectives at the following website: <http://www.workingforamerica.org/documents/Factsheets/factsheet13.htm>.

More specifically, tools courses are designed to prepare members for an active role in the unions and through this in their workplace through the representation of the needs, interests and perspectives of workers as a whole. Mostly, these courses are targeted to current or future activists and thus represent education for a minority of members. They include such subject areas as effective leadership, grievance procedures or collective bargaining. These subjects teach skills and knowledge that relate directly to the way that work is organized, the way that workers' perspectives are represented as well as the way that tensions within the work process are resolved on a day-to-day basis.

Issues courses are more broad. They include subjects such as workplace reorganization strategies, racism or sexism in the workplace, technological change, and even training or apprenticeship development policy. Like tool courses the skills and knowledge developed in these courses relate directly to how work is organized, but unlike tools courses they provide a more general framework for understanding the issues that affect the workplace environment. Labour studies courses provide the broadest framework of all for union member's learning. These courses are often taught by university professors, and in many cases, lead to a state-recognized diploma or post-secondary school degree. Subjects include sociology, political economy and history with a focus on organized labour and its role in society. These courses have more distant and general effects on the way work is accomplished in organizations, but it would be a mistake to say they do not play an important role in shaping the directions that local collective bargaining and other forms of labour activism take in the workplace.

At the same time, it is worth noting that there have been other models of labour education which have thought more expansively. For example, in the 1970s and 80s many writings on labour education reported on worker education including 5, rather than 3, basic categories: i) basic skills; ii) union role skills; iii) social, economic and political; iv)technical and vocational; v) cultural and artistic (p.20). Hopkins (1985) elaborated on this with comments on how the distribution of union educational resources differed from country to country. That is, "developed" countries tend to invest the most resources in the union role skills with commitments to cultural and artistic activity varying by nation and many of the other categories being taken up by various governmental and private bodies;

and, in "developing" countries (with lower resource levels generally) the focus tends to be on role skills as well as social economic and political education with much less attention to technical and vocational issues, and an absence of any formal cultural programming. Interestingly despite the fact that time has eroded their influence, Hopkins (1985) points to the relatively substantial investments that unions in communist countries tended to make in cultural and artistic programming. In general, we would say that it is important to draw on a more, rather than a less, expansive model of labour education when attempting to assess the complete range of effects that unions have on workers and work.

Before proceeding farther, it is important to move briefly beyond curricular matters to address the emerging practice of "e-learning" within the union movement, which has grown significantly. In 1995, for example, unions scarcely had a "cyber" presence, whereas now the internet has become a standard organizational feature. Tangible gains are difficult to document at this early stage and there are many skeptics. Lee (1997, 2000) notes that the internet may allow organized labour to share information and increase communication within and between organizations,

> [T]he skeptics are right. All the thousands of pounds invested so far in fancy websites have not produced even a fraction of the promised results. That is absolutely true – and also absolutely wrong. It is wrong because it is a snapshot instead of a video. The important thing about understanding the net and the unions is that everything is in motion. Snapshots tell us nothing. (p. 1)

Skepticism aside, through the use of "digital signatures" the internet has allowed some online union recruiting as well as balloting (which has been done on a limited basis in the USA). In Canada, unions like the CAW have been quick to adopt policies and educational programs related to the Internet. Interestingly, it may be in the area of learning and education that cyber-technologies are most rapidly realizing their potential. This can be seen in the International Labor Organizations development of the "Union Course Reader" software (Belanger, 2001), while one of the best summaries of the brief history of e-learning in the union movement can be found in the collected work of Taylor (e.g. 1996a, 1996b, 2002; Briton and Taylor, 2000) and Shostak (1999). Supplementing these programs and general reviews are research initiatives as seen in Briton and Taylor (2000), Sawchuk (1998; 2002). More directly related to technology and the labour process, in places like Sweden (e.g. Ehn and Kyng, 1987; Ehn, 1988) and Canada (e.g. Henessey and Sawchuk, 2003), pro-labour scholarship has directly sought to contribute to soft- and hard-ware development and re-development cycles adding yet another layer to the way that unions affect work and learning in relation to computers. As in discussions of internal union education efforts above, e-learning generally affects change in workers including the ability to actively and effectively participate in the workplace and to represent labour interests across the many dimensions of work.

No matter what type of training offered, traditional distance education, learning circles, e-learning or face-to-face courses, the goal of the training is the same: to increase the ability of unions to represent workers and shape work and learning from the standpoint of labour. To be clear, the union movement doesn't just teach *about* work and the role of unions, all courses, even those as seemingly self-contained as "Effective Stewarding" or as abstract as "Political Economy for Trade Unionists" are meant to develop workplace union leaders or cadres and to mobilize workers *to affect change* in the workplace and beyond as well. Toward this end, all union education is undertaken with collective rather than strictly individualistic purposes in mind. This is expressed in the expectation that all course participants upon completion return to their workplace and share their new found skill and knowledge with others. To the degree this is a major distinction between learning in schools or in traditional employer-based training, this exemplifies the importance of informal learning processes for union-based workplace learning (an area we first discussed in Chapter 3 and to which we shall return below).

Stirling (2002) and Gereluk and Royer (2001) provide useful reviews of the education delivered by unions around the world. Stirling (2002) draws on earlier work (e.g. Bridgford and Stirling, 1988; Bridgford and Sterling, 2000) and reports from the European Trade Union College, all sources worth visiting in their own right, to offer an excellent summary of the different political economic contexts pre and post European Union for fifteen different countries. He characterizes union education in Europe as having "suffered two decades of hostile attacks and increasing pressures for change," and adds, "It is now emerging from this gloom with greater self-reliance and professionalism ... " (p.26). At the same time Stirling problematizes the "professionalism" taking root in the 1970s as a possible subversion of the traditional orienting principles of trade unionism based in solidarity and collective action (cf. Heery and Kelly, 1994). He specifically identifies workplace learning issues such as "skills-based competencies" development and understanding the organization of the labour process as two of the most dominant educational themes for unions. These themes play themselves out in different forms and with different foci in different countries. Across Europe we see the development and co-sponsorship by unions of "European Works Councils" (EWC's) mediate such things as time-off for training and funding. And, drawing on various national reports we see workplace learning themes emerging in such forms as negotiations over industrial relations regimes (e.g. in Greece; Kouzis, 2000), "Codes of Practice" regarding training (e.g. in Ireland; O'Brien, 2000), understanding and shaping the labour process (e.g. in Norway; Birkeland, 2000), computer literacy initiatives (e.g. in Germany; Romer-Karrasch, Gehrmann and Hanns, 2000), the development of workplace "training representatives" (e.g. in the U.K.; Ross, 2000; Munro and Rainbird, 2000) and so on. Wills (2001) and Miller (2002) add considerable depth to the discussion of EWC's specifically providing the background of their emergence in the mid-1990s as a means for unions (though officially employees *not* unions are participants) to mediate work as well as learning practices across multi-national corporations (see also Hall, 1992). He reports that by 1999, works councils had been initiated in 700 of the 1200 multi-national companies operating in Europe. Effective training for representative participation in these councils is supported by the European Trade Union College[1] and, in an indirect way, is an important means through which the worker's learning (as representatives) comes to shape the practices and agendas of workplaces. Specifically, EWC's offer a forum for negotiation of, among other matters, health and safety, vocational training, technological change and labour standards which *directly* shape the learning of workers at the establishment level.

It is worth mentioning particularly inventive and expansive approaches to understanding union-based workplace learning in Gereluk and Royer (2000; 2001) as well as work carried out through the combined efforts of the International Labor Organization (ILO), the International Confederation of Free Trade Unions (ICFTU), and the Organization for Economic and Cooperative Development's Trade Union Advisory Committee (TUAC)(organizations which together represent over 155 million workers worldwide). These approaches combine analyses of "sustainable workplace and environmental development" and issues of learning and effective change initiatives under a basic, but important, rationale:

> [t]he origins of the union movement itself can be traced to collective action that was taken against unsustainable forms of production that appeared during the First Industrial Revolution. By unionizing, workers gained protection, integrated with a limited right to participate in workplace governance, giving birth to the field of occupational health and safety ... [unions] are contributing to a cultural shift towards sustainable development, which increasingly affecting decision-making by workers, community groups and business. (Gereluk and Royer, 2001, p. 536)

Gereluk and Royer go on to say that the principle informing this type of union-based work and learning framework is that, as the ICFTU argues, "union-led activity in the workplace ... is the training ground for the democratic leadership which is needed in our society" (p.537). This work-based educational world-view is possibly best represented in the ILO's "Workers' Education and Environment Programme" (ILO/ACTRAV, 1996) launched in 1991. In this program, participants from around the world learned to respond to the needs of their fellow workers and communities through workplace action. In many ways, the expansiveness of this type of approach represents the next generation of critical, integrated theories of workplace learning in a global context with respect to the role of workers and their organizations.

REFLECTIVE QUESTION

At different periods around the world particular union struggles are instructive for what they have to tell us about the complex relationship between work, learning and political change. Two very different instances present themselves in the form of the South African labour movement and the labour movement in Los Angeles, USA. Explore literature on these two contexts and consider the following: What factors explain the contrast between these two situations? What is the role of union education as well as informal learning amongst union members?

TRAINING AND VOCATIONAL EDUCATION

Training is clearly on the agenda of public policy and political life. The reasons are many. Training is central to current management initiatives for the restructuring of work. It is also critical for politicians, as a substitute for a coherent industrial strategy. Most important, training has a powerful impact on the lives of working people, but it can be either friend or foe, depending on how it is done. (Beckerman, Davis and Jackson, 1992, p.iii).

Training is a tool of political struggle in the workplace (Dunk, McBride and Nelson, 1996; Kincheloe, 1999). Unions, such as those in the UK have enthusiastically attempted to build a union agenda in terms of training and lifelong learning (Trades Union Congress, 1996; Monks, 1999; Munro and Rainbird, 2000). Indeed, workplace learning today is enmeshed within a range of programs, slogans and initiatives that revolving around the need to develop a learning organization, and a knowledge-based, information economy. Moreover, the dominant view is that the barriers to achieving this type of 21st century workplace are found in workers themselves rather than in workplaces. Berg (1972), Carnoy and Levin (1985) and more recently David Livingstone (1999), Lowe (2000) and Wolf (2001), offer devastating critiques of the basic logic of this view. In different ways, they suggest that the problem is not workers, but rather the irrationality of *laissez faire* labour markets and the hierarchical, as opposed to democratic, organization of work and society.

Union involvement in forms of training policy debates has a significant international tradition. Canadian union educator D'Arcy Martin (1998) offers one of the most insightful, personal accounts of this role for unions. He describes in detail the challenges of this process, emphasizing the difficulties that many union movements have in dealing with what is called "open-field bargaining"; an approach in which unions, government and business come together to negotiate training policy. In broader terms, however, we see that organized labour is playing a key role in mediating training and various forms of vocational education through its influence on their respective national industrial relations regimes and through direct collective bargaining at the establishment, sectoral, national and international levels. Unions play a key role in establishing a normative, institutional and financial infrastructure that shapes training frameworks, resulting in an organized, pro-democratic voice on vocational and apprenticeship education.

> ### STUDY TIP
>
> A variety of useful resources for understanding the labour move-ment and workplace learning can be found on the Web. For exam-ple, the International Labor Organization's Training Centre in Italy <http://www.itcilo.it/english/bureau/turin/index.htm> offers a range of valuable resources that represent a labour standpoint on training issues. Foremost among them is the publication "Design, Management and Evaluation of Open/Flexible Training." The world's first survey of "informal learning" was done in Canada by the New Approaches to Lifelong Learning Research Network. This is also an important empirical source. A summary of this publica-tion can be found at <http://www.oise.utoronto.ca/~dlivingstone/ iage/index.html>. To better understand the research of informal learning, try the online survey on which this research was based at <http://www.oise.utoronto.ca/depts/sese/csew/nall/learn4.htm>. And finally, one of the most intensive studies of "union learning" in North America has recently been completed by Jeff Taylor at Athabasca University (Taylor, 2001). The website that accompa-nies this book is full of useful information as well as audio visual resources (see <http://unionlearning.athabascau.ca>).

Conventional wisdom, particularly in North America and Australia considers that employers and the state are responsible for vocational train-ing. However in other parts of the world, in distinct ways, organized la-bour plays a more active role in these matters. Some of the most progres-sive discussions in this area are found in Europe, particularly since the late 1980s with the establishment of the "Community Charter of the Funda-mental Social Rights of Workers" and related elements of the European Union's (EU) charter of rights framework. This policy framework states explicitly that "every worker of the European Community must be able to have access to vocational training and to benefit there from throughout his [*sic*] working life," and this basic element has been interpreted as requir-ing the involvement of public authorities, companies and trade unions as key participating partners. Situations vary according to national contexts, but at the present time, Australia (despite its relatively progressive history), the UK (despite recent changes), and North America do not have comparable, labour-inclusive structures. Some researchers (e.g. Hyman, 2001c) are skeptical of the real transformative value of these developments, nevertheless the EU's 1997 "Employment Summit" gave shape to these principles by urging partners to actively establish formal agreements to enhance training, traineeships, work-based experiential learning and lifelong learning capacity. Driving the process, as mentioned above, was the apparent need to develop a genuine knowledge economy, and despite contention over what this term might actually mean, it seems evident that "training" is one of the few areas where employer and worker interests converge. Public policy supportive of this shared interest quickly emerged in relation to the construction of the EU political framework centred on forms of collective bargaining.

These types of progressive training structures pre-date the establishment of the EU, however. ILO reports show that in the 1970s employer and union federations in France entered into central inter-sectoral agreements, which would become law in France, institutionalizing the rights of workers to ongoing training during working hours, financed through an employer levy system, and regulated by bipartite, labour/employer, bodies. Other countries, such as Belgium and Spain, offer similar examples of negotiated employer levy systems, while still others such as Finland, Austria, and Germany, have ongoing traditions of offering rights for worker representation on firm, sector or inter-sectoral level bodies. These examples are important to mention because this is where the negotiation of the actual content and specific access to training took place. These initiatives, along with firm-based collective bargaining, laid the groundwork in many ways for the emergence of the European Works Council system (see Miller, 2002) in its current form. Over time, they created a significant example of the way that organized labour influences workplace learning overall.

As mentioned earlier, a contrasting situation exists in Australia, according to Ewer (2000), where after promising activities in the late 1980s the union movement has found its national training reform strategy in tatters under the pressures of steady "marketization of vocational training" through which business has gained ever increasing control over design, delivery, access and assessment. Indeed, writers like Abrahart and T'Zannos (2000) confirm a general trend in Australia to break union involvement in vocational as well as apprenticeship learning. In contrast with most EU countries we see that in the UK employer intransigence is particularly strong (see, for example, Claydon and Green, 1994; Millward et al., 1992; Steedman, 1998). This despite the fact that research in the UK demonstrated that where unions are most active, better training and wider access to training for workers exists (Green and Wilkinson, 1996). These types of conclusions support the classic "exit/voice" research as well as analysis of union participation in "high performance" and "Quality" workplaces generally (e.g. Bender and Sloane, 1998; Freeman and Medoff, 1984; Kincheloe, 1999; Mishel and Voos, 1992; Osterman, 1995; Turner, Bertelli, and Kaminski, 1996; Shaiken, Lopez and Mankita,1997). This research argues convincingly that unions help establish better man-agement practices in organizations, and better communication patterns between workers and management as well as more relevant and more ef-fective workplace programs, including those involving training. Moreo-ver, as Elias (1994) has established, lower worker turnover (i.e. greater "voice" / fewer "exits") conform to the idea that knowledge can be accu-mulated better in unionized workplaces as well. Overall, there is good evi-dence for these indirect, as well as more direct roles (Heyes, 1993; Stuart, 1994; Wies, 1985) that unions play in issues of the character of and access to workplace training and organizational learning.

A very different model from the EU has emerged in South America, in particular in Brazil, where the historical development of political and eco-nomic institutions as well as labour processes make the region distinct from Europe, Australia or North America. According to Posthuma (1998) and Lopes (2002), through the 1990s and up to the present time the Brazillian vocational training system has undergone important changes as a result of direct popular and union pressure from below. While direct union involvement in occupational training dates back to the 1970s in Bra-zil (particularly in the steel, metal trades, and manufacturing), new mo-mentum for popular and union mediation of vocational and apprenticeship learning has surfaced. As Lopes outlines, the Third National Confedera-tion of Metalworkers of the Unified Central Labour Union Congress held in 1995 marked an important turning point in which occupational training took centre stage in the union agenda. "New institutionalities" in regard to participatory governance of vocational training structures have begun to be put in place, and will, in all likelihood continue to develop under the governance of the recently elected Workers' Party leadership.

APPRENTICESHIPS AND LEARNING

Apprenticeship training, is of course, linked closely to formal vocational education. It has been said that the earliest forms of the labour movement can be traced to the organization of journeymen craftworkers. Such groups formed to protect their skills and wages, as well as acquire the situated experience and sociocultural knowledge on which they built their craft (Schön, 1987; Wright, 1908; Unwin and Fuller, 2001; Taylor, 2001). Carpenters, shoemakers, stonemasons, cabinetmakers and a range of trades people took great pride in their work. As Wren (2002) outlines,

> The development of apprenticeship in any regulated form during the 19th century was closely related to the development and strength of the trade unions and collective bargaining. Construction Unions in Britain proposed reforms that included the attachment of apprentice to industry rather than to an individual employer .... (p. 7)

Contemporary researchers show that unions continue to play a positive role in shaping apprenticeship-based workplace learning. According to recent research in the USA (e.g. Berik and Bilginsoy, 2000; Castellano, 1997), unions are also playing an important role in facilitating greater gender equity in terms of retention and attrition probabilities in joint union-management apprenticeship training programs. Indeed, these studies indicate that union involvement raises women's graduation rates above those of both women *and* men in employer-only sponsored apprenticeships.

Key analyses of apprenticeship systems in Finland (e.g. Kivinen and Peltomaki, 1999), Germany (Streek and Hilbert, 1987; Culpepper, 1999) and the UK (Gospel, 1997) are instructive for understanding the tensions and dynamics of change as regards the role of unions as well. In general terms, apprenticeship systems and the strategies of unions in relation to them are undergoing change in the face of global capitalism. In Germany, a traditional stronghold of union-mediated apprenticeship system, the "long-term" view of skills development that has marked sustained productivity gains is in jeopardy, and with it the relative levels of equity experienced in the German labour market. Moreover, as Richard Hyman (2001a, 2001b) discusses in his review of the post re-unification German trade union scene, a complex form of union politics has emerged. Central to this scene is the need for renewed union mobilization in the context of rising unemployment and disruption of the traditional industrial training system. Among other things, this has led to a new "jobs alliance" strategy. This should be reviewed carefully for understanding models of union tactics in relation to vocational and apprenticeship learning.

ADULT BASIC EDUCATION

An additional element concerns labour's role in issues of literacy, numeracy and language development (i.e. work-based "basic education'). Unions have traditionally been interested in the need to increase these types of core skills among workers all over the world, though it is only in the last two decades that major public policy and employer interest has emerged in a sustained way. From a labour perspective, basic education not only increases the portability of worker's skills and knowledge, it also contributes to their ability to individually and collectively defend their economic and political interests through their unions. In sum, basic education is thought of as central to increasing equity in the workplace, the labour market and beyond.

Reflecting on the Canadian context, labour educators like Ian Thorne (2001) point out that issues of labour adjustment (i.e. workers being laid-off and having to relocate/retrain for new jobs) as well as immigration patterns associated with global trade agreements have helped spike concerns by unions over the issue of basic education. In response, through the 1980s and 1990s the labour movement in Canada has developed a range of programs at all levels: Basic Education for Skills Training (BEST; though now discontinued) in Ontario and Workers' Education for Skills Training (WEST) in Saskatchewan, run by provincial federations; basic skills programs run by the Canadian Steel Trade and Employment Congress, a sectoral council; and innovative programs run by unions such as the United Food and Commercial Workers, Canadian Union of Public Employees, and the Communications Energy and Paperworkers. Moreover, since the late 1990s the Canadian Labour Congress's Workplace Literacy Project (see Levine, 2002; http://www.clc-ctc.ca) has represented one of the most sophisticated models of critical adult basic education in the North American union tradition.

One of the most relevant, general summaries in regard to basic education and unions can be found in Holland and Castleton (2002). These authors set the stage for a comparative understanding of initiatives around the world, while providing a detailed analysis of the UK and Australian contexts. They note the prevalence of a narrow, economic/functionalist perspective that prevails in the area of most government and employer-based perspectives, programs and policies. Inherent in these, they say, is the presumption that workers, not funding, access and program content, are the problems. An important example they outline is an initiative in Australia in the early 1990s called the "Workplace Language and Literacy" program (WELL), that, like so many progressive attempts, collapsed under the pressure of sustained attack and the dismantling of progressive industrial relations laws by the government of the day. WELL was a policy plan through which trade union councils as well as individual trade unions were able to influence basic education programs through various forms of tripartite committees. A more recent initiative, the UK government's "Adult Basic Skills Strategy," also makes room for union involvement. This occurred through the establishment of the "Union Learning Fund" involving the central labour federation (the Trades Union Congress (TUC)) (see Monks, 1999). Importantly, however, Holland and Castleton (2002) note that this basic education agenda is inseparable from contemporary employer agendas for workplace restructuring:

> It is the impact of the Total Quality Management discourse and accompanying changing work practices and accountability requirements that have provided the greater impetus for workplace literacy programs, rather than equipping members to cope with the demands of industrial relations issues and enterprise bargaining. (p. 94)

Indeed, the TUC, like other labour bodies before it, finds itself treading an increasingly fine line between balancing the needs of members and employers, encouraged by the trust it places in the Labour government. What these and other examples and analyses show, is that labour has played an important role in work-based, basic education, but that this role has important political implications.

PEL AND PLAR

Another element of union involvement in training and continuous vocational education are initiatives to allow workers to take time from work to become more educated (e.g. Paid Educational Leave (PEL)) as well as allow them to get formal credit for the everyday learning they develop informally (e.g. Prior Learning Assessment and Recognition (PLAR)). PEL operates in the realm of formalized learning. Union-negotiated PEL (as distinct from forms of PEL offered by the governments such as the innovative policies of Sweden) links a great deal of the discussion of vocational education with the workplace directly. In the USA, the United Autoworkers have been leaders in this regard, where the PEL program is currently under the direction of the committees at the UAW-GM Centre for Human Resources. This educational programs is broad, including courses in economics, politics and technological studies relevant both to work as well as the collective bargaining process in which the content as well as access has been actively negotiated. Participants travel to various parts of the country to meet with experts in all areas, and programs are delivered by both union and employer representatives. In the UK, a coalition of unions, labour federations, and other progressive social groups has formed to establish the "Paid Educational Leave Campaign."[2] In Canada unions have negotiated the inclusion into their collective agreements such elements as the Canadian Autoworkers' "Tuition Refund Plan for General Motors Hourly-Rate Employees," the Ontario Public Service Employees Union's "Work Related Tuition Reimbursement" clause, or the Canadian Union of Postal Employee's "Educational Leave" clause (see specific contract language in Beckerman et al., 1992: Appendices).

In the realm of informal work-based learning unions have been actively considering the potential uses of PLAR (alternatively called Accreditation of Prior Learning (APL) in the UK; Validation d'Acquis Professionnel (VAP) in France; Recognition of Prior Learning (RPL) in Australia, and so on) as a means of influencing patterns of (and credit for) workplace learning as well. The Canadian Labour Congress's Training and Technology Committee, for example, produced one of the world's first "Statement of Labour Values" regarding PLAR (2000). The potential of PLAR is that it will provide workers with recognition of their skills as well as support for entering into further educational opportunities. However, from the perspective of unions, PLAR comes with some dangers. A labour perspective on PLAR is summed up nicely by Laurell Ritchie (1999) (an official of the CAW) in which she articulates several core concerns revolving around issues of confidentiality (e.g. who controls the information gathered in PLAR?); privatisation of educational work (e.g. will educational workers be downsized as result of PLAR); erosion of apprenticeships; punitive results for workers not participating; the downloading of training costs onto the backs of workers; and so on. Likewise, in Sawchuk (1998a; 1998b) similar concerns are expressed by rank-and-file union manufacturing workers in the Canadian chemical industry. From the perspective of organized labour, workplace learning in the areas

of PEL and PLAR is as highly politicised and contentious as other vocational education, training and apprenticeship issues.

UNION EFFECTS ON EVERYDAY LEARNING AT WORK

> [T]he organization of work settings and work processes has always
> represented a – if not the – dominant influence in the formation of
> re-formation of knowledge, skills, abilities and psycho-social char-
> acteristics of working adults. This influence extends beyond the
> adult workers themselves to their families and socio-cultural life
> contexts. Thus the organization of work can be regarded, in the
> broadest sense of the term education, as playing an educative role
> vis-à-vis workers … Despite the widespread acceptance of the old
> adage that "experience is the best teacher," little attention has been
> paid to what the experience of work is teaching workers.
> (Schruman, 1989, pp. 42-43)

Workers learn a great deal informally through the course of the everyday experience of the labour process, whether unionized or not. As we
discussed in Chapter 3, the way paid work is designed (task variety, flexibility, decision-making, etc.) represents a type of informal "pedagogy"
complete with overt as well as hidden forms of curriculum. Through their
varying levels of involvement in control over the production system, unions influence this learning experience and shape its curriculum, in many
cases generating a curriculum of their own.

Schurman emphasizes that research pays little attention to the everyday experience of work as a form of "education." Now, over a decade
later, the issue is emerging as an important theme of the workplace learning literature. At the same time, one of the most important schools of
analysis of work processes known as "labour process theory" (see Chapter 3) has been slow to theorize everyday learning and the ways unions
shape this process. Thus, careful research combining a solid understanding of social and economic dimensions of work, learning, control and resistance has suffered. Peter Sawchuk (2002; 2003) offers insight into how
the union movement plays an educational role *vis-à-vis* the labour process. In some cases (see Sawchuk, 2001a), we see examples of unions constituting a parallel working-class "learning organization" at the local level
complete with its own unique modes of knowledge production. Indeed,
unionization provides workers with a fundamentally different foundation

for interpreting their experiences of work, and gives them a greater sense of agency concerning their involvement in work. In the final instance, workers still may not have much meaningful control over how work is formally organized, but the sense of agency that unions can provide may be directed toward forms of active disengagement and so on. We should bear in mind that the basic "curriculum" of the capitalist labour process is not a particularly positive one for the majority of workers. In the absence of formal union intervention and/or informal forms of resistance, workers everyday participation in work teaches them that they do not have control, and, in the worst case scenarios, that they have only their sweat and tolerance to "dumbed down" tasks to offer.

Understanding how unions shape workers' everyday learning can be difficult, but fortunately, there is a set of literature that provides some important clues. A critical point of relevance for unions is whether or not work teaches workers to act in individualist or collective ways, and whether or not unionization can affect these patterns (see Peters, 2001 for a provocative theoretical discussion of unions, management systems and personal autonomy). The labour movement, founded on collective action, obviously sees the development of the capacity for collective action as vital. These studies are only rarely framed in terms of collective and individual learning processes *per se*; nevertheless, the evidence is international, richly documented and, when viewed through a "workplace learning lens," relevant for our purposes.

REFLECTIVE QUESTION

In a book on union perspectives on training (from Beckerman et al., 1992, p.2), Canadian union activist/educator Jim Turk provides useful exercise. He writes, "Surprisingly, when you ask workers if they can do their jobs well, you get an almost uniform answer – "Yes." When you then ask whether they were trained by their employer to do the jobs – the most common answer is "No." Try this out yourself on your friends." If Turk is correct, what does this say about future strategies for workplace learning? If the majority of training takes place informally, what kind of strategies does this suggest for unions, management and policy-makers? What kind of factors contribute to quality informal learning at work?

To summarize the recent research in the area, we can begin with work in the Danish context by Madsen (1997) as well as Bild, Jorgensen, Lassen and Madsen (1998), which shows that the organization of work does shape workers' sense of agency and willingness to engage in collective behaviour. The 1998 study specifically adds that forms of collective bargaining also seem to have important effects in these terms. Research with Finnish (e.g. Jokivuori, Ilmonen, and Kevatsalo, 1997; Ilmonen, 1998) and Swedish trade unions (e.g. Allvin and Sverke, 2000) suggests that the type of work (white collar vs. blue collar) as well as gender, age and prior education mediate this type of learning. Biographical research from Australia (e.g. Western, 1998) confirms similar relationships between the organization of work and individual behaviours and beliefs in terms of collective action. Studies of the UK financial services (unionized call centre workers) show the inter-linkages of unionization and resistance in the face of new forms of work intensification. A particularly interesting analysis of union activity in the UK provides a detailed taxonomy of practices including "trade union collectivism," "workplace collectivism" as well as a more diffuse "social collectivism of everyday life" (Stephenson and Stewart, 2001) citing the mediating role of work organization. Comparative research in the banking sectors in the UK and France (Thornley, Contrepois and Jefferys, 1997) and the manufacturing sector in the UK and Spain (Ortiz, 1999) show stubbornly intact worker attitudes towards collective action despite new forms of work organization. In the USA, interesting analyses of unionized workers actively constructing their own cultural/economic environments (including the progressive and less progressive results of this; see Herod, 1997) also demonstrates the relations of everyday life and its effect on workers' behaviour/learning. Even the effects of fledgling, post-communist trade unions in the Russian mining industry (Ashwin, 1997) show how unions can and do mediate everyday conflict resulting in changes in worker attitudes and practice. What is clearly documented in these studies in the fact that the way work is organized can have important "learning" effects for workers. To the degree unions influence the organization of work, they simultaneously influence the learning lives of workers. We should note that few of these studies have used "learning processes" as opposed to "skill," "behaviour change," "resistance," etc. as the unit of analysis, providing rich opportunities for workplace learning scholars and practitioners to engage in secondary analysis.

CAMPAIGNS, CULTURE AND COMMUNICATION: THEIR AFFECTS ON WORKERS AND WORK

Raymond Williams, one of the seminal writers on working-class culture, remarked that the greatest cultural achievement of the working-class is the creation of the labour movement. As we briefly discussed in Chapter 3, when we examined team learning from a critical perspective, strikes are a powerful form of workplace learning for union members, and this learning reverberates throughout the workplace long after the strike is over. A workplace is never the same after a strike, and this is the result of more than simply a collective agreement won or lost, and financial costs sustained by workers, their unions and companies. A strike affects the workplace through the lessons, large and small, it teaches workers. Social science literature provides detailed examinations of strikes to which a range of learning analyses can be applied: from analyses of Poland's solidarity strikes (Barker, 2001), the UK's 1984-85 miners' strike (e.g. Allen, 2001), the strike of South African Sarmcol workers (Bonnin, 1999); to a variety of detailed analyses on strikes, both old (e.g. Johnson, 2000) and more recent (e.g. Beckwith, 2000) in the USA and Denmark (Mikkelsen, 1998). These studies show how strikes create intense learning opportunities for workers with long-term effects. Union campaigns also teach a great deal, and are increasingly thought by union intellectuals to be an effective form of active, direct learning for members (Cooper, 1997; Mantsios, 1998; Wong, 2002).

Electronic media and labour arts are among the elements of union life most often ignored in terms of their educational value, and even more so in terms their contribution toward the representation of workers' interests in the workplace. Trade unions have had limited involvement in television and radio productions; in Canada, for example, there have been such recent attempts as "Working TV" (British Columbia) or the Canadian Labour Congress's "Union Wave" radio broadcasts. Garment workers in New York fought to establish radio programming in the 1930s (e.g. Godfried, 2001), and in Australia there has been an attempt to establish Internet radio telecasts (e.g. "Wobbly Radio'). An excellent example of a study of mass media and its direct effects on workers' union learning, work organization and strike activity is by Roscigno and Danaher (2001). The authors analyze the effects of radio on textile workers in the southern USA between 1929 and 1934, and clearly demonstrate how such learning contexts emerge. Learning analyses focussing on the effects of mass media and unions on the workplace remain rare, however, and in this sense the area is an untapped focus of systematic research.

Labour arts, broadly conceived, provide some of the most engaging sources of learning for workers. Hansome, writing in 1931, commented on the importance of "festivities, theatricals, choral societies, sports and recreational events under labor auspices ... which conduce to morale, group loyalty, [and] solidarity" (p.62). However, Michael Denning, an American cultural historian, wrote "[w]ork itself resists representation ... Stories, after all, come from travels, adventures, romances, holidays, events: interruptions of the daily grind" (1998, p. 244). Taylor (1988) writes that the complex of "work" seems to defy analysis in many ways with the "[n]ovelists and imaginative writers have done rather better than psychologists and sociologists in describing what has [been] sacrificed (p.206). And, it is perhaps these facts that make the arts so relevant to the workplace learning process for workers. The connections between workplace learning and the arts can be thought of in terms of a number of key categories, though many overlap and few seek to address issues of the labour process in isolation from the more general sensibilities and experiences of workers' lives. Art, and particularly visual and performance art, by its very nature can represent the complex and contradictory reality of work from a working-class standpoint. There is long history of great artists associated with radical politics and unions, some of the most prominent being the Spanish painter Pablo Picasso, the Mexican muralist Diego Rivera, the African-American singer Paul Robeson, and the German dramatist Bertholt Brecht. Important international examples of labour arts initiatives include the "Art and Working Life" program (Australia), the "Bread and Roses" program (USA), "Mayfest" events in Glasgow (UK) as well as the formalized governmental/union cultural programs in Sweden. In the past, initiatives such the Federal Theatre Project in the USA (O'Connor, 1973; O'Connor and Brown, 1978), interwoven with the largest wave of strikes in US history and significant international events such as the Spanish Civil and the rise of fascism, were at the centre of one of the most progressive and energetic periods of union activity in North America (1930-40s).

Beverage and Johnston (1999) note that Frederick Taylor was one of the first painters to exhibit in a union hall, specifically in 1944 at the International Association of Machinists hall in Montreal. Many Canadian writers directly addressed themes of work and working-class life and politics, including Gabrielle Roy, Ted Allen, Irene Baird, Donald Durkin and others. According to Beveridge and Johnston (1999), one of the most important, early instances of arts, labour action and, we could add learning was seen in the 1950s in Sudbury (Ontario, Canada). There a remarkable union tradition emerging from the Industrial Workers of the World (IWW) and the radical International Union of Mine, Mill and Smelter Workers, led by Weir Reid (hired as recreational director of for Mine Mill in 1952), taught and mobilized workers in the 14,000 member union local 598. Later, unions such as the United Steelworkers of America, with their "Going Public: The Steelworkers Communication Policy" (1985), adopted explicit arts policies. Although these activities are not *only* educational, their educational value for understanding work and society are indisputable. The fact that some of the most progressive work reforms were initiated by such locals as Mine Mill 598, and others developing sophisticated cultural/educational programs, is no coincidence.

The Canadian union movement continues to offer a full range of artistic forms directed at helping workers cope with and transform the workplace. Novels, short-stories and poetry (e.g. the work of Canadian Auto Worker activist/writer Ron Dickson or the recitations presented at the Mayworks Festival's "Woman Talk" events) put the labour perspective and key issues for workers into words. Sculpture, photography and videography organized by the "Working Image" exhibits at the Mayworks festival, embody the experience of, and contradictions within, the workplace. Painting, such as the works of United Steelworker activist Charlie Stimac or Carl Wesley Jean (Canadian Union of Public Employees), "educate" on a similar level as does dance (e.g. the work of dancer/choreographer and International Brotherhood of Boilermakers activist Tom Brouillette), and drama (e.g. the work of the Queer Artists Union Collective). Music continues to be central to the way worker perspectives on work and life are shared, with the "Music in the Workplace" program of the Mayworks festival being an important example.

In educational terms, there are few more powerful and more immediate means of building awareness and understanding of a complex social reality than those offered by visual art. And, though it is not conventionally thought of as either "labour education" or "workplace learning," the representation of art that expresses workers' perspectives on work is a vital form of learning practice with unique powers to mobilize and inform.

'Hearts starve as well as bodies, Give us bread, but give us roses."
When workers develop collective strength, many outsiders assume that the driving force is wages – bread ... To the degree that the labour movement has survived and thrived, it has been on issues of equity, dignity, fairness, the broader social vision – the roses. Without that vision, it is harder to imagine an alternative ...." (Beveridge and Johnston, 1999, p. ix)

SUMMARY

In this chapter we have provided an overview of the many ways unions shape learning associated with paid work. We emphasized from the start that the purpose of the union movement is to represent the interests and worldview of workers. In this sense, the goals of workers and their unions may overlap as well as run in opposition to those of management. For the union movement, managerial notions of productivity and cost-cutting run second place to the development of skills and knowledge at work. Unions seek to shape learning for the purposes of building a quality workplace with greater participation in work and work planning, and more creative, humane and healthy conditions.

We began our discussion with how labour unions develop themselves internally through various types of skills courses, issue courses as well as broad "labour studies" education. This is the most organized expression of what the union movement believes are the skills and knowledge its members need in order to effectively intervene within the world of work, a world in which bosses formally control how work is organized and carried out.

We turned our attention to literature, analysing the roles unions have played in the realms of vocational education, training, apprenticeship, basic education, PEL and PLAR programs. Central to this was discussion of the many past and currently emerging organizational structures at the workplace, at sectoral, national and international levels. Collective bargaining as well as forms of "open-field bargaining" are important means by which unions shape the patterns of learning we see in workplaces around the world.

Finally, we drew on a diverse array of literatures other than those that explicitly reference learning, training or education for work. Industrial relations, history and sociology research shows that the organization of work shapes the everyday learning experiences of workers, and that unions play an important role in mediating these effects. We explored cultural studies, history, media and arts research to discuss the role of mass media, communications, and labour-based arts. These arts have unique powers to shape agency, understanding and learning related to work and workers' lives.

REFLECTIVE QUESTION

This chapter has dealt with research on learning and the labour movement, but little has been said about how one goes about doing this research. There are of course a variety of ways, but in the book *Hidden Knowledge: Organized Labour in the Information Age* (Livingstone and Sawchuk, 2003 – Garamond Press) the authors comment that there is an "easy way" and a "hard way" to carry out educational research in partnership with labour unions. The hard way involves careful consultation and involvement of both individual union members in the research process but also integration with the union's organizational structure. Review this text and ask yourself: How might the "hard way" contribute to the types of learning purposes and goals of the labour movement as described at the beginning of this chapter?

In our view, to understand fully workplace learning requires a critical awareness of the social perspective of workers and the functions of their organizations. The union movement has an incredible capacity to shape the character and experience of learning at work. Unions function in many different ways (e.g. business, service and social movement unionism), delivering courses, creating training structures and policies at all levels, negotiating with governments and employers. Most importantly, however, unions sustain a cultural life in the workplace and beyond that, through its diversity, positively expresses the unique economic and political standpoint of workers.

Notes

1. As Miller indicates, see www.etuco.org/etuco/en/projects for a sense of how this has been accomplished.
2. www.paid-educational-leave.org.uk

CHAPTER 6

Adult Education, Learning and Work

Labour will come into its own when workers discover better motives for production and finer meanings for life. (Lindeman, 1926, p. 27)

Contemporary thinking and research about work and learning generally suffer from narrow conceptions of both phenomena . . . The only effective solutions to current underemployment problems ... include work redistribution and workplace democratisation. (Livingstone, 2001, p.60)

The second quote (from a leading Canadian sociologist of education) helps us shift our focus from *managing* the workplace for economic efficiency to *freeing* the workplace for participatory democracy, a theme further elaborated in the final chapter. Our concern with democracy and freedom in the contemporary workplace is but a recent expression of an age old trend in the adult education movement. This gives us the courage to know our strength, and the confidence to interpret workplace learning as a part of a broader and deeper movement.

Most of the current workplace learning literature focuses on the job site in which managers explore ways of managing workers or in management parlance, "human capital." If we expand the notion of work beyond the job site and incorporate our life's purpose and vocation (that may or may not be directly related to our job, that is "paid work"), inquiry into workplace learning is considerably enriched. David Livingstone stretches our frame of reference further with these words:

In economically advanced societies, there are at least three distinguishing spheres of work (paid employment, housework and community volunteer work) . . . the relations between paid work, housework and community work may represent major dimensions of future economic change." (2001, p. 2)

From an adult education perspective, we argue that conventional understandings of work and workplace learning are too narrow in the face of growing complexities in all aspects of life (Hart, 1995). At the most basic level, work cannot be understood solely as what we do for pay since much of the important "work" that is done in the world is unpaid. By expanding our definition of workplace, we are free to locate workplace learning within many and diverse traditional adult education settings including the home, places of worship, service clubs and voluntary groups. We would extend Livingstone's notion of "housework," for example, away from an edifice where we engage in domestic chores to a space in which we accomplish "motherwork" (Hart, 1995) encompassing the nurturing work that is part of our essential humanity. Furthermore, it is our view that even the "job-place" cannot be thought of as isolated from broader social life and social struggle; this opens for us a view of learning within new social movements which is also attracting attention in the literature (Foley, 1998). In fact, few of these "expansive" perspectives are new to adult education. As we demonstrate below, the adult education movement has frequently affiliated itself with progressive activities in the "informal economy," most often those linked with such groups as the cooperative movements, the feminist movements, the farmers' movements as well as the various peace movements. The concept of workplace learning has been an integral part of adult education from its formation as a distinct field of study and practice commencing in the early years of the twentieth century. Therefore, we feel it is essential that a book about workplace learning makes explicit the past as well as contemporary connections between the informal economy, social movements and adult education traditions, connections largely ignored in the emerging literatures of "workplace learning" proper.

What are our assumptions as we commence this journey? To begin with, we know precious little about learning as a phenomenon itself. What we do know is increasingly contested (Fenwick, 2001). At its most basic, learning is something taking place in our body, mind, or in our social environment, that we cannot see and which we take for granted. At the base of this "taken-for-granted," but central term are notions of knowledge, experience, judgement, skill and competence. Adult educators ask: What is knowledge and whose knowledge has value? We assume there are three broad categories of knowledge – official knowledge representing the state, expert knowledge representing the professions and people's knowledge representing themselves. Alternatively we could say there is declarative and non-declarative knowledge; technical and practical knowledge; formal and tacit knowledge (Beckett and Hager, 2001; Fenwick, 2001; Ileris, 2002). People's knowledge incorporates concepts generated from such phenomena as women's ways of knowing (e.g. Luttrell, 1997), working-class street smarts (e.g. Sawchuk, 2003) and indigenous knowledge (e.g. Dei, 1996). The works of two Canadians spring to mind. Smith's (1990) discussions of the "social organisation of knowledge" as well as the pioneering thoughts of Michael Polyani (1967) on "tacit knowledge" are important texts that expand our understanding of knowledge. Park's (2001) reflective knowledge, relational knowledge and representational knowledge is a recent contribution to our understanding of basic forms. Peter Reason's (1998) typology includes experiential knowing, presentational knowing, propositional knowing and practical knowing. Who owns knowledge? The emergence of "knowledge management" (KM), for example, raises important ownership and governance issues for management; how to convert the tacit knowledge of works into a managerially controlled "corporate" good. As McKinlay writes, "The audacity of KM is breathtaking. To appropriate and codify not just the specificities of individual experience, but also the reflexive meditation of workgroups on their collective activities and perceptions" (2002, p. 77). Do workers own their knowledge, do their organisations, or do they share? Keep these questions in mind as you continue reading.

REFLECTIVE QUESTION

What are your assumptions about adult learning theory as you begin this chapter?

After sketching the evolution of some theoretical approaches, we highlight six critical points for our understanding of learning theories for the twenty first century. The six are: recovering our multiple selves; embracing new forms of knowledge; living with complexity, uncertainty, accelerated change and the possibility of chaos; understanding power; acting upon that power; and, celebrating democracy. These points are evolving as we collectively write, but on a broader disciplinary scale have also been evolving since the modern adult education enterprise began taking shape early in the twentieth century. We are assisted in understanding this evolving phenomenon by action research methodologies, especially participatory action research (PAR) outlined below. And finally, in this chapter we make another assumption. We assume that freedom is a fundamental human need. The question is – from a liberatory tradition perspective in the adult education movement – how do we see our struggle for freedom playing out in/at the workplace/job-place?

CHAPTER OBJECTIVES:

After reading this chapter, you should be able you:

1. Identify the key features of the evolution of the adult education movement in the 20th century as they pertain to workplace learning;

2. Identify the research strategies compatible with critical inquiry into learning in the workplace;

3. List the six critical trends guiding current inquiry into adult learning theory as they pertain to workplace learning.

This chapter places into historical context the current fixation with the concept of workplace learning as an extension of trends in the modern adult education movement that commenced in the early part of the twentieth century. This opens up our understanding of workplace learning beyond our position in previous chapters where we introduced the possibility of the ideology of workplace learning serving the economic needs of business organisations and strengthening managerial hegemony. Here, we introduce the "possibility of the impossible" (Woodcock, 1992) – workplace learning as a vehicle for practising democracy in the workplace.

Firstly, where did the liberatory tradition originate? Where do we see it in our work? If we call ourselves adult educators, we should know what this means and what our traditions are. Without tradition, without memory, we function blindly and are open to any fad or fashion, including workplace learning.

REFLECTIVE QUESTION

Can you imagine a rootless tree, a rudderless boat, a thoughtless action?

NATURE OF THE ADULT EDUCATION MOVEMENT

Adult educators in this century have been aligned with a variety of social movements which is part of the liberatory tradition. Canadian examples are: Moses Coady with the co-operative movement of the 1920s and 1930s; Ned Corbett with the social democratic movement of the 1930s and 1940s; Roby Kidd in the community development movement in the 1950s and 1960s; Catharine Warren with the women's movements of the 1970s and 1980s; Budd Hall and Darlene Clover with the environmental movement of the 1990s. There are many references to the adult education movement as a social movement in itself although this is never explained. Malcolm Knowles' (1977) history of the movement does not make clear if the movement was social, political or philosophical, or all or none of these. For others, the movement has been described as a "point of view" impacting social movements and institutions. Two American philosophers suggested: "Adult education is not so much a separate movement carried on by specific institutions as a point of view which is beginning to permeate institutions and practices" (Overstreet and Overstreet, 1941). Mitchell advanced a similar notion in 1967:

The neglect of adult education as an important segment of history stems from its nature. Although it is not a social institution, it permeates every institution as a marginal function and activity. It is not a social movement yet it is a part of every movement, and indeed is often the principal force that makes a social movement move. It is not a significant event because it permeates the whole structure of society and its significance in history is obscured by the events it produces (Mitchell in Hardy, 1967, p. xii).

This notion reflects well the amorphous nature of the adult education movement and still emphasises the significance of the movement as an important influence on social movements. We find it helpful to define the adult education movement as a social philosophy permeating society with the notion of learning as a lifelong process. This process must be facilitated by social institutions and organisations through provision of opportunities for all adults to continue their education throughout life in order to achieve individual self-actualisation, and create a better social order. Provision of educational opportunities throughout life is the means to the ends of individual and social transformation, criteria of which vary with time and place. The dual goals of the movement were first articulated in

The 1919 Report wherein the purposes of adult education in Britain were identified as "personal development" and "social service." The British adult education tradition is lengthy – the first history of adult education in Britain was published in 1850 – and has strongly influenced adult education in all English speaking countries.

The historical imagination locates threads over time that are woven into historical narratives with the careful touch of a storyteller. For our purposes, we are concentrating on the 20th century in preparation for what is coming in the 21st, not a straightforward task. Many of our individual and collective contributions to social movements remain untold and undervalued in mainstream adult education. Welton (1987) has been documenting contributions of men and women working for justice for working people, but there are many stories yet to be heard. We eagerly await histories of the various women's movements of the century interpreted as "social movements permeated by adult education." According to Lerner (1990):

> What is history? We must distinguish between the unrecorded past – all the events of the past as recollected by human beings – and History – the recorded and interpreted past. Like men, women are and always have been actors and agents in history. Since women are half and sometimes more than half of humankind, they always have shared the world and its work equally with men. Women are and have been central, not marginal, to the making of society and to the building of civilisation. Women have also shared with men in preserving collective memory, which shapes the past into cultural tradition, provides the link between generations, and connects past and future. This oral tradition was kept alive in poem and myth, which both men and women created and preserved in folklore, art and ritual. (p. 10)

Lerner's image of the power of women's knowledge expressed through narrative as a fundamental part of life is in keeping with trends within all disciplines wanting to democratise knowledge-making in the new century. It is as if we are preparing for a new age of knowledge-making accessible as never before to large numbers of people. Perhaps this is what Lincoln (1995) had in mind when she wrote: "there is a quiet revolution going on out there, a revolution where even ordinary people can be reconnected to the questions which drive their lives" (p.51). She links this revolution to the increasing attention given to qualitative research.

> Qualitative research does seem to have the power to enable people of all stripes to engage the questions, which are addressed. If this means an alteration – or even an expansion – of what is considered *scientific discourse* then we will have enfranchised a goodly number of everyday people. (p. 51)

What she means is that your voice and ours – voices of "ordinary" citizens, people's knowledge – are as valid as those of experts and professionals. This democratising imperative is a prominent thread in the modern adult education movement (Newman, 1999; Foley, 2001) and one on which we focus in our interpretation of workplace learning as a potential "satisfier" (Max-Neef, 1991) of the fundamental need for freedom.

While trying to explain the late 20th century's "sudden" interest in life-long learning, learning organisations and related concepts, we are convinced there is something to the notion of the "underground" nature of adult education (Mitchell, 1967). As we start the new century, signs indicate a major role for adult education. However, because adult education has long championed the individual learner, societal recognition of these values may simply emerge in broader social trends such as "workplace learning" and not be associated with a particular field such as adult education. Indeed, as adult education "permeates the whole structure of society," its very success renders it indistinguishable from the whole. Could this be ultimate success for the adult education movement – societies celebrating lifelong learning as a core value in all their workings simply as a matter of routine? Yet again, if we fade into the woodwork, do we forget who we are and where we've come from? Do we lose our memory? Do we lose sight of our "work" and lock ourselves into jobs that are becoming less secure? Is losing memory of our work another consequence of flexible capitalism (Sennett, 1998)?

THE LIBERATORY TRADITION: ITS ORIGINS AND CHALLENGES

At its core, the liberatory tradition in adult education encourages us to act in support of each other to remove barriers to our individual and collective freedom while creating an environment wherein we can be free to express ourselves and act to change our social realities. This desire is found in all societies going back to ancient times. Recently, historically conscious adult educators are articulating it at home and abroad. Michael Welton (1997) draws upon Canadian adult education traditions to resurrect our collective passion.

> I believe that many of our forefather and foremother educator of adults in farm, women's, worker and co-operative movements would be shocked and dismayed at the extent to which the modern practice of adult education has capitulated to a technocratic ideology, market-driven logic and rampant individualism. They understood adult education as part of the resistance movement to capital's maniacal drive to break into bits and create "possessive individualists" out of us all. They knew, to use the language of adult education in the Canadian farm movement, that "combined intelligence" enabled us to command our life-situations. Left to our individual resources, we would not be strong enough to counter those forces fracturing us – each against the other, class against class, men against women, group against group, region against region. (p. 31)

Welton founded the history sub-group of the International Council for Adult Education (ICAE) which has created the "Liberatory Moments History Project." He explained that the Project "has its spiritual origins in the heart-felt belief that we need the lessons and insights from many national and cultural traditions to know how to fashion practicable emancipatory projects and to articulate our dreams of justice and goodness into the longed-for 21st century" (Welton, 1993, p.3).

International examples of the liberatory tradition are particularly well illustrated in a 1993 issue of *Convergence*, the journal of the Canadian based ICAE. Here we see the principles of liberatory adult learning in the context of political education in the Zimbabwe liberation war, the protest tradition in Nigerian adult education, the Ulster People's College fight against sectarianism in Northern Ireland, the Soloman Mahlangu Freedom College in Tanzania and the Highlander Centre's continuing work with organised labour in the United States. Griff Foley (1998) has contributed to the tradition in a passionate and critical study of the learning taking place within emancipatory social movements. He draws on a basic historical materialism critique and case studies from U.S. working class women, Zimbabwean guerrillas, Australian environmentalists, and Brazilian and

Australian women. Berndt Gustavsson (1997) also focuses on social movements and learning.

> One of the main features of popular education is that learning takes place in social movements, amongst people in action. These movements and their role in the production of knowledge and learning processes are often crucial to the discussion of lifelong learning. Many people have their central insights and starting-points from studies and experiences rooted in social movements (p. 242).

This interest in social movements and learning should produce new adult learning theories. Work must be understood as representing a continuum of human activity, and specifically as more than what goes on in the "job-place" of paid employment. These startling, often heroic, examples of social movements help draw our attention to this fact. In this context, we suggest these activists are engaged in work. Indeed, it is work of a particularly important kind in that it attempts to add value to individual and collective human life directly, against formidable opposition.

STUDY TIP

As noted, the liberatory tradition has deep historical roots. It is associated with the progressive ideals contained in a diverse range of writers and social activists from the "Ranters" and "Diggers" of 17th century England to intellectuals associated with the French and American revolutions, on to Proudhon, Kropotkin and the Industrial Workers of the World. Examine one or more of the works in this area and suggest ways that the basic principles might inform progressive adult education today. (Black Rose, Montreal have published most of Kropotkin's books including the seminal anarchist work *Mutual Aid*.)

It is important to briefly register that adult educators, such as Welton and others, have settled on the word "liberatory" to convey specific historical linkages to the radical intellectual movements that emerged in Europe during the 19th century from which we borrow many of our ideas about liberty. However, the older and respected term "libertarian" that once referred to radical expressions of freedom – epitomised by the anarchists – has, to some degree, been co-opted by North American neo-liberals, who espouse "rugged individualism," an ideology easily morphed into an ultra-conservative agenda. It is appropriate to settle on the word "liberatory" if we keep an eye on its traditional philosophical origins, despite the pressures of co-optation.

Mainstream adult education today tends to avoid the political dimensions of adult learning, but the liberatory tradition of adult learning in the informal economies of social movements encourage our direct and active involvement in collective, democratic action. Unlike the famous struggles of adult educators such as Father Jimmy Tompkins (leading the poor in the Canadian Maritimes) or Myles Horton (helping to organise strikers in the Appalachians of the United States) or Paulo Freire (organising/educating rural peasants in Latin America) – in most core capitalist countries, at least, we are seldom called upon to engage in such open struggle. For most of us, it means petitioning our MPs to legislate tough laws against child abuse, sitting on the Board of a local association to improve community living, encouraging learners in our classrooms to get involved in democracy directly, and so on. This is changing, and we are entering a new era where direct action may be required if we are to honour our traditions. For example, we need to take a position regarding the universal protests to global capitalism illustrated by the organised protests against the emerging market hegemony of "free trade" arrangements. At its core, adult education of all kinds is the translation of knowledge into action. Writing in 1926 about the meaning of adult education, Eduard Lindeman cautioned: "Once we lose the sense of active participation in affairs, we sink to the level of inaction, or what is worse, silent opposition" (p. 37). For him, "adult education specifically aims to train individuals for a more fruitful participation in those smaller collective units which do so much to mould significant experience" (p. 38). Moreover:

> Experience is, first of all, doing something; second, doing something that makes a difference; third, knowing what difference it makes. Our personalities count for something; we enjoy experiences in proportion to the effectiveness of our actions. (p. 87)

These actions are not random or thoughtless, they are critical and disciplined as is adult education in its most progressive form. As the social context underwent change in the depression of the 1930s Lindeman's approach could be understood to mean "learning" for direct social action for fundamental changes in the social system itself.

Many Canadian and American adult educators today, specifically in the area of workplace learning, are unaware of the social action component of our field as it evolved in the 1930s through the 1950s, when in the face of emerging post-war prosperity and McCarthyism, there emerged the urge amongst leaders in the field to establish adult education as a "legitimate discipline." Social action and political concerns and activities became threatening in a new age of intolerance (prominent leaders like Eduard Lindeman were "red circled" by the new inquisitors) and writers sought the political safety of academic discipline. Some of the most articulate statements about adult education as a social force appeared as part of the "Social significance series" published by the American Association for Adult Education during the late 1930s and early 1940s. An International League for Social Commitment was formed in 1984 led by European and American adult educators (Hoghielm, 1984), an example of periodic attempts to revive the old passion.

On the whole, the social change element in the adult education movement seems to have faded as most adult educators support the status quo – flexible capitalism (Sennett, 1998) – by concentrating on becoming a "respectable" academic discipline. Some voices have spoken out occasionally against this preoccupation. Writing in 1953 in a British journal, even as the Cold War hardened the hearts of many, Verner warned of the enormous changes occurring and of the possibility of the redundancy of all educational institutions. If this occured, it made no sense to bolster up fading institutions. Verner (1953) declared:

> This makes a mockery of our efforts to resist changes and maintain the *status quo* and of arguments over university standards in adult education. We might better spend our time in some group planning on the future role and forms of the [adult education] movement. (p. 37)

For his part, Verner directed his attention to championing the community development method of adult education as the means of supporting democracy directly and with commitment. His advice to universities was clear and direct, and included the first statement in the adult education literature about the potential value of action research – an approach to knowledge making committed to immediate application of what is being learned.

Existing university personnel cannot provide this kind of training unless they too become a part of it through action-research with adult groups. Has traditionalism so pinioned our university departments that they are incapable of creating an adequate university curriculum for adult educators? (p. 41)

The liberatory tradition of adult education has the potential to offer an important alternative to mainstream ways of thinking about work and learning. Indeed, following Verner's lead, we should ask the same questions about the relationship between learning and change-making today. To see how one leading adult educator coped with changing political conditions, it is helpful to take a closer look at Verner's professional career. He seemed to reflect broader trends in adult education as a field of study and practice, and as the scholarly tradition of workplace learning emerges, his interrogation of the purposes of adult education during its emergence into "respectability" is instructive. He was born in the United States (in the state of Virginia he would be quick to remind people). After taking a post in 1961 at the University of British Columbia to set up the first Canadian doctoral studies program in adult education, he became a Canadian citizen. Like many North American adult educators, he started out as a rural sociologist, and this led him into community development work with Jean and Jess Ogden at the University of Virginia prior to World War II. He was attracted to the social change dimension of the adult education movement and wrote a good deal about the notion of education in preparation for social action (see Pyrch, 1983). He joined with Ralph Spence in the early 1950s to show how learners could be prepared for an educational approach to social issues – in this case to racial desegregation – by "helping them recognize issues, anticipate change and acquire the knowledge essential for an intelligent approach to action" (Spence and Verner, 1953, p. 42). Verner declared that adult education was concerned directly with educational processes leading to social action. These ideas projected an active though non-directive role for adult education in the processes of social change, and were accepted by many adult educators during the 1950s. However, the times were changing and a new era of intolerance created by a fear of communism shifted adult educators away from social action.

Verner continued his investigation of community development and in 1959 offered a distinction between the education and action components

(Pyrch, 1983). He suggested that community development was an educational method leading to co-operative community action and should not be confused with the action itself. A year later, he stated that learners required education in order *to adjust* to change while preserving the social order. That position inferred more of a passive role for learners in social change processes than the active role articulated during the 1930s, though Verner offered no explanation for his change of perspective. In 1953, he had written about adult education preparing learners *to anticipate and make* change. This notion of change invited more active forms of input for learners than his passive framing of "adjusting" to change. Perhaps he reflected the mood of the 1950s, intolerant of ideas seeking to amend the social order (Pyrch, 2002). For his part, Verner re-directed his scholarly efforts to building a distinct discipline of adult education. For an understanding of the evolution of the liberatory tradition, his shift in research focus in face of neo-conservative societal pressures associated with the Cold War may indicate a broader trend we see today. This trend, which we challenge in this book, was to see mainstream adult education move toward a human resource development and business focus and away from a commitment to democracy and freedom. Why is the dominant adult education literature business management focused, and why does the term workplace more often than not mean job-place? What happened to our liberatory work?

Evolution of Adult Learning Theories

During the 1960s, the U.S. Commission of Professors of the Adult Education Association undertook the first all-inclusive effort to detail adult education as an academic discipline. The way that a "discipline" was constructed through the commission debates and research tells us a great deal about workplace learning as a discipline, and many of the emerging debates in workplace learning research today derive from this earlier work. Commission member Max Birnbaum defined two major schools of adult education:

> The term "Traditionalist" will be used to denote all those who see mental functions or cognition as the central phenomenon in learning, who stress content as against method, who see their task as the liberal education of the individual, who stress the development of a mature value system, and who would, moreover, make

substantial use of the content of past civilizations, for example, the Great Books.

The term "Psychological" will include those who stress the importance of the emotions in learning, who are impressed with the influence of the unconscious in human behavior, the powerful educational value of group learning, the role of experience in learning, and the frequent conflict between values and attitudinal systems. (p. 35)

Led by the Commission of Professors, the search for adult learning theory had commenced.

To understand the emergence of "workplace learning" as a field of inquiry it is extremely relevant to see North American adult education in context. What were societal conditions in Canada and the United States at the time and how did they influence adult learning theory? There was a move away from the lengthy concern with social change issues that had included a strong focus on collective action in community-based democracy which had dominated the 1930s and 1940s. At the same time, there was a return to the individual as the centre of attention, perhaps not the "rugged-individualism" of earlier times, but something like it. The Cold War coincided with "McCarthyism" and anti-communist purges of the 1950s, and social change and collective action could be too easily come under investigation by hysterical "witch-hunts" on both sides of the border.

Through the 1960s and 1970s mainstream adult education continued to emphasise the individual with the focus on self-directed learning associated with the work of Alan Tough (1971), Malcolm Knowles (1975) and Cyril Houle (1961). These perspectives are well summarised by Merriam (1993). Despite this, though submerged by the dominance of the focus on the individual, critical questions were raised by such writers as Freire and Thompson about adult education's support of a liberal/conservative status quo. Close on their heels, Welton (1995) added a radical perspective drawing on critical theory, especially the work of the German philosopher Jürgen Habermas. Newman (1999) has recently visited the critical tradition in adult education by directing our attention back to our critical roots as advocates of adult education for social change. In a similar vein, Foley (1998) celebrates the critical tradition by demonstrating how we learn while participating in social movements.

Without implying anything like a linear model of progression, we nevertheless wish to see if there are themes running throughout the many theoretical perspectives that have emerged and receded over time, to see if adult educators have asked similar questions about the human condition and if these patterns continue into the workplace learning discourse. Historical inquiry – particularly in the genealogical, poststructuralist approaches inspired by Michel Foucault – in the contemporary globalized political economy has abandoned many of the pretences of forming a grand narrative of purposeful social progress, despite the fact that basic economic principles of capitalism remain in place. There is certainly a diverse array of traditions in adult education. David Boud (1989) refers to four main traditions of learning theory in adult education: training and efficiency in learning; self-directed learning or andragogy; learner-centred or humanistic; and critical pedagogy and social action. These traditions reflect different perceptions of freedom that closely parallel at least one of the foundational books in adult education. According to Lindeman (1926):

> Those individuals are free who know their powers and capacities as well as their limitations; who seek a way of life which utilizes their total personalities, who aim to alter their conduct in relation to a changing environment in which they are conscious of being active players . . . Freedom can never be absolute. None of us is self-determined. Self is relative to other selves and to the inclusive environment. We live in freedom when we are conscious of a degree of self-direction proportionate to our capacities. (p. 50)

Adult educators have been struggling to understand our roles and responsibilities in the search for freedom, and have often struggled to create the liberatory tradition in adult education, referred to in this chapter. We are now in a better position to pose and offer some answers to the question, but how does this tradition play itself out in the workplace? Clearly, one answer presents itself in the form of the basic approaches to the researching of work and learning.

Much research in adult education as a field, has been multi-disciplinary in the sense that psychology, sociology, anthropology, philosophy and so on have all contributed. One's disciplinary background becomes evident in the concepts with which one frames reality. In the past, classifications such as Verner's (1962) separated methods into the dimensions of individual, group and community. Recent classifications, influenced by organisational behaviour studies commencing in the 1950s, tend do something similar, replacing "community" with "organisation," implying an artificial/formal relationship rather than an organic one.

> **STUDY TIP**
>
> Distinguishing between community and organisation is a well established sociological practice. You may want to seek out the classic study written by Ferdinand Tönnies where he distinguishes between *gemeinschaft* and *gesellschaft* human associations.

Adult education research shows an interdisciplinary face when traditional disciplines "dialogue" together to create a hybrid result. The authors of this book are examples, bringing the views of scholars trained in industrial relations, organizational studies, sociology, history and adult education together in the text. This dialogical relationship fits within some of the earliest conceptions of the field of adult education, and is obviously suited to the field of workplace learning. In our collective writing effort, we consciously give and take from each other as we systematically draw upon our disciplinary experiences to create our interpretation of workplace learning. In this sense, we are putting into practise a form of action research.

PARTICIPATORY ACTION RESEARCH

The "action research community of inquiry" has branches in all of the social sciences and related fields such as education, management, medicine, engineering and social work (Pyrch, 1998). It insists on an action component in research to bring research to bear directly on current challenges facing humanity. Research must be practical; it must put into practice what is learned as soon as possible, without abandoning a critical eye. In the context of the liberatory tradition in adult education, and the linkage that is made between it and workplace learning research, action research is manifested in part in participatory action research (PAR) which grew out of resistance movements in Latin America to the neo-colonial policies of the U.S. during the 1950s and 1960s. This explains PAR's overt political agenda based on broad-based democracy and social change. With the emergence of international adult educators as leading spokespeople for PAR during the 1970s and the inclusion of PAR as a central theme of the

ICAE, the adult education movement easily took up this newer expression of older beliefs. In a way, we are recovering the meaning of adult education articulated by Lindeman in the 1920s. He had insisted adult education be responsive to the immediate needs of people, while encouraging us to take direct action to improve our own conditions.

Members of the Action Research family share insistence on the practical nature of meaningful knowledge. The philosopher of science Stephen Toulmin (1996) wrote:

> … the outcome of action research is. . .practical wisdom not theoretical grasp. In such knowledge, timeliness is essential: what is known is what needs doing here and now to handle a given situation. (p. 210)

This notion is a cornerstone of the adult education movement. Toulmin's concern with knowledge for a given *situation* leads us back to 1926 when Lindeman introduced his *situation*-approach to learning:

> The situation-approach to education means that the learning process is at the outset given a setting of reality. Intelligence performs its functions in relation to actualities, not abstractions. (p. 122)

These two American philosophers writing seventy years apart were saying similar things as they commented on the value of practical knowledge – the sort of knowledge adult education is all about. In this way, they represented the pragmatic philosophy of John Dewey. Linking these three philosophers illustrates the practical side of historical knowledge. It is helpful to know that important issues facing us in the 21st century have been a focus of the adult education movement for generations. Adult educators today are at the centre of knowledge creation rather than isolated in the "marginal" position in the world of education we once knew.

The adult education liberatory tradition figures prominently in the first international Handbook of Action Research (Reason and Bradbury, 2001). Amongst the many other perspectives in the Handbook, feminist voices appear, including a chapter on "feminism" (Maguire, 2001) in the section representing the "groundings" of Action Research. Maguire (2001) writes: "Feminist-grounded action research opens knowledge creation conditions to scrutiny, attempts to unsettle and equalize power relations between researchers and participants, facilitates conditions for empowerment and reciprocity, wrestles with dilemmas of representation and interpretation, and experiments with polyvocal research accounts" (p. 66). Maguire's interpretation clearly links feminist inquiry to our liberatory tradition. This leads us to wonder if the liberatory tradition might be interpreted as a feminine phenomenon, if not feminist. There are many feminist perspectives in the adult education literature (Tisdell, 1993), but are there perspectives that interpret adult education itself as a feminine concept? If adult education is a feminine concept, could this explain why adult education has been a marginal player in educational institutions, basically paternalistic cultures celebrating "power over" relationships? "Power with" relationships like interdisciplinary and transdisciplinary inquiry are still rare in the academy. If adult education celebrates femininity including a nurturing interconnectedness, our influence may be hidden behind the dominant culture's focus on individuality and aggressive competitiveness – flexible capitalism. If this is true, we can understand more fully why adult educators are marginal at best and perhaps anathema to an educational establishment wanting to remain in control of the "learning business," and to the management establishment's preoccupation with the "bottom line." Can we create new metaphors to celebrate the fluid, organic and free nature of adult learning? Can these metaphors facilitate workplace learning as a democratic process? How might we combine our liberatory tradition with the burgeoning interest in action research? How can we reconnect with our work and not be overwhelmed by our job?

STUDY TIP

PAR is an alternative methodology to the once dominant positivist or quantitative based approach in the social sciences. It stands in opposition to narrow modes of scientific thought. In the *Handbook of Action Research* (2001), several authors argue the strength of PAR as scientific methodology. After reading this section, outline an argument for or against PAR as an appropriate methodology for workplace learning. As a start, you may wish to read the introductory chapter in the *Handbook*.

CRITICAL TRENDS IN LEARNING THEORY

We now discuss six critical trends in adult education theory and practice that will directly shape the future of workplace learning scholarship.

Beyond Self

As we enter the new century, there is an emerging understanding in the adult education literature of multiplicity as the normal state of adult learners and a moving away from the domination in adult learning theory of the unitary model of self (Clark, 1999). Clark (1999) suggests a "nonunitary" model of adult learners. Emphasis on the individual self is at the centre of the concept of andragogy with its focus on self-directed learning originating in the work of Knowles (1970). These concepts have been critiqued on a number of fronts (Collins, 1998; Usher, Bryant and Johnston, 1997) but still appear prominently in main stream adult education. The assumptions of self-directed learning view the learner as having the power and the intellectual capacity to diagnose, plan, implement and evaluate their own learning. One consequence of this is the isolation of individuals into themselves cut off from the support and care of collectives like community, union and social class.

As we move beyond "self" into "selves," we unmask the myth of the individual self in our culture. Concluding a lengthy critique of the concept of self-directed learning, Chovanec (1998) asks: "If meaning is a socially constructed and mutually shared understanding, does the absence of an accepted definition within the discipline of adult education render the term *self-directed learning* meaningless" (p. 312)? Adult education has moved beyond the fiction of the generic adult learner. Cunningham (1993) comments on the myth that we are learner-centred and that we empower learners:

> We are often in fact domesticating, not educating, our students. We have bought into the myth of education as a liberating experience to enhance and increase life choices. In actuality, those who had life choices before they came to our classes or program continue to have about the same life choices on completion . . . Our values of individualization teaches our students to blame themselves because success depends on the individual. (p. 3)

We consider learner-centredness to be a naïve position that does not come close to approximating the political and ethical dilemmas, the contradictions, and the possibilities of collective action.

As we are moving away from the focus on the individual self towards the collective, there are trends directing us to explore more deeply in another direction. We are encouraging each other to search within ourselves to locate our spirtuality, our soulful self, seeking our "power from within" (Park, 2001). Looking at research practices in adult education, Usher, Bryant and Johnston (1997) suggest these practices can be viewed as simultaneously writing the self and the world. This indicates an autoethnographic (Ellis and Bocher, 2000) approach, an approach encouraging us to locate our authentic self. More than that, if we journey to and realise our authentic self, we will come to understand we are connected to an authenticity that extends far beyond our individual lives. This presents new opportunities for dialogical relationships. Flecha (2000) contributes to our understanding of these relationships through his seven principles of dialogic learning – egalitarian dialogue, cultural intelligence, transformation, instrumental dimension, creating meaning, solidarity and equality of differences. His theory and practice of dialogic learning evolved from a lengthy association with literary circles comprised of low-literacy adults reading the great literature of our times.

Expanding Voices

We are assisted in the recovery of ourselves collectively and reflectively by a concomitant recovery of other forms of knowledge – other voices. For example, until now, adult education literature has been dominated by Euro-American worldviews. This is being challenged more and more by Afro-centric perspectives (Alfred, 2000), indigenous science (Colorado, 1988) and a wide range of interests grouped under the banner of "popular education." Alfred notes that the Afro-centric feminist perspective is based on four assumptions: first, concrete experiences as a criterion for meaning; second, the use of dialogue in assessing knowledge claims; third, the ethic of caring; and fourth, the ethic of personal accountability. Colorado created an epistemological foundation for Native North American peoples explaining that "through spiritual processes, it synthesizes information from the mental, physical social and cultural/historical realms" (p. 50). Other powerfully creative and passionate voices are struggling to be heard. Dian Marino (1997) tells us about the language of silence:

> Those who want to understand injustice, or be in solidarity with the silenced, must learn to listen carefully to the language of silence. Silent resistance needs to be transformed into stories of resistance. Hidden cracks in our social consent need to be made visible. Per-

sonal stories and social histories of resistance and change, the failures no less than the successes, need to be widely shared. Otherwise we are left with the impression that community issues and struggles are born out of nothing – or that only extraordinarily heroic peoples can get involved and make a difference. (pp. 30-1)

Some of these voices have organised themselves into the North American Alliance for Popular and Adult Education that held its founding general assembly in Alberta in 1994. In attendance were anti-racist groups, environmentalists, farmers, First Nations and Native Americans, gays and lesbians, grass roots organisations, labour educators, people of colour, unions, youth and women organisations. They exchanged stories about resistance and success organised by various social movements. It may be that oppressed voices express themselves in subtle ways even in the face of their oppressors and the "arts of resistance" far more powerfully at work than first meets the eye (Scott, 1990).

Until recently, men have written the dominant literature. This has changed rapidly during the past two decades as many feminist perspectives have emerged, although there are feminists who believe much more needs to be done to overcome decades of neglect of women's voices in the literature. The question about the feminine nature of the adult education movement itself, posed earlier, may expand inquiry into the question of gender.

REFLECTIVE QUESTION

In terms of workplace learning, to what extent is the workplace characterised by masculine culture? How can the gendering of work help us understand how workplace learning is structured and practised in contemporary workplaces?

The growing power and confidence in the realm of qualitative research recently described in a new edition of the *Handbook of Qualitative Research* (Denzin and Lincoln, 2000), supports the expansion of authoritative voices in the world of knowledge-making. Foley's (2001) book on "strategic learning" includes ethnography and story-telling at the workplace as key aspects of his strategic learning methodology. In her most recent celebration of the power of the narrative, Bateson (2000) reflects on the power of story telling:

I believe that the choices we face today are so complex that they must be rehearsed and woven together in narrative. The decisions we make cannot be those of "economic man," rationally and short-sightedly pursuing self-interest, but those of an artist, composing a future of grace and truth. We will need new kinds of listening and looking to be open to new styles and harmonies. (p. 247)

In searching out the hidden transcripts of oppressed and oppressor alike, James Scott (1990) privileges the issues of dignity and autonomy rather than material exploitation.

However, there are forces ranged against these new contributions to the liberatory tradition. Richard Sennett (1998) writes: "The conditions of time in the new capitalism have created a conflict between character and experience, the experience of disjointed time threatening the ability of people to form their characters into sustained narratives" (p. 31). And as Flecha (2000) demonstrates, most people possess the requisite abilities. It is paradoxical that in these times of the recovery of hidden voices, we confront new tyrannies in the lack of time, opportunity and willingness to engage with these voices. In terms of workplace learning, our recovery of abilities surrounding us is offset by "managerialist" forces. Is there a down side to the acceptance of many voices? Do these many voices result in cacophony, or do they celebrate democracy?

Complexity and Chaos

At the same time, we are becoming comfortable with "learning within the unknowable" (Flood, 1999) as an expression of a challenge for the future in which adult learners are skilled players of the infinite game (Carse, 1990). This means something more than interpretations of the learning organisation concept stressing continuous innovation in an environment of constant change (Watkins and Marsick, 1993). New metaphors are needed to prepare the workplace for free and creative learning opportunities. Usher, Bryant and Johnston (1997) sub-title their book "learning beyond the limits." They suggest adult education thrives best in an atmosphere of uncertainty and lack of clear direction. We would argue that the liberatory tradition gives us the grounding to thrive in uncertainty, in the moorland that has replaced the field of adult education. The attempt to clarify the nature of adult education in the past partly included distinguishing between the field of practice and the field of study. With the arrival of postmodern discourse in adult education, some "were prepared to abandon the security of the bounded "field" of adult education for the rugged and open "moorland" of adult learning" (Usher, Bryant and Johnston, 1997, p. 26).

Marshall (1999) advances the notion of living life as inquiry meaning that "I hold open the boundary between research and my life generally" (p. 160). Does this describe her work? Does living life as inquiry mean that life itself is her workplace? This frees her to explore beyond the box-like "job-place." Her approach is strongly process and people-centred rather than outcome-based, "looking to devise something that would provide information and opportunities for learning as it went along, rather than a blueprint for perfection" (p. 164). Her notion of "living life as inquiry is a continuing unfolding process" recalls Lindeman's concept of lifelong learning.

We might view workplace dialogue as an open circle, compared to the closed box image of monological relationships. A few individuals may engage at any one time others will come and go, and this is fine. Ideally, control is shared and no one person takes over. The circle grows in the workplace and, if strong, will outlast any one individual or group. This encourages workplace democracy, and builds civil society more broadly, as we learn how to treat one another respectfully and joyfully while experiencing emancipatory learning. This is especially valid when thinking of motherwork and voluntary work although, perhaps, not as welcome in the dominant job-place. Foley (1998) argues that the unlearning of dominant discourses and the learning of resistant discourses is central to emancipatory learning.

> Consciousness and learning are central to the processes of cultural and social reproduction and transformation. The unlearning of dominant oppressive ideologies and discourses and the learning of insurgent, emancipatory ones are central to processes of emanciptory change. But these processes of emancipatory learning and action are not straightforward; they are complex, ambiguous, contradictory. (p. 16)

Complexities, ambiguities and contradictions should not overwhelm us. Indeed, these are simply routine factors in the current state of knowledge making in the various parts of the action research family influenced by complexity theory and other attempts to explain our world. There is a liberating aspect to the notion of learning within the unknowable (Flood,

1999) and embracing contraries (Elbow, 1986). We are liberated from the oppressive expectation of always being correct. We also are liberated from the myth of the "global project" intending to standardise human activity for the convenience of the financial and economic elite's of the world (Esteva and Prakash, 1998). It may be within the small, human scale, relationships that we can hope to discover meaning and joy in life, whether in community work, motherwork or paid employment.

In terms of facilitation, the question is, can we help each other enter the circle between the boxes? The circle configuration seems a good way to express interdependence and mutuality, to feel the organic nature of this kind of learning. The image we see is an open circle where there is continuous change and learning. Individuals enter and leave depending upon work's/life's demands. The circle continues as we come and go. As new individuals arrive, they are introduced to the protocols – as members return they are brought up to date. In this way we all are learners and teachers. While in the circle, we engage in a narrative – dialogue even – to give shape and meaning to our life, suggesting reasons why things happen, showing their consequences and agreeing to take action directly to improve matters. We need this to heal what Sennett (1998) refers to as the corrosive effects of flexible capitalism.

In Chapter 3 we offered a critique of team working and so-called "flexible capitalism." Similarly, Sennett (1998) exposes a controlling quality in the concept of flexibility. Garrick (1998) agrees and adds that "becoming "more flexible" can be coded language for workers having to accept additional responsibilities, perhaps having to work different (more extensive) hours, but being paid no more" (p. 8). Garrick and Usher (2000) identify an unspoken dimension of learning in the workplace; "a hidden curriculum where what is learned is flexibility itself – a set of values and attitudes which stress adaptability, continual modification and an acceptance of fluidity and uncertainty as a permanent condition of subjectivity" (p. 10). Garrick (1998) earlier had something to say about the power of the hidden curriculum and what we might do about it. He wrote:

> If conceptions of training are to be better, they will have to take
> seriously the contested status of knowing/knowledge and include
> the characteristics of self-negation, irony and doubt. This means a
> high degree of tolerance for unanswered questions, uncertainty,
> ambiguity and difference. By definition, therefore, some prob-

lems will never be fully resolved, indicating new demands upon mental life. (p. 79)

What John Garrick is saying sounds a lot like the need for critical thinking/doing that is missing from our educational system. An inability to deal confidently with issues of power and control in everyday life is one consequence of being poorly prepared, and devoid of a healthy scepticism and a critical eye. We require considerable mental strength, faith and mutual support in order to maintain a sense of freedom within the turbulence Garrick sees in the contemporary workplace. This notion may fit within the liberatory tradition as, like adult educators of old, we work subversively in the face of controlling trends. We render transparent issues of power and control in adult education settings like the workplace.

Instead of transparency, we search for translucence where energy is generated and shared, and we can detect the glow generated by the energy. The energy is diffuse, protected from being seen too clearly, and open to co-optation. Given the traditional role of management discussed in Chapter 2, can we imagine a situation where workers collectively assist the goals of the organisation while retaining their integrity as workers whose collective power is shared, but is uncontrollable? Is this the very essence of an ideal relationship? In terms of learning, can workers learn best how to contribute to organisational goals – company and union – while retaining their own individual integrity? Can we conceive of a condition of "mutual empowerment"? Our liberatory tradition is a useful compass in this journey, helping us become proficient in the arts of resistance (Scott, 1990).

Nature of Power

Adult educators show signs of understanding the political nature of learning and working, and consequently, we are obliged to explore the nature of power in our learning theories. According to Cervero and Wilson (1999), "adult education cannot be a neutral activity in the continual struggle for the distribution of knowledge and power in society." They continue:

Adult educators must always ask that timeless political question: Who benefits? Necessarily tied to this question is the ethical one: Who should benefit? The increasing importance of adult education in the constitution of social, economic, and cultural life demands no less. (pp. 36-7)

At the heart of their adult education practice should be a vision linking adult education, power and society. How does this play itself out in the workplace? John Garrick (1998) writes: *To Release from control*

> In the discourse of experiential learning are questions seldom addressed about whether "emancipatory intent" and so-called "liberating" reform processes merely lead to other forms of control. For example, what are the goals of empowerment underlying learning at work? What are the ethics of "other directed" experiential learning activities *set up* by trainers, line-managers, coaches and mentors to he experiential? A serious consideration of the ethics of "other directed" experiential learning events at work is relatively undeveloped in the literature. (p. 27)

Our liberatory tradition encourages us to ask critical questions so that workplace learning is not co-opted by agendas governed by "power-over" rather than "power-with" intentions.

REFLECTIVE QUESTION

What does a critical thinker actually do?

We seem to have discovered "critical thinking" recently. Why does it seem to be new? What have we been doing till now – thinking uncritically? We might answer in the positive if we think of critical thinking as critiquing the social order. Newman (1999) has a clear image in mind when he describes a critical thinker:

> The writers or speakers are clear-sighted and frank about their own values, assumptions and ideologies. They assume responsibility for what they say and the actions implied by or associated with what they say. They make judgements. They analyse, state a case, and lay the blame. They locate their analyses within social and political contexts. They see these contexts in terms of conflicts of interests and perceptions, and they examine the conditions, people, institutions, and emotions that mediate these conflicts. They communicate the sense of being at the meeting point of the past and a number of possible and significantly different futures, at a moment intensely of the present. (p. 33)

He also has in mind a clear understanding of what adult education for critical thinking means:

> Adult education for critical thinking is concerned with the positions we adopt, the sides we take, the alliances we form and the solidarities we enter into. This kind of adult education is not detached and dispassionate. It helps us explain how knowledge, consciousness and power are generated and controlled; and then examines how knowledge, consciousness and power can be generated and controlled in ways that will enable of us to live in equitable, peaceful and sustainable ways on a habitable planet. Adult education for critical thinking is constructed on an ethical stance. It is a form of education by and for those wanting to understand the world in order to change it. It is education for social justice. (p. 56)

The authors of this books subscribe to this adult education theoretical position in our vision of workplace learning. Newman's position is in keeping with the liberatory tradition and early voices in the contemporary movement such as Lindeman and the priests of the Canadian Antigonish Movement. The liberatory thread remains intact.

Action Imperative

Understanding power is necessary, but insufficient. Workplace learning, as we conceive it, encourages us to put our understanding of power relationships in a complex and rapidly changing society into direct action, so that we can build a more democratic and equitable life. The old notion of "knowledge is power" is faulty. Information and knowledge are incomplete without implementation. Implementation is power; knowledge sharing is power. Taking part in any research activity that produces behaviour or attitude change constitutes action. Toulmin (1996) explains action research as "aimed at practical effects, not theoretical rigor: both seek the kind of knowledge Aristotle called phronesis ("practical wisdom") more than episteme ("theoretical grasp")" (p. 3). This kind of research is judged by practical results, not by theoretical propriety. Action research calls not just for explanations, but for improvements – change now rather than some time in the future. Gustavsen (1996) would agree:

> A major point is that, today, the chief research issue in action research and related forms is *change itself*: the nature of change proc-

esses, their forces and elements, their evolutionary logics, the role of knowledge, etc. Other issues can be placed on the agenda as well, i.e. issues from "theory of organization," "socio-technical design," "socio-ecology," "skills formation" and many others; but inasmuch as a main theoretical topic can be identified in today's development research, it is the issue of change itself. (p. 23)

In Scandinavia, this change manifests itself in trends to introduce industrial democracy as a social imperative, trends most compatible with our liberatory tradition and its democratising intentions. How might this play itself out in the workplace?

There is great variety within the Action Research extended family as clearly illustrated in the first international handbook on the subject (Reason and Bradbury, 2001). Where one places oneself on the continuum depends on personal philosophy and practical expediency. If you align yourself with the liberatory tradition in the adult education movement, as we do, you commit yourself to social justice in the workplace. If you extend that commitment to direct action in the workplace, you function politically and join the PAR branch of the extended family. Cunningham (1993) would agree: "For me, adult education is about critically assessing our reality, to name that reality, to devise strategies through adult education to change that reality, and to help students to do the same thing" (p. 12). For her, as for us, facilitating democratic processes within the adult educational culture is simply a given.

Creating Democracy

PAR is committed to democratising knowledge making. Other members of the Action Research family are more or less also committed to opening up the world of knowledge making to a wider range of voices, as we noted earlier (Gaventa and Cornwall, 2001; Lincoln, 1995; Park, 2001;). This opening up, the political aspect of PAR and others in the broader family, is what threatens the positivist hold on the social sciences and not the smoke screen of questionable scientific rigour (Greenwood and Levin, 1998). Gustavsen (1996) writes:

Although we can theorize about democracy, democracy is not a theory but a family of practices linked to a set of ideas. However ambiguous and many-sided this cluster of ideas and practices may possibly be, it is the only set of premises outside ourselves – with historical legitimacy – to which we can link our striving to do better research. (p. 26)

In searching for adult education theories for workplaces of the future, we need "a family of practices" – reflected in the six critical trends outlined in this chapter – "linked to a set of ideas" in the form of the liberatory tradition in the adult education movement. Gustavsen encourages us to move beyond adult learning theories unless they help us to function in immediately practical ways, a notion familiar to Lindeman in 1926. That practice must be democratic, and as such, it will have radical consequences in workplaces unused to critical inquiry and dialogical relationships inferred by the democracy we envision.

REFLECTIVE QUESTION

Can you create an image of what participatory democracy might look like in your workplace and job-place?

As we can see through our recovery of so many "quiet" voices, there is enormous wealth in the human condition ready to contribute new knowledge if we as adult educators are bold enough to acknowledge this knowledge and act upon it. This is demonstrated in the work of Flecha (2000) with low-literacy adults grouped together in literacy circles to read the great writers of the world. He proves that "without degrees or money, people can understand and enjoy great literature if they find a setting that encourages rather than destroys them" (p. 105). With this kind of approach to learning, workplace learning can be conceived in broadly democratic terms. Closer to home and drawing on data from the first national survey of informal learning conducted in 1998, Livingstone (2001) concluded:

> The only effective solutions to current underemployment problems are likely to be found in economic reforms that encourage our highly educated labour force to make fuller use of their skills and knowledge in paid workplaces. The most feasible reforms include *work redistribution* and *workplace democratisation.* (p. 60; our emphasis)

He also concluded that underemployed Canadians continued to be active lifelong learners despite their inferior position in the economy caused by that underemployment. His finding is similar to Flecha's in the sense that the potential marginalization of citizens because of low-literacy and underemployment measures does not infer these citizens are not engaged in or are incapable of learning. In fact, both Canadian and Spanish researchers conclude that these very citizens are active and productive contributors to the learning society. These citizen-learners are active in their workplace even as their job-place might be weak, uncertain or absent.

Our historic commitment to democracy has been expressed in a concern for a responsible and active citizenship in voluntary community settings. Usher, Bryant and Johnston (1997) focus on adult learning for citizenship in the postmodern world and look to "new social movements." "The argument is that such movements, coalescing around concerns of feminism and anti-racism as well as peace, environmental issues, gay rights, "grey" issues and other alternative identities, visions and lifestyles have the potential to organise at the local level around issues of (social) consumption in respect of, for example, housing, education and health" (p. 45). If your workplace is in one of these social movements, democracy is an essential part of your work. They go on:

> A key area which affects everyone, is central to the idea of citizenship and allows meaningful connections between the societal macro and the educational micro, is the changing nature of work. . . A broader, more critical economic and welfare focus in education for citizenship in relation to work can help to extend and challenge the more circumscribed economic empowerment associated with the discourses of competence and consumerism at the same time as giving more specific meaning to the idea of pursuing social empowerment for learner/citizens. (pp. 48-9)

In place of the discourses of competence and consumerism, we envision the discourses of democracy and social justice, and position them in society in broadly defined work settings in order to reflect the realities of work and learning in the new century. Livingstone concluded from the 1998 survey that "the strongest positive relationship between work and learning is found in voluntary community settings appears to support the thesis that greater discretionary control or self-management can lead to fuller use of work-related skills and knowledge" (p. 61). "In short," he concludes, "greater democratization appears to be the most suitable way of reducing underemployment in the workplace" (p. 61). We would argue, supported by Sennett (1998) and our liberatory tradition, that those democratic processes require us to regain a collective sense of communal responsibility, and to act accordingly.

> ### REFLECTIVE QUESTION
>
> Assuming your reading is proceeding more or less sequentially, as you end this chapter, how does your understanding of adult learning theory relate to the assumptions you recorded when you commenced reading?

SUMMARY

At the beginning of this chapter, we said our focus was moving from "managing the workplace" for economic efficiency, (a focus critically examined in Chapters 2, 3 and 4) to "freeing the workplace" for participatory democracy, a theme we have examine in this chapter and explicitly and implicitly in Chapter 5. In this last part in our journey we have surveyed the extensive international adult education learning theory literature guided by a commitment to the liberatory tradition in the adult education movement. Our vision for workplace learning is to move beyond the commodification of all aspects of life directed by notions of flexible capitalism and organization efficiency into a future respectful of our social, political, economic, cultural, and spiritual needs. Our vision of the workplace, broader than where one simply has one's job, opens our creative imaginations to celebrate adult education's great potential for drawing from a rich past, understanding the present, and shaping the future.

CHAPTER 7

Toward the Future of Workplace Learning

The whole of life is learning, therefore education can have no endings. (Lindeman, 1926, p. 5)

The challenge presented at the outset of *Workplace Learning: A Critical Introduction* was to address to several bodies of literature directly – Management Strategies, Group/Team Learning, Organizational Learning, Unions and Learning, and Adult Education – that together define the core issues of the emerging field of workplace learning. These different bodies of literature are fields of study and practice in their own right, but in the context of this book they become partners and sub-fields in a broader discussion. The underlying assumption is that these fields have something to teach each other, and that no single one can fully grasp the phenomenon of workplace learning alone. Inter-disciplinary dialogue is not only mutually rewarding but also essential for the full development of the field.

Across each of these bodies of literature we drew out mainstream and critical perspectives, as a requirement for generating inter-disciplinary dialogue. We have been insistent that differing perspectives are necessary for proper analysis of workplace learning. Moreover, notions of contrasting perspectives underlay the determination of relevant/non-relevant, reproduction/transformative and even legitimate/illegitimate notions of work and learning. We maintained principles of supporting open, adult learning, including the expansion of perspective and understanding of the diversity of approaches; the encouragement of independent thinking and critical inquiry; and the attempt to make the topic more open to reader's own interests and experiences. In the final instance, we aimed to encourage the reader, through reflective questions and study tips, to investigate the major lines of argument presented and undertake further inter-disciplinary inquiry. In this closing chapter we want to step back and take a birds-eye view, to stimulate broad, and in some cases difficult questions, and suggest a "tool-box" of concepts and themes to assist the reader in future inquiry.

CHAPTER OBJECTIVES:

After reading this chapter, you should be able to:

1. Describe different ways in which the preceding chapters relate to one another, and how these different ways of readings figure possible futures for workplace learning as a practice and as a field of inquiry;

2. Expand the possibilities for understanding workplace learning in all its forms and from a variety of different standpoints;

3. Discuss the five conceptual themes/tools that are aimed to help to critically evaluate workplace learning literature across multiple traditions and perspectives.

Before examining the relationship between the different chapters, and the five core themes/tools for future inquiry, it is important to spend a moment situating the field broadly and testing the appropriateness of the concepts on which it relies the most. As a core principle of inquiry we should first ask ourselves: Why "workplace learning" now? What has led us as students, scholars and as a society to this contemporary concern for "workplace learning," at this point in history, in this way? Positive evaluations of trends in the world of work, such as the optimistic perspectives presented in Castells (1996) and Beckett and Hager (2002), largely cast work as a world of continued job creation, economic progress, and more knowledge-intensive and satisfying; in general, the realization of the promise of a post-Fordist, post-industrial, even a postmodern information socio-economy. Such approaches suggest that workplace learning represents a discourse of "humanization" in the world of paid work, or the emergence of human learning as a cornerstone of economic activity. Under this rubric the "learning organization," is warmly welcomed and seen as confirming of the progression of human society in the area of work and learning. The need for organizational learning emerges from an analysis of future trends, e.g. Castells (1996), as such accelerated change, new communication technologies and globalized competition, cited as inevitable and more or less positive influences on human development. Many readers find the writing of scholars like Senge (1990) genuinely uplifting. Emanating from the hymn book of organizational change, this literature's consistent claim is that the central barrier to the realization of a productive, competitive as well as more humane workplace lies in organizational leadership practices which need to transcend narrow forms of thinking. With its secularized images of salvation, sacrifice and saviours, Senge's work relates to western audiences in general for its familiar themes, and indisputably strums a chord with an increasing number of Human Resource professionals, management consultants, and managers. The message calls for people to contribute their greatest human capacities to the community of work as the most meaningful step toward meeting the challenges of the future together.

However, this is not the only way to address the question "Why workplace learning now?" There are more historicized and critical approaches; authors such as Rifkin (1996) and Aronowitz and DiFazio (1994), for example, suggest a more troubling future for work. This perspective argues that there are more conflictual, historical dynamics that account for the emergence of the burgeoning interest in workplace learning. It suggests that the attempt to expand our conceptualization of workplace learning arises from social struggles involving, the ongoing contradictions of capitalism and what sociologist Smith (1990) refers to as the reproduction of the "relations of ruling." Relations of ruling refer to that conglomerate of social and institutional (class, gender and race-based) mechanisms that produce and reproduce socio-economic order, including the forms of inequity and conflict it relies upon the most (see, for example, Andersen and Collins, 2004). Following this perspective there is a distinct possibility that our concern for workplace learning, similar to the emergent concern for "lifelong learning," represents a historical "conjuncture" in the capitalist production process; a "conjunction," according to Antonio Gramsci (1971), being defined as the immediate terrain of struggle over which forces of opposition organize (p.178). The emergence of the discourses of workplace learning, scholarly and practical, may be a very real and specific flashpoint for the wider social struggles that characterize these relations of ruling and the forces of historical development in our society. In other words, the discourse of workplace learning, as a mechanism of control may represent a an unprecedented level of penetration by the relations of ruling into the lifeworld of human communities. Such a process would account for the realization of new heights of market-rationalization of human activity. In different ways, writers such as Boud and Garrick (1999), Garrick (1998), Garrick and Usher (1998) have noted a similar dynamic, in the case of the latter, marking the emergence of the notion of the "enterprising self." That is, the colonization of the self (identity/subjectivity).

STUDY TIP

From a critical perspective, this notion of "relations of ruling" expands upon a focus on relations of paid work and capitalism more broadly to include the tensions of contradictions in society generally. Smith's work is grounded in a feminist critique and is theoretically rich, though fairly complex for a general audience. The concept of relations of ruling informs most if not all of Smith's work but for a short introduction see Smith (1996).

This penetration is intimately linked with theories of human capital discussed implicitly and explicitly in the book. Increasingly sophisticated conceptualizations of workplace learning from this critical perspective orient us to the possibilities, dangers and extent to which people's learning is interpreted through the lens of exchange value and profit-making, versus meeting human needs directly.

UNDERSTANDING THE ARGUMENTS ACROSS CHAPTERS

Workplace Learning: A Critical Introduction has presented a detailed look at core definitions, theories, historical development and contemporary lines of argument on workplace learning within the separate traditions of Management Strategies, Group/Team Learning, Organizational Learning, Union-based Learning, and Adult Education. Each chapter draws out key points of contact between the specific sub-field and the realm of workplace learning. In this section we review core findings in these chapters and discuss how the chapters relate to and inform one another. In doing this we present two possible ways of reading and understanding the text, that is meta-readings, and the general arguments that each type of reading initiates.

In Chapter 2, we began with mainstream managerialist perspectives that emphasized the development of human assets, commitment to an organization's goals, the pursuit of flexibility, and sustainable competitive advantage. It is important to note that we focused on understanding the wider context of workplace learning by examining employment strategies (HRM) and techniques from the perspective of those who design and control work arrangements: managers. Empirical studies and theoretical models concerning these issues in the paid workplace were seen to *be* increasingly *interested in* learning as a core activity, perhaps even a definitive asset for organizations. Older methods of organizing the labour process, so the literature stated, had to recognize this fact in order to meet the challenge of a new economic environment. From this perspective, theoretical models help managers to understand how to heighten the capacities of workers to learn and to help them become engaged with organizational goals around innovation and change. Post-bureaucratic work regimes we argued seek to create types of mutually dependent, community relationships thought to be most suitable to the development of creativity and the ability to respond positively to accelerated change.

In the same chapter, we introduced a more critical perspective on these major management theories and HRM models. We noted explicitly that these models do not necessarily represent the perspective of workers or their trade unions satisfactorily, but rather they interpret positive dimensions of workers' agency emerging through successfully meeting the needs of the organization. Mainstream managerial approaches do not represent the unevenness of the work experience for participants. And we explained that neither does mainstream management scholarship focus much attention on the vast majority of those jobs in advanced capitalist countries, let alone around the globe, that have been, and continue to be, "dumbed-down" and systematically dehumanized. The dynamic that emerged was one of trade-offs: greater productivity and wealth of the firm made the prospect of employment more likely and possibly more secure and satisfying, but this came at a price – heightened "cultural control" of workers rather than genuine empowerment to pursue their own unique goals; the expansion of insecure, non-standard work amidst "flexible specialization" and knowledge work; and work intensification interwoven with a mixed prospect for the growth in the quality of working-life.

Chapter 3 saw us further develop literature on the relations of the paid workplace, though here we expanded beyond a strict concern for individual learning. We began by theorizing work teams, including inherent paradoxes in work-based regimes, and proceeded to examine issues of collective learning in the paid workplace. However, we moved beyond traditional team learning issues and introduced the notion that collective action is a type of informal "pedagogy" (a topic developed more fully in Chapter 5). In reviewing two leading theories of team learning, we explained key managerialist and HRD/M approaches. A range of empirical work has been completed on these phenomena, and we outlined how group and team learning is subject to a variety of internal developmental stages, as well as a range of modifying factors, including individual orientations, organizational contexts, and complex social relations. A key theme in this chapter was echoed in Chapter 6 where we outlined trends for future research and practice. Analyses of learning are moving beyond the individual, and becoming more sophisticated and effective in explaining behaviour and outcomes in consequence.

Moving from concerns for learning amongst individuals, groups and teams toward broader notions of learning in whole organizations, Chapter 4 provided discussion of one of the most popular and influential bodies of literature in the field of workplace learning: learning in terms of organizations. In this chapter we drew an important distinction between analytical tools and the development of prescriptive programs for workplace change. This was largely embodied in the important distinction we made between the learning organization and organizational learning. A major argument we presented is that this literature is diverse and in support of this we demonstrated the many tensions and contradictions, again with reference to the idea of dominant and critical perspectives. Building on the type of analysis we applied in earlier chapters we saw how the individual and collective needs of workers can be submerged by the needs of the organization. This brought into view the tensions of both individual-organizational relationships, and also implicitly signaled the need to address the conflict inherent in the capitalist employment relationship.

Chapter 5 took up the theme of employee/employer relations, outlining the myriad ways that workers and the union movement shape learning in the workplace. Our argument depended on the notion that we must expand our assumptions around the purpose of work to include the idea that workers wanted more than to merely contribute to the success of a firm. From the standpoint of workers issues of productivity and profitability were secondary on the list of purposes of work and learning. Foremost are safe and healthy workplaces, workplaces that help them to develop prospects for better work in which they developed as creative, full human beings, and are above all, workplaces that were equitable. Learning within their unions as well as at various inter-firm, sectoral, national and even international levels was discussed with an emphasis on the types of bargaining and organizational structures that are put in place to allow workers a say in workplace learning. We discussed training, vocational education and apprenticeships with an eye to the ways that unions shape and contribute to their development. Finally, we looked at the most wide-spread (but unfortunately also the most neglected in terms of empirical research) forms of learning that unions play a role in shaping, that is everyday learning, both in the labour process but also in the realm of mass communications and the arts.

We explored the perspective and literature of adult education in Chapter 6. We expanded our conceptualization of work considerably, beginning with the juxtaposition of workplace and "job-place." We discovered the historical trajectory of the field, and from a liberatory adult education perspective, we learned that work-based learning can be a tool to serve individuals, groups and communities directly by drawing on examples of community action and learning in social movements. We compared the emergence of the field of workplace learning from this liberatory perspective by looking back at the way adult education itself emerged to legitimate status in North America in the post World War II era. We personalized this emergence by tracing the development of a particular educator, Verner, who found himself at the centre of this emergence in many ways. Empirical findings, concepts and theories examined in Chapter 6 challenged the prevailing hegemony with regard to legitimate work and learning. Here we suggested that legitimate workplace learning should not be narrowly construed to mean that which meets only (if at all) the needs and interests of business. In the paid workplace, this drew our attention to issues of portability, and the development of individual and collective potentials outside the exigencies of profit-making. In the community and social movements it draws our attention to how important learning and action takes place both at home and away, and is not readily separated from the forces of paid work and economy. The liberatory tradition of adult education, we suggested, points to how equity and justice are important elements of workplace learning, broadly conceived. Equity, justice and meeting the direct needs of people arose in our brief methodological discussion involving the "action research" community, and finally in our announcement of six key themes or conceptual trends that we felt were central to understanding workplace learning, from a liberatory tradition, into the 21st century.

From this chapter-by-chapter review we now summarize what we see as some of the most central issues and assumptions. Building on our discussion above, as well as the foundational arguments of Waring (1988), Spencer (1998), Livingstone (1999; 2001) and others, we feel it is important that readers in the field of workplace learning seek to expand upon the dominant conception of work. As we have said, work takes place beyond the "job-place." Moreover, activity on the job is greatly influenced by learning in the home, community and other organizations and *vice versa*. We all take part in forms of activity in the household and community that produce use-value, that are essential for our survival, and for the reproduction of our paid work, and that provide quality of life.

Linking with our discussions of various emerging discourses of workplace learning, nowhere is the nature of the distinction between paid and un-paid labour more clear than in contemporary thought around work and learning. In a recent collection of readings on workplace learning, Barnett writes, "work has to become learning and learning has to become work" (1998, p. 42). Whereas informal job-place learning was once a taken for granted feature of work, it is now often considered a key job activity and perhaps even a major asset of the corporation. Popular writers like Peter Senge (1990) and contemporary empirical surveys such as Gordon Betcherman et al (1994) both seem to confirm this type of shift in thinking.

As David Livingstone (2001) argues, it is not simply notions of "work" that suffer from narrow conceptualization. Critical formulations of "learning," in all its forms and for all its purposes, continue to suffer narrow conceptualization as well. Simplistic notions of "self-direction" and individual cognition have been seriously challenged of late, but attempts to understand how this learning overlaps and crosses institutional boundaries of the home, community, paid workplace, community groups, trade unions, and so on have not been seriously attempted to date. In our view, such an expansion holds the key to understanding how the full range of historical and cultural dynamics affect workplace learning and, in turn, how workplace learning affect them.

REFLECTIVE QUESTION

Have we over-stepped the boundaries of "workplace learning" proper? For example, can labour education, or learning in social movements be considered legitimate topics within the study of workplace learning? These questions are open for debate and the debate must certainly begin in earnest for the study of work and learning to have continued relevance. We have described dominant, mainstream perspectives and have presented an alternative perspective. The alternative perspective will hopefully contribute to this debate, however a reasoned response, negative or positive, is precisely the reaction this text was designed to instigate.

Having reviewed the core arguments of the chapters, we can now examine the different ways the themes and contents relate to one another. This will help us think more deeply about the current state of workplace learning as a field of inquiry, and it will help us understand how we might contribute to its future development. There are many ways one can go about reading this text, but we want to engage you, the reader, directly by asking: "How would you have organized the chapters of this book?" We ask this directly because we feel that the question has the power to reveal presumptions about the nature of workplace learning as an integrated field of study, rather than simply the sum of its separate parts. For our part, we identified and critiqued our own different meta-readings. When we first began to write this book, for example, we had placed Chapter 6 first. We felt we should begin with first principles, the adult learning process. As we wrote about the field of adult education, however, we found its roots actually disturbed this initial story-line, and finally we decided to alter the order. At first glance, this is another type of conventional reading. It represents an organization of the information on the basis of an "individual-group-organization-movement" progression. In placing Chapter 2 at the beginning, however, we realized we were displaying yet another set of presumptions. This time, we seemed to implicitly privilege both individual and managerial approaches, suggesting that the individual is the foundation of theory and practice in workplace learning, and those in control are the people we should be concerned with overall. What lies behind these presumptions? What does it say about our common sense beliefs about the nature of work and the learning process? What do we legitimize and obscure through these beliefs? What goals of work are legitimate? Is it possible to understand the learning that goes on in the "job-place" without understanding the learning and social dynamics beyond it? It is true that our goal in this concluding chapter is to pose as many questions, rather than to give as many answers, as possible. Indeed, we found that by asking ourselves the questions listed above we gained a deeper understanding of the field of workplace learning than we ever had before. If we were to tell a different story than we have, for example by rearranging the chapters, or by including additional or different chapters, how might we do it?

A "TOOL-BOX" FOR STUDYING WORKPLACE LEARNING

In this closing section, we want to suggest a kind of analytic "toolbox" for future readings in the inter-disciplinary world of workplace learning literature. These tools help to answer some of the very first questions we posed in the book about the impact of new forms of work, such as the meaning of the HRM paradigm, the role of worker organizations in the paid workplace, and so on.

Drawing on a theme common to several chapters, a clear understanding of the *tensions inherent to the capitalist employment relationship* is essential for the development of a critical eye regarding the range of workplace learning literature. Having presented grounded discussion of workplace learning in a variety of forms and contexts, we can draw attention more clearly to an important distinction that should inform future discussion of workplace learning. To begin with, tension in the employer-employee relationship should not be confused with tension in the group/organizational-individual relationship. Though in reality inseparable, analytically they represent two relatively distinct sets of dynamics. The distinction is essential for expanding notions of paid work, and also relates to the role of trade unions in workplace learning. As we pointed out perhaps most directly in Chapters 3 and 4, tensions that emerge from individual participation in group, team or organizational contexts are related to human individuality, the burdens of negotiating scarce resources, and conflicts arising from interdependency within work structures and processes. These forms of tension have a close relationship with what organization theorists call the "horizontal tensions" within organizations. Though they can also involve tensions related to hierarchy, they tend to emerge from the relationship between the individual and the group or organization, where individual agency meets collective needs and social structures. Strictly speaking, these tensions can emerge in any form of collective activity (e.g. in social movements, community groups, non-profit work, trade unions, etc.).

The tensions that arise in the context of the employer/employee (or capital/labour) relationship necessarily involves tensions inherent in the individual and group/organizational relationships, but provide a distinct set of additional tensions more or less unique to life under capitalism. These tensions revolve around a specific class-based form of what could be called a "vertical" tension within specific work organizations and in society in general. This set of relationships and tensions is rooted in the process of "appropriation" where capital accumulation requires control over surplus value be placed in private hands mediated by market exchange, technological development, and inter-capitalist competition, rather than direct human need. Resnick and Wolff (1987) have argued this set of relationships is further enhanced by private control over the process of "distribution" (e.g. distribution of wages, investment as well as marketing resources, media campaigns and so on) as well. The employer/employee tension is therefore rooted in specific processes (appropriative and distributive) that are interwoven with, though distinct from, the types of horizontal tensions discussed above. These and other distinctions draw our attention to the essence of the central contradiction and lines of tension that define the employer and employee relationship under capitalism.

The concern to distinguish between different forms of tension outlined above relates to an ongoing, broad interest that runs throughout this text. It involves a concern for understanding and testing *definitions, concepts and theories*. At their core, these represent the symbolic tools or metaphors that allow us to meaningfully understand workplace learning and begin to illuminate diverse standpoints and lines of tension inherent in it. What is the difference between education, training and learning? What is the significance of HRD versus HRM; liberatory as opposed to non-liberatory traditions in adult education; "groups" and "teams"; organizational learning versus the learning organization; and so on? Is the source of a concept or theory's usefulness its ability to simply describe reality, or is it also a tool to mediate, organize and, in a sense, create reality? Which set of notions "works for you" as a reader, as an employee, as an educator, as a manager? Definition, and specifically the struggle over the boundaries that define different categories of phenomena, represent a filter that will sort out relevant from non-relevant information. These tools bring certain relationships into view and obscure others, and in so doing set the boundaries of legitimate and illegitimate work and learning.

Differing *standpoints* in the social world, particularly those that define the major social divisions in society, give rise to different perspectives, which in turn define different sets of relevancy and legitimacy. What may be legitimate learning in the social movements discussed in sections of Chapter 3 is illegitimate learning to the institutions they oppose, and what may be legitimate learning to a home-partner raising children is trivialized by the institutions of paid work, and so on. The two general standpoints that were presented consistently through each chapter were managerialist, mainstream and/or orthodox on the one hand, and critical, radical and/or liberatory on the other. Realizing how standpoints relate to seemingly contradictory claims, foci and conclusions of research is not only central to understanding this text, but is also an important tool for interpreting the diverse range of literature in the field of workplace learning.

STUDY TIP

The conceptual notion of standpoint has been developed in a variety of forms of philosophy and social theory. The form to which we mean to draw attention is with the process of "dialectic analysis," generally associated with the work of G.W.F Hegel but developed by others, including Karl Marx and, more recently, writers collectively referred to as having developed "Feminist standpoint epistemology" (Hartsock, 1983; Harding, 1986; Haraway, 1991; Stanley and Wise, 1993). For an accessible and engaging look at the theory of standpoints within dialectical analysis see B. Ollman's text *Dialectical Investigations* (1993).

Understanding the importance of social standpoints also allows readers to understand and identify the *unevenness* of the effects of new and old dynamics of paid work and learning. We see unevenness through the course of an individual working life and workplace when we compare the conditions of, for example, temporary clerical staff and professional or upper management. We seen unevenness across different sectors of mature versus emerging industries, and we see gross unevenness within work and learning relationships across different parts of the world. In this context, it will be valuable to acknowledge the "postmodern," knowledge-based tasks of the "virtual" entrepreneur, keeping in mind that there are also many more data-entry clerks, some working in prisons and third world countries. While many workplaces can be described as post-industrial, perhaps even post-modern, the vast majority of work that is done for pay takes place in the context of labour processes that are not governed by less postmodern principles. Any relevant and robust theory of workplace must contend with this unevenness, either implicitly or explicitly.

Central to the insights of each chapter, and forming the final element of our tool-box is the explanation of historical *trajectories,* providing a sense of the origins of the key topics. The issues, concerns and problematics discussed – no matter how new the specific variation –all have deep historical roots. Whether it is the apparent "discoveries" of workplace culture (largely pre-figured in the Hawthorne studies, if not earlier), the value of informal learning (well understood in apprenticeship systems of the middle ages and the forms of craft production proceeding industrial capitalism), the co-existence of coercive/cooperative forms of leadership (at least 5000 years old), the problematics of workplace learning research are rarely new, despite the fact that they do often play themselves out in unique ways. Workplace learning is emergent. It has few, if any, "seminal" texts in the conventional sense. Indeed, students and scholars from different disciplines are frequently and understandably unfamiliar with the approaches and core theorists that inform each other's work. In a field of inquiry so variable, so wide-ranging and divergent, workplace learning is difficult to understand in terms of a classic paradigm model, and it is precisely this fact that makes its potential so great.

STUDY TIP

An introduction to the historical treatments of adult education and learning, beyond what we have provided in individual chapters, can be found in chapters by Welton and Solar in Scott, Spencer and Thomas's collection, *Learning for Life: Canadian Readings in Adult Education* (1998). A key text on past and current trends in the area of literacy, education and training relating to paid work can be found in P.E. Barton (2000). Systematic and critical treatments of the histories of "work" are much easier to come by. For a focus on core North American readings on the transformation of work and political economy in the 20th century we suggest : Montgomery *Worker's Control in America*, Gordon, Edwards and Reich *Seg-*

mented Work, Divided Workers; Sabel and Piore *The Second Industrial Divide*; and, Edwards *Contested Terrain: The transformation of the workplace in the 20th Century*. For a recent discussion of the future of work in Canada specifically see Betcherman *et al.* and Lowe (1994; 2000).

FINAL COMMENT

Workplace Learning: A Critical Introduction goes beyond a collection of readings devoted to workplace learning toward preliminary attempts at encouraging interdisciplinary discussion. This concluding chapter has sought to crystallize the arguments over disciplinary boundaries of the field, and in so doing we have necessarily embraced discussions of the legitimate definition of "work" and "learning." We have tried above all to pose key questions for the field of workplace learning, and provide analytic tools for answering these important questions.

Readers seeking to avoid the undertow of the successive waves of best-sellers and the "snake-oil salesmen" that characterize so much of the popular discourse of management, workplace change and learning must seek to develop awareness of critical perspectives and expertise in grasping a range of different forms of empirical work. In this context, readers will continue to be well served by concentrating on unraveling contradictions and unevenness in the field, continuously building an historical perspective on work, learning theory, and broader social/political dynamics, and always posing the question; from whose standpoint does this text speak? In this final section we have raised many questions related to the nature and future direction of research on workplace learning. As Eric Hobsbawn (1997) mused, it is easier to formulate questions than answers, and we have taken the easier route rather than the more difficult. But asking questions, especially about assumptions underpinning workplace learning theory and the experiences of workers, is not a worthless exercise. Our aim throughout this book has been to ask the type of questions that stimulate reflection and increase understanding of learning in the workplace.

Glossary

Autonomy The extent to which a job allows employees freedom and discretion to schedule their work and decide the procedures used to complete it.

Briefing groups Groups called together on a regular and consistent basis so that organization decisions and the reasons for them may be communicated. Group members may in turn meet with another briefing group so that information is systematically communicated down the management line.

Bureaucracy An organizational structure marked by rules and procedures, hierarchy of authority and division of labour.

Competencies Underlying characteristics of a person which result in competent or effective performance taking into consideration the nature of the tasks and the organization context.

Communication The process by which information is exchanged between a sender and a receiver.

Community of practice Informal groups or teams bound together by shared history, expertise and interest for a particular activity, interest or job.

Core workforce Workers with organization-specific skills and high discretionary elements in their work.

Critical perspective An approach to workplace enquiry aimed at exploring inequality and the power relations underpinning work organizations.

Culture The set of values, understandings, and ways of thinking that is shared by the majority members of a work organization and is taught to new employees as correct.

Downsizing Laying off of employees to restructure the business.

Emergent learning Learning derived by interaction with evolving situations such as dealing with customers; used in the formation and formulation of strategy.

Employee involvement (EI) Processes providing employees with the opportunity to influence decision-making on matters which affect them.

Empowering Limited power sharing; the delegation of power or authority to subordinates.

Ethics The code of moral principles and values that governs the behaviour of an individual or group with respect to what is right or wrong.

Fordism The application of Taylorist principles of job design to work performed on specialised machines, usually based on flow-line production assembly work. First applied by Henry Ford.

Foucauldian analysis refer to the application of Michel Foucault's concepts of taxinomia, mathesis, examination and confession to HRM. The hypothesis is that HRM practices play a key role in constituting the self, in defining the nature of work, and in organizing and controlling employees.

Guided learning The process of participative learning through which more experienced workers assist others through joint problem-solving and encouraging the less experienced into thinking and acting, rather than instructing them didactically.

Group technology The grouping of machines and workers to form a logical "whole task" which can be performed with minimum interference.

Groupthink The tendency of members of a highly cohesive group to adhere to shared views so strongly that they totally ignore external information inconsistent with these views.

Human capital theory A theory that seeks to explain economic outcomes from paid work by reference to the quantity and quality of requisite qualifications, skills and work experiences.

Human relations movement A movement which grew out of the Hawthorn experiments conducted by Elton Mayo in the 1920s which emphasizes the psychological and social aspects of job design.

Human Resource Development (HRD) A term used to indicate training and development as an organization's investment in the learning of its people as part an HRM approach.

Human Resource Management (HRM) That part of the management process that specializes in the management of people in work organizations.

Informal learning Learning, sometimes unconsciously, from the context and everyday life experiences.

Japanization A term used to encapsulate the adoption of Japanese-style management techniques such as team or cellular production, just-in-time and total quality control systems in western organizations.

Job Characteristic Model A job design model developed by Hackman and Oldham (1976) suggesting that five core job characteristics – skill variety, task identity, task significance, autonomy and feedback – result in positive work experience.

Job design The process of combining task and responsibilities to form complete jobs, and the relationships of jobs in the organization.

Job enlargement The horizontal expansion of tasks in a job.

Job enrichment Processes that assign greater responsibility for scheduling, coordinating and planning work to the employees who actually produce the product.

Knowledge management KM concerns the conversion of tacit or covert knowledge of individuals and workgroups into explicit knowledge so that it can be shared with others, and managerially regulated.

Labour process The production process at work, including job design and the authority relationships therein.

Learning The process of constructing new knowledge and its ongoing reinforcement.

Learning climate Physical and psycho-social variables in an organization which affect the efficiency of employees in realising learning potential.

Learning organization A concept representing an ideal of whole organization learning by all employees and the use of learning to transform the organization.

Learning cycle A modern view of learning emphasising learning as a continuous process. Usually linked to the work of Kolb (1984).

Learning transfer Learning from HRD activities transferred to workplace behaviour and performance.

Managerial prerogative A belief that management should have unilateral control within an organization.

Managerialist perspective An ideology concerned primarily with the maximization of employee commitment and motivation through the adoption of appropriate HRM practices.

Normative model A theoretical model that describes how managers *should* make choices and decisions and provides guidelines for reaching an ideal outcome for the organization.

Organizational communication The systematic provision of information to employees concerning all aspects of their employment and the wider issues relating to the organization in which they work.

Organizational politics Those activities that are not required as part of a manager's formal role, but that influence the distribution of resources for the purpose of promoting personal objectives.

Paradigm A framework of thinking based on fundamental assumptions providing explicit and implicit views about the nature of reality.

Peripheral workforce Workers outside the core workforce (e.g. temporary or casual workers).

Pluralist perspective A view of workplace relations which assumes that management and employees have different goals but seeks a reconciliation of such differences.

Post-industrial society/organization The thesis that posits that the modern western industrial society is moving into a "post-industrial" era, where traditional manual work will disappear and large bureaucratic work organizations will be replaced by smaller organizations "adhocracies," characterized by high levels of flexibility and participation in decision-making.

Power A term denoting the ability to influence others' behaviour.

Psychological contract A metaphor that captures a variety of largely unwritten expectations and understandings of the two parties – employees and their organization – about their mutual obligations.

Quality of Working Life A movement in job design advocating employee participation, autonomy and collaboration with management over work issues. The term, QWL, applied to job enrichment and participation schemes in the 1970s.

Reengineering A cross-functional initiative by senior management involving fundamental redesign of business processes to bring about changes in organizational structure, culture, information technology, job design and the management of people.

Reinforcement Events and interactions that strengthen the links between particular activities and responses.

Reliability A statistical measure of the extent to which a selection or assessment technique achieves consistency in what it is measuring over repeated use.

Scientific management A process of determining the division of work into its smallest possible skill elements and how the process of completing each task can be standardized to achieve maximum efficiency. Also referred to as Taylorism.

Self-managed team (SMT) A group of employees with difference skills who rotate jobs and assume managerial responsibilities as they produce an entire product or service.

Situated cognition An approach that views learning as a process of enculturation, whereby people consciously and subconsciously adopt the behaviour, language, norms and belief systems of a social group.

Synergy The concept that the whole is greater than the sum of its parts. The condition that exists when a group interacts and learns and produces a group outcome that is greater than the sum of the individuals acting alone.

Taylorism A management control strategy named after F.GW. Taylor. A systematic theory of management, its defining characteristic has been the identification and measurement of work tasks so that the completion of tasks can be standardized to achieve maximum efficiency (see also Scientific Management).

Transformational leadership The ability of leaders to motivate followers to believe in the vision of organizational transformation or reengineering.

Union recognition strategy A management strategy to accept the legitimacy of a trade union role and of collective bargaining as a process for regulating the employment relationship. This contrasts with union exclusion, a strategy to curtail the role of trade unions, and union opposition, a strategy to maintain a non-union company.

Unitarist perspective A view of workplace relations which assumes that management and employees share common goals.

Validity A statistical measure of the extent to which a selection or assessment technique actually measures what it sets out to measure. Criterion Validity measures the results of technique against criteria such as present success of existing employees (Concurrent Validity) and future performance of recruits (Predictive Validity).

Work Physical and mental activity that is carried out at a particular place and time, according to instructions, in return for money.

Bibliography

Abernathy, W., Clark, K. and Kantrow, A. (1983). *Industrial Renaissance: Producing a Comparative Future for America,* New York: Basic Books.

Abrahamson, E. (1996). "Management Fashion" *Academy of Management Review*, 21, pp. 254-285.

Abrahart, A., and T'zannatos, Z. (2000). "Australia" in I. Gill, F. Fluitman, and A. Dar (eds.) *Vocational Education and Training Reform: Matching Skills to Markets and Budgets*. New York: Oxford University Press.

Adams, F. (1975). *Unearthing Seeds of Fire: The Idea of Highlander.* Winston-Salem: John F. Blair.

Agashae, Z. and Bratton, J. (2001). Leader-follower Dynamics: Developing a Learning Organization. *Journal of Workplace Learning,* 13 (3), 89-102.

Alexander, A. (1997). *The Antigonish Movement.* Toronto: Thompson Educational.

Alfred, M. (2000). "The Politics of Knowledge and Theory Construction in Adult Education: A Critical Analysis from an Afro-centric Feminist Perspective" in *Proceedings of the 41st Annual Adult Education Research Conference*, Vancouver, 6-10.

Allvin, M. and Sverke, M. (2000). "Do New Generations Imply the End of Solidarity? Swedish Unionism in the Era of Individualization" *Economic and Industrial Democracy*, 21(1), pp. 71-95

Alvesson, M., and Berg, P.O. (1992). *Corporate Culture and Organizational Symbolism*. Berlin: de Gruyter.

Alvesson, M. and Y. Billing (1992). "Gender and Organization: Towards a Differential Understanding" *Organization Studies,* Vol. 13, No. 1, pp. 73-103.

Amit, R. and Shoemaker, P.J.H. (1993). "Strategic Assets and Organizational Rent" *Strategic Management Journal*, Vol. 14, pp. 33-46.

Andersen, M.L. and Collins, P.H. (2004). *Race, Class and Gender* (5th Ed.). Belmont, CA: Thomson/Wadsworth.

Anthony, W.P. (1978). *Participative Management*. Reading, MA: Addison-Wesley.

Argyris, C. (1973). *On Organizations of the Future*. Beverly Hills [Calif.]: Sage Publications.

—— (1982). *Reasoning, Learning, and Action: Individual and Organizational*. San Francisco,CA: Jossey-Bass.

—— (1993). *Knowledge for Action: A Guide to Overcoming Barriers to Organizational Change*. San Francisco: Jossey-Bass.

Argyris, C. and Schön, D. (1978). *Organizational Learning: A Theory of Action Perspective*. Reading, MA: Addison-Wesley.

Aronowitz, S. and DiFazio, W. (1994). *The Jobless Future: Sci-tech and the Dogma of Work,* University of Minnesota Press, Minneapolis, MN.

Ashton, D. and Felstead, A. (2001). "From Training to Lifelong Learning: the Birth of the Knowledge Society?" pp. 165-189 in J. Storey (ed.) *Human Resource Management: A Critical Text.* (Second Edition). London: Thomson Learning

Ashwin, S. (1997). "Shopfloor Trade Unionism in Russia: The Prospects of Reform from Below" *Work, Employment and Society*, 11(1), pp. 115-131.

Baldry, C., Bain, P. and Taylor, P. (1998). "'Bright Satanic Offices': Intensification, Control and Team Taylorism." In P. Thompson & C. Warhurst (eds). *Workplaces of the Future* (pp. 163-183), London: Macmillan Press.

Barker, C. (2001). "Fear, Laugher, and Collective Power: The Making of Solidarity at the Lenin Shipyard in Gdnask, Poland, August 1980" pp. 175-194 in J. Goodwin, J. Jasper and F. Polletta (eds.) *Passionate Politics: Emotions and Social Movements*. Chicago: Univ. of Chicago Press.

Barney, J. B. (1991). Firm Resources and Sustained Competitive Advantage, *Journal of Management,* 17 (1) : pp. 99-120.

Bate, P. (1990). "The Cultural Paralysis of Innovation" in *7th International Conference on Organization, Symbolism and Corporate Culture*. Saarbrucken, Germany.

Bateson, M. (2000). *Full Circles, Overlapping Lives*. New York: Random House.

Beckerman, A., Davis, J. and Jackson, N. (eds.) (1992). *Training for What? Labour Perspectives on Job Training*. Toronto: Our Schools / Our Selves.

Beckett, D. (2001). "Hot Action at Work: A Different Understanding of 'Understanding'" in Tara Fenwick, (ed.) *Socio-cultural Perspectives on Learning Through Work (*pp. 73-84) San Francisco, CA: Jossey-Bass.

Beckett, D. and Hager, P. (2002). *Live, Work and Learning: Practice and Postmodernity*. London: Routledge.

Beckwith, K. (2001). "Ender Frames and Collective Action: Configurations of Masculinity in the Pittston Coal Strike" *Politics and Society*, 29 (2), pp. 297-330.

Beer, M. *et al.* (1984). *Managing Human Assets*, New York: Free Press.

Bélanger, M. (2001). *Union Course Reader Initiative*. Turin, Italy: International Labor Organization.

Bender, K. and Sloane, P. (1998). "Job Satisfaction, Trade Unions, and Exit-Voice Revisited" *Industrial and Labor Relations Review*, 51 (2), pp. 222-240.

Benders, J. and Van Hootegem, G. (1999). Teams and Their Context: Moving Team Discussion Beyond Existing Dichotomies, *Journal of Management Studies*, vol 36, no. 5, pp. 609-628.

Bendix, R. (1956). *Work and Authority in Industry*, New York: Harper and Row.

Berik, G. and Bilginsoy, C. (2000). "Do Unions Help or Hinder Women in Training? Apprenticeship Programs in the United States" *Industrial Relations*, 39 (4), pp. 600-624.

Betcherman, G., McMullen, K., Leckie, N. and Caron, C. (1994). *The Canadian Workplace in Transition*. Queen's University, Kingston,Ontario: IRC Press.

Beveridge, K. and Johnston, J. (1999). *Making our Mark: Labour Arts and Heritage in Ontario*. Toronto: Between the Lines Press.

Beynon, H. (1984). *Working for Ford* (2nd Ed.). London: Pelican.

Bierema, L.L. (2001). "Women, Work and Learning" in Tara Fenwick, (ed.) *Socio-cultural Perspectives on Learning through Work (*pp. 53-62). San Francisco, CA: Jossey-Bass.

Bild, T., Jorgensen, H., Lassen, M. and Madsen, M. (1998). "Do Trade Unions Have a Future? The Case of Denmark" *Acta Sociologica*, 41(3), pp. 195-207.

Billett, S. (1999). "Guided Learning in the Workplace" in D. Boud and J. Garrick (eds.) *Understanding Learning at Work* (pp. 151-164). London: Routledge.

—— (2001). *Learning in the Workplace: Strategies for Effective Practice*. Crows Nest, AUS: Allen & Unwin.

—— (2003). Workplace Mentors: Demands and Benefits. *Journal of Workplace Learning,* 15 (3), pp. 105-113.

Boje, D.M. (1994). "Organizational Storytelling: The Struggles of Pre-modern, modern and Postmodern Organizational Learning Discourses" *Management Learning,* 25 (3): pp. 433-462.

Boje, D.M. and Winsor, R. (1993). "The Resurrection of Taylorism: Total Quality Management's Hidden Agenda" *Journal of Organizational Change Management*, 6 (4): pp. 57-70.

Bonnin, D. (1999). "'We Went to Arm Ourselves at the Field of Suffering': Traditions, Experiences and Grassroots Intellectuals in the Making of Class" *Labour, Capital and Society*, 32 (1), pp. 34-69.

Booth, A. (1989). "The Bargaining Structure of British Establishments" *British Journal of Industrial Relations*, 27 (2), July, pp. 225-234.

Bouchard, P. (1998). "Training and Work: Myths About Human Capital" in S. Scott, B. Spencer and A. Thomas (eds.) *Learning for Life: Canadian Readings in Adult Education*. Toronto: Thompson.

Boud, D. (1989). "Some Competing Traditions in Experiential Learning" S. Weil and I. McGill (eds.) *Making Sense of Experiential Learning*. Milton Keynes, Open University Press.

Boud, D. and Garrick, J. (1999). *Understanding Learning at Work*. London: Routledge.

Bowen, L. (1982). *Boss Whistle: The Coal Miners of Vancouver Island Remember*. Lantzville, BC: Oolichan Books.

Boxall, P. (1992). "Strategic Human Resource Management: Beginnings of a New Theoretical Sophistication?" *Human Resource Management Journal*, 2 (3).

—— (1996). "The Strategic HRM Debate and the Resource-based View of the Firm" *Human Resource Management Journal*, 6 (3), pp. 59-75.

—— (1992). *Japanization at Work: Managerial Studies for the 1990s*, London: Macmillan.

—— (1999). "Gaps in the Workplace Learning Paradigm: Labour Flexibility and Job Redesign" *Proceedings of the First International Conference of Researching Work and Learning*. Leeds University, England.

—— (2001). "Why Workers are Reluctant Learners: The Case of the Canadian Pulp and Paper Industry" *Journal of Workplace Learning*, 13 (7/8), pp. 333-343.

Bratton, J. and Gold, J. (2003). *Human Resource Management: Theory and Practice*. (Third Edition), London: Palgrave-Macmillan.

Bratton, J. and Sawchuk, P.H. (2001). Editorial, *Journal of Workplace Learning,* Vol. 13 (7/8): 269-273.

Bratton, J. and Waddington, J. (1981). *New Technology and Employment*. London: Workers' Education Association.

Braverman, H. (1974). *Labor and Monopoly Capital*, New York: Monthly Review Press.

Briton, D. and Taylor, J. (2000). *Online Workers' Education: How Do We Tame the Technology?* (Progress report of the "Union-Based Telelearning Project") Athabasca University, AB, Canada.

Brookfield, S. (1986). *Understanding and Facilitating Adult Learning*. San Francisco: Jossey-Bass.

Brown, J.S., Collins, A. and Duguid, P. (1989). "Situated Cognition and the Culture of Learning" *Educational Researcher,* 18 (1): pp. 32-42.

Brown, J.S. and Duguid, P. (1991). "Organizational Learning and Communities-of-practice: Toward a Unified View of Working, Learning and Innovating" *Organization Science*, 2, pp. 40-57.

—— (1996). "Organizational Learning and Communities of Practice: Towards a Unified View of Working, Learning and Innovation" In M. Cohen and L. Sproull (eds.) *Organizational Learning*. Thousand Oaks, CA: Sage.

Buchanan, D. (2000). "An Eager and Enduring Embrace: The Ongoing Rediscovery of Teamworking as a Management Idea" in S. Procter and F. Mueller (eds.) *Teamworking*. London: Macmillan.

Burawoy, M. (1979). *Manufacturing Consent: Changes in the Labour Process Under Monopoly Capitalism*. Chicago: Chicago University Press.

Burgoyne, J. and Jackson, B. (1997). "The Arena Thesis: Management Development as a Pluralistic Meeting Point" in J. Burgoyne and M. Reynolds (eds.) *Management Learning: Integrating Perspectives in Theory and Practice*. London: Sage.

Burgoyne, J., Pedlar, M. and Boydell, T. (1994). *Towards the Learning Company: Concepts and Practices*. Maidenhead, UK.

Canadian Labour Congress (2000). *Prior Learning Assessment & Recognition (PLAR): A Statement of Labour Values. <http://www.oise.utoronto.ca/depts/sese/csew/nall/plar.htm>* Ottawa: CLC.

Cappelli, P. and Singh, H. (1992). "Integrating Strategic Human Resources and Strategic Management" in D. Lewin (ed.) *Research Frontiers in Industrial Relations and Human Resources*.

Carse, J. (1986). *Finite and Infinite Games*. New York: Ballantine.

Carter, B. (2000). "Adoption of the Organising Model in British Trade Unions: Some Evidence from Manufacturing, Science and Finance (MSF)" *Work, Employment and Society*, 14 (1), pp. 117-136.

Case, P. (1994). "Virtually the End of History: A Critique of Business Process Re-engineering" in *Modernity/Postmodernity Conference*. Oxford Brookes University, Oxford.

Castells, M. (1996). *The Rise of the Network Society,* Blackwell Publishers, MA.

Champy, J. (1996). *Reengineering Management: The Mandate for New Leadership*. New York: Harper-Business.

Chovanec, D. (1998). "Self-Directed Learning: Highlighting the Contradictions" in S. Scott, B. Spencer and A. Thomas (eds.) *Learning for Life*. Toronto: Thompson.Clarke, L. (1997). "Changing Work Systems, Changing Social Relations" *Relations Industrielles/Industrial Relations,* Vol. 52., No. 4, pp. 839-861.

Clawson, D. and Clawson, M. (1999). "What has Happened to the US Labor Movement? Union Decline and Renewal" *Annual Review of Sociology*, 25, pp. 95-119.

Clegg, S. and Dunkerley, D. (1980). *Organization, Class and Control*, London: RKP.

Cohen, M. and Braid, K. (2000). "Training and Equity Initiatives on the British Columbia Vancouver Island Highway Project: A Model for Large-Scale Construction" *Labor Studies Journal* 25 (3), pp. 70-103.

Cohen, M., and Sproull, L. (eds.) (1996). *Organizational Learning*. Thousand Oaks, CA.: Sage.

Collins, M. (1998). "Critical Returns: From Andragogy to Lifelong Education" in S. Scott, B. Spencer and A. Thomas (eds.) *Learning for Life*. Toronto: Thompson.

Colorado, P. (1988). "Bridging Native and Western Science" *Convergence*, 21 (2/3), pp. 49-72.

Conference Board of Canada (2002). *Performance and Potential 2002-03,* Ottawa, Ontario: Conference Board of Canada.

Cooper, L. (1998). "From Rolling Mass Action to 'RPL': The Changing Discourse of Experience and Learning in the South African Labour Movement" *Studies in Continuing Education*, 20 (2).

Coopey, J. (1996). "Crucial Gaps in the 'Learning Organization'" in K. Starkey (ed.), *How Organizations Learn*, London: International Thomson Business Press.

Craig, J. and Yetton, P. (1993). "Business Process Redesign: A Critique of Process Innovation by Thomas Davenport as a Case Study in the Literature" *Australian Journal of Management,* Vol. 17, No. 2., pp. 285-306.

Cressey, P. (1993). "Kalmar and Uddevalla: The Demise of Volvo as a European Icon" *New Technology, Work and Employment,* Vol. 8 No. 2. pp. 88-90

Crouch, C. (1982). *Trade Unions: The Logic of Collective Action*. London: Fontana.

Cully, M., Woodland, S., O'Reilly, A. and Dix, G. (1999). *Britain at Work*. London: Routledge.

Culpepper, D. (1999). "The Future of High-Skill Equilibrium in Germany" *Oxford Review of Economic Policy*, 15 (1), pp. 43-59.

Cunningham, P.M. (1993). "The Politics of Worker's Education" *Adult Learning*, 5, pp. 13-14.

—— (1993). "Let's Get Real: A Critical Look at the Practice of Adult Education" *Journal of Adult Education*, 22 (1), pp. 3-15.

Cyert, R. and March, J. (1959). "A Behavioural Theory of Organizational Objectives" pp. 76-90 in M. Haire (ed.) *Modern Organization Theory*. New York: Wiley.

—— (1963). *A Behavioural Theory of the Firm*. Englewood Cliffs, N.J.: Prentice-Hall.

Daft, R. (2001). *Organization Theory and Design*. (7th Edition). Cincinnati, OH: South-Western.

Deaton, D. and Beaumont, P. (1980). "The Determinants of Bargaining Structure: Some Large Scale Survey Evidence for Britain" *British Journal of Industrial Relations*, 28, pp. 202-216.

Dei, G. (1996). *Anti-Racism Education Theory and Practice*. Halifax: Fernwood Publishing.

Denison, E. F. (1967). *Why Growth Rates Differ,* Brookings Institute: Washington DC.

Denzin, N. and Lincoln, Y. (2000). *Handbook of Qualitative Research (Second Edition)*. Thousand Oaks, CA: Sage.

Department for Education and Employment (DfED) (1998). *The Learning Age: A Renaissance for a New Britain.* London: Stationary Office.

Dex, S. (1988). "Gender and the Labour Market" in D. Gallie (ed.) *Employment in Britain*, Oxford: Blackwell

Dickens, L. (1998). "What HRM Means for Gender Equality" *Human Resource Management Journal*, 8 (1), pp. 23-38.

Dixon, N. (1992). "Organizational Learning: A Review of the Literature with Implications for HRD Professionals" *Human Resource Development Quarterly*, 3, pp. 29-49.

Dunk, T., McBride, S. and Nelsen, R. (1996). *The Training Trap: Ideology, Training and the Labour Market*. Halifax, NS: SSS/Fernwood Publishing.

Durkheim, E. (1997 [1933]). *The Division of Labour in Society*. New York: Free Press.

Easterby-Smith, M., Thorpe, R. and Lowe, A. (1991). *Management Research: An Introduction*. London: Sage.

Easterby-Smith, M., Burgoyne, J. and Araujo, L. (eds.) (1999). *Organisational Learning and the Learning Organization*. London: Sage.

Ehn, P. (1988). *Work-Oriented Design of Computer Artifacts*. Arbetslivscentrum, Stockholm.

Ehn, P. and Kyng, M. (1987). "The Collective Resource Approach to Systems Design" in G. Bjerknes, P. Ehn and M. Kyng (eds.) *Computers and Democracy*. Avebury, Aldershot, UK.

Elbow, P. (1986). *Embracing Contraries*. Oxford: Oxford University Press.

Elkjaer, B. (1999). "In Search of a Social Learning Theory" in M. Easterby-Smith, J. Burgoyne, and L. Araujo (eds.) *Organizational Learning and the Learning Organization*. London: Sage.

Ellis, C. and Bochner, A. (2000). "Autoethnography, Personal Narrative, Reflexivity: Researcher as Subject" in N. Denzin and Y. Lincoln (eds.) *Handbook of Qualitative Research*. Thousand Oakes: Sage.

Engeström, Y. (1987). *Learning by Expanding: an Activity-theoretical Approach to Developmental Research*. Helsinki: Orienta-Konsultit.

—— (1994). *Training for Change: New Approaches to Instruction and Learning.* Geneva: International Labour Organization.

—— (2001). Expansive Learning at Work: Toward an Activity Theoretical Reconceptualization, *Journal of Education and Work.* 14 (1), pp. 133-156.

Esteva, G. and Prakash, M. (1997). *Grassroots Postmodernism.* London: Zed Books.

Ewer, P. (2000). "Trade Unions and Vocational Education and Training: Questions of Strategy and Identity" *Labour & Industry*, 10 (3), pp. 37-56.

Felstead, A. and Jewson, N. (1999). "Flexible Labour and Non-Standard Employment: An Agenda of Issues" in A. Felstead and N. Jewson (eds.) *Global Trends in Flexible Labour*, pp. 1-20. London: Macmillan.

Fenwick, T. (1998). "Questioning the Concept of the Learning Organization" in S. Scott, B. Spencer and A. Thomas (eds.) *Learning for Life.* Toronto: Thompson.

—— (2001), (ed.) *Socio-cultural Perspectives on Learning through Work.* San Francisco, CA: Jossey-Bass.

Flecha, R. (2000). *Sharing Words: Theory and Practice of Dialogic Learning.* Lanham, Maryland: Rowman & Littlefield.

Flood, R. (1999). *Rethinking the Fifth Discipline.* London: Routledge.

—— (2001). "The Relationship of 'Systems Thinking' to Action Research" in P. Reason and H. Bradbury (eds.) *Handbook of Action Research.* London: Sage, pp. 133-44.

Foley, G. (1995). *Understanding Adult Education and Training,* Sydney: Allen & Unwin.

—— (2001). *Strategic Learning: Understanding & Facilitating Organizational Change.* Sydney: Centre for Popular Education.

Fombrun, C., Tichy, N.M. and Devanna, M.A. (eds.) (1984). *Strategic Human Resource Management,* New York: Wiley.

Forrester, K. (1999). "Work-related Learning and the Struggle for Subjectivity" in K. Forrester, N. Frost, D. Taylor and K. Ward (eds.), *Proceedings of First International Conference: Researching Work and Learning.* Leeds, England: University of Leeds.

Forrester, K., Payne, J. and Ward, K. (1995). *Workplace Learning Perspectives on Education, Training and Work.* Aldershot: Avebury.

Foss, N. J. (ed.) (1997). *Resources, Firms and Strategies.* Oxford: Oxford University Press.

Foucault, M. (1979). *Discipline and Punish:The Birth of the Prison.* New York: Vintage.

—— (1983). "The Subject and Power" in H.L. Dreyfus and P. Rabinow (eds.), *Michel Foucault: Beyond Structuralism and Hermeneutics* (2nd Ed.) pp. 208-26. Chicago: UCP.

Fox, A. (1966). *Industrial Sociology and Industrial Relations.* London: HMSO.

Francis, R.D., Jones, R. and Smith, D. (1988). *Destinies: Canadian History Since Confederation.* Toronto: Holt, Rinehart and Winston.

Freeman, R. and Medoff, J. (1984). *What Do Unions Do?* New York: Basic Books.

Galbraith, J.R. (1996). "Designing the Innovative Organization" in K. Starkey (ed.) *How Organizations Learn.* London: International Thomson Business Press.

Garavan, T. (1997). "The Learning Organization: A Review and Evaluation" *The Learning Organization*, 4, pp. 18-29.

Garrick, J. (1998). *Informal Learning in the Workplace.* Routledge: London.

—— (1999). "The Dominant Discourses of Learning at Work" in D. Boud and J. Garrick (eds.) *Understanding Learning at Work.* London: Routledge.

Garrick, J. and Usher, R. (2000). "Flexible Learning, Contemporary Work and Enterprising Selves" *Electronic Journal of Sociology.* <www.sociology.org>

Gaventa, J. and Cornwall, A. (2001). "Power and Knowledge" in P. Reason and H. Bradbury (eds.) *Handbook of Action Research* London: Sage, pp. 70-80.

George, C.S. Jr. (1972). *The History of Management Thought.* New Jersey: Prentice-Hall.

Gersick, C.J. (1988). "Time and Transition in Work Teams: Towards a New Model of Group Development" *Academy of Management Journal,* Vol. 31, pp. 47-53.

Giroux, H. A. (1994). "Reading Texts, Literacy, and Textual Authority" in David Richter, *Falling into Theory: Conflicting Views on Reading Literature,* pp. 63-73. Boston: St. Martin's Press.

Glenday, D. (2001). "Off the Ropes? New Challenges and Strengths Facing Trade Unions in Canada" in D. Glenday, A. Duffy (eds.) *Canadian Society: Meeting the Challenges of the Twenty-First Century,* pp. 3-37. New York: Oxford University Press.

Godard, J. (1991). "The Progressive HRM Paradigm: A Theoretical and Empirical Re-Examination" *Relations Industrielles/Industrial Relations,* vol. 46, no.2, 378-399.

—— (1994). *Industrial Relations: The Economy and Society*, Toronto: McGraw-Hill Ryerson.

Godfried, N. (2001). "Struggling Over Politics and Culture: Organized Labor and Radio Station WEVD during the 1930s" *Labor History*, 42 (4), pp. 347-369.

Gospel, H. and Littler, C.R. (eds.) (1983). *Managerial Strategies and Industrial Relations*, London: Heinemann.

Graff, H.J. (1976). "Respected and Profitable Labour Literacy, Jobs and the Working Class in the Nineteenth Century" in G. Kealey and P. Warrian (eds.) *Essays in Canadian Working Class History,* Toronto: McClelland and Stewart.

Gramsci, A. (1971). *Prison Notebooks*. New York: International Publishers.

Greene, A-M and Kirton, G. (2002). "Advancing Gender Equality: The Role of Women-Only Trade Union Education" *Gender, Work and Organization*, 9 (1), pp. 39-59.

Greenwood, D. and Levin, M. (1998). "Action Research, Science, and the Co-optation of Social Research" *Studies in Cultures, Organizations and Societies*, 4 (2), pp. 237-61.

Grevatt, M. (2001). "Lesbian/Gay/Bisexual/Transgender Liberation: What's Labor Got to Do with It?" *Social Policy*, 31 (3), pp. 63-65.

Grint, K. and Willcocks, L. (1995). "Business Process Re-engineering in Theory and Practice: Business Paradise Regained?" *New Technology, Work and Employment,* Vol. 10, No. 2, 99-108.

Guest, D. (1997). "Human Resource Management and Performance: A Review and Research Agenda" *The International Journal of Human Resource Management*, Vol. 8, No. 3, 263-276.

—— (1990). "Human Resource Management and the American Dream" *Journal of Management Studies,* 27 (4).

Gustavsen, B. (1996). "Development and the Social Sciences" in S. Toulmin and B. Gustavsen (eds.) *Beyond Theory: Changing Organizations through Participation.* Amsterdam: John Benjamins.

Hackman, J. and Oldham, G. (1980). *Work Redesign.* Reading, MA: Addison-Wesley.

Hager, P. (2003). "Lifelong learning in the workplace? Challenges and issues" *Proceedings of the 3rd International Conference of Researching Work and Learning,* pp. 24-35. Tampere, Finland.

Hamel, G. and Prahalad, C.K. (1993). "Strategy as Stretch & Leverage" *Harvard Business Review*, March April: pp. 75-84.

Hammer, M. and Champy, J. (1993). *Reengineering the Corporation.* Nicholas Bealey: London.

Hannah, J., Fischer, M. and Bueno, C. (1998). "Learning About Globalization: A Comparative Study of the Role of Trade Union Education in Britain and Brazil" *International Journal of Lifelong Education*, 17 (2), pp. 121-30.

Hansome, M. (1931). *World Workers' Educational Movements*. New York: Columbia University Press.

Hardy, N. (1967). *Farm, Mill and Classroom.* Columbia: University of South Carolina.

Hart, M. (1992). *Working and Educating for Life: Feminist and International Perspectives on Adult Education.* London: Routledge.

Hawkins, P. (1994). "Organizational Learning: Taking Stock and Facing the Challenge." *Management Learning*, 25, pp. 71-82.

Hearn, J., Sheppard, D.L., Tancred-Sheriff, P. and Burrell, G. (eds.) (1989). *The Sexuality of Organizations.* London: Sage.

Heery, E. (1998). "Campaigning for Part-Time Workers" *Work, Employment and Society*, 12 (2), pp. 351-366.

Helms Mills, J.C. (2000). "Making Sense of Organisational Change: A Strategic Use of Weick's Sensemaking approach to a Case Study of Nova Scotia Power Inc., 1983-1999" in *Behaviour in Organisations,* pp. 406. Lancaster, UK: University of Lancaster.

—— (2003). *Making Sense of Change.* London: Routledge.

Hendry, C. and Pettigrew, A. (1990). "Human Resource Management: An Agenda for the 1990s" *International Journal of Human Resource Management,* Vol. 1 No. 1, pp. 17-44.

Henessey, T. and Sawchuk, P. (2003). "Technological Change in the Canadian Public Sector: Worker Learning Responses and Openings for Labour-centric Technological Development" *Proceedings of the 3rd International Conference of Researching Work and Learning,* pp. 111-119. Tampere, Finland.

Herod, A. (1997). "From a Geography of Labor to a Labor Geography: Labor's Spatial Fix and the Geography of Capitalism" *Antipode*, 29 (1), pp. 1-31.

Hertog, J.F. and Tolner, T. (1998). "Groups and Teams" in M. Poole and M. Watner (eds.) *The Handbook of Human Resource Management,* pp. 62-71. London: International Thomson Business Press.

Hobsbawm, E. J. (1997). *On History,* London: Weidenfeld & Nicolson.

Hoghielm, R. (ed.) (1984). *Rekindling Commitment in Adult Education.* Stockholm: Institute of Education.

Houle, C. (1961). *The Inquiring Mind.* Madison: University of Wisconsin.

Huber, G. (1991). "Organizational Learning: The Contributing Processes and the Literature" *Organization Science,* 2, pp. 88-115.

Hutton, W. and Giddens, A. (2000). *On the Edge: Living with Global Capitalism,* London: Jonathan Cape.

Huysman, M. (1999). "Balancing Biases: A Critical Review of the Literature on Organizational Learning" in M. Easterby-Smith, J. Burgoyne, and L. Araujo (eds) *Organizational Learning and the Learning Organization,* pp. 59-74. London: Sage.

Hyman, R. (1973). *Marxism and the Sociology of Trade Unionism.* London: Pluto Press.

—— (1975). *Industrial Relations: A Marxist Introduction,* London: Macmillan.

—— (1997). "The Geometry of Syndicalism. A Comparative Analysis of Identities and Ideologies" *Relations Industrielles/Industrial Relations* 52 (1), pp. 7-38.

—— (2001a). *Understanding European Trade Unionism: Between Market, Class and Society.* Thousand Oaks, CA: Sage.

—— (2001b). "A Small Crisis in Germany" *Work and Occupations,* 28 (2), pp. 176-182.

—— (2001c). "European Integration and Industrial Relations: A Case of Variable Geometry?" *Antipode,* 33 (3), pp. 468-483.

Ichniowski, C., Kochan, T., Levine, D., Olson, C. and Strauss, G. (1996). "What Works at Work: Overview and Assessment" *Industrial Relations,* vol. 35, no. 3, pp. 299-333.

Ileris, K. (2002). *The Three Dimensions of Learning: Contemporary Learning Theory in the Tension Field between the Cognitive, the Emotional and the Social.* Copenhagen: Roskilde University Press.

Ilmonen, K. (1998). "Collectivism and Individualism. The Different Members of the Finnish Trade Union Movement" *International Sociological Association.* (ERIC).

International Labor Organization (1976). "Workers' Education and its Techniques" Geneva: ILO.

Jackson, B. (2001). *Management Gurus and Management Fashions.* London: Routledge.

Järvinen, A. and Poikela, E. (2001). "Modelling Reflective and Contextual Learning at Work" *The Journal of Workplace Learning,* Vol. 13 No. 7/8, pp. 282-289.

Jones, O. (1997). "Changing the Balance? Taylorism, TQM and the Work Organization" *New Technology, Work and Employment,* Vol. 12, No. 1., pp. 13-23.

Johnson, D.W. and F.P. Johnson (2000). *Joining Together: Group Theory &Group Skills (7th ed).* Boston: Allyn & Bacon.

Johnson, V. (2000). "The Cultural Foundation of Resources, the Resource Foundation of Political Cultures: An Explanation for the Outcomes of Two General Strikes" *Politics and Society,* 28 (3), pp. 331-365.

Jokivuori, P., Ilmonen, K. and Kevatsalo, K. (1997). "Collectivism and Individualism" *Sociologica,* 34 (2), pp. 113-124.

Kamoche, K. (1996). "Strategic Human Resource Management Within a Resource-Capability View of the Firm" *Journal of Management Studies,* 33 (2) pp. 213-233.

Kanter, R.M. (1989). *When Giants Learn To Dance.* London: Simon & Schuster.

Kasl, E., Marsick, V. and Dechant, K. (1997). "Teams as Learners", *Journal of Applied Behavioral Science,* 33 (2), pp. 227-246.

Katzenbach, J.R., and Smith, D.K. (1993). *The Wisdom of Teams.* Boston: Harvard Business School Press.

Keenoy, T. and Anthony (1992). "HRM: Metaphor, Meaning and Morality" in P. Blyton and P. Turnbull (eds), *Reassessing Human Resource Management,* London: Sage.

Keep, E. (1989). "Corporate Training Policies: The Vital Component" in J. Storey (ed.) *New Perspectives in Human Resource Management.* Routledge: London.

Kett, J. (1994). *The Pursuit of Knowledge Under Difficulties: From Self-improvement to Adult Education in America (1750-1990).* Stanford, CA: Stanford University Press.

Kieser, A. (1997). "Rhetoric and Myth in Management Fashion." *Organization,* 4, pp. 49-74.

Kivinen, O. and Peltomäki, M. (1999). "On the Job or in the Classroom? The Apprenticeship in Finland from the 17th Century to the 1990s" *Journal of Education and Work.* 12 (1), pp. 75-94

Klein, J. (1994). *Maintaining Expertise in Multi-Skilled Teams: Advances in Interdisciplinary Studies of Work Teams* 1: pp. 145-65.

Kline, T. (1999). *Remaking Teams.* San Francisco, CA: Jossey-Bass.

Knights, D. and Willmott, H. (1986). (eds.) *Gender and the Labour Process,* Aldershot: Gower.

Knowles, M. (1970). *The Modern Practice of Adult Education.* New York: Association.

—— (1977). A History of the Adult Education Movement in the United States, 2nd edition Revised. New York: Krieger.

Kochan, T. and Dyer, L. (1995). "HRM: An American View" in J. Storey (ed.) *Human Resource Management: A Critical Text.* London: Routledge.

Kochan, T., McKersie, R. and Cappelli, P. (1984). "Strategic Choice and Industrial Relations Theory" *Industrial Relations,* 23 (1), pp. 16-39.

Kok, J. (ed.) (2002). *Rebellious Families: Household Strategies and Collective Action in the Nineteenth and Twentieth Centuries.* New York: Berghahn.

Kolb, D.A. (1984). *Experiential Learning,* Prentice- Hall: Englewood Cliffs.

Korsgaard, O. (1997). "The Worlds of the Hand and of the Mind" in S. Walters (ed.) *Globalization in Adult Education & Training.* London, Zed.

KPMG (1996). Learning Organisation Benchmarking Survey, KPMG:London

Larson, S. and Nissen, B. (eds.) (1987). *Theories of the Labour Movement.* Detroit, MI: Wayne State University Press.

Lave, J. and Wenger, E. (1991). *Situated Learning: Legitimate Peripheral Participation,* Cambridge, UK: CUP.

Lawler, E.E. (1992). *The Ultimate Advantage: Creating the High Involvement Organization.* San Francisco, CA: Jossey-Bass.

Lee, E. (2000). "What has the Web ever done for us?" November 16, <http://www.actionforsolidarity.org.uk>.

Legge, K. (1995). *Human Resource Management: Rhetorics and Realities.* London: Macmillan.

—— (1996). *On Knowledge, Business Consultants and the Selling of TQM.* University of Lancaster, UK.

Lerner, G. (1990). "Writing Women into History", *Women of Power,* 16, pp. 8-12.

Levine, T. (2002). "Learning in Solidarity: A Union Approach to Worker Centred Literacy" *Just Labour,* 1, pp. 19-28.

Levitt, B. and March, J.G. (1988). "Organizational Learning." *Annual Review of Sociology,* 14, pp. 319-340.

Lindeman, E. (1926). *The Meaning of Adult Education.* New York: New Republic.

Linton, T.E. (1965). *An Historical Examination of the Purposes and Practices of the Education Program of the United Automobile Workers, 1936-1959.* Ann Arbor: University of Michigan School of Education.

Littler, C.R. (1982). *The Development of the Labour Process in Capitalist Societies.* London: Heinemann.

Littler, C.R. and Salaman, G. (1984). *Class at Work: The Design, Allocation and Control of Jobs,* London: Batsford.

Livingstone, D.W. (2001). *Working and Learning in the Information Age: A Profile of Canadians.* Ottawa: Canadian Policy Reseach Network.

—— (2001). "Expanding Notions of Work and Learning: Profiles of Latent Power" in T. Fenwick (ed.) *Sociocultural Perspectives on Learning through Work,* pp. 19-30. San Francisco, CA: Jossey-Bass.

—— (1999). *The Education-Jobs Gap.* Toronto: Garamond Press.

London, S., Tarr, E. and Wilson, J. (eds.) (1990). *The Education of the American Working-Class.* New York: Greenwood.

Lopes, F.A.M. (2002). "Programa Integrar in Brazil: Union Intervention in Employment, Development and Education" in B. Spencer (ed) *Unions and Learning in a Global Economy: International and Comparative Perspectives,* pp.120-128. Toronto: Thompson.

Lorge, I., Jensen, G., Bradford, L. and Birnbaum, M. (1965). *Adult Learning.* Washington: Adult Education Association.

Lowe, G. (2000). *The Quality of Work: A People-Centred Agenda*, New York: Oxford University Press.

Lowe, G. and Krahn, H. (1993). *Work in Canada: Readings in the Sociology of Work and Industry.* Scarborough: Nelson.

Lyman, S.M. (ed.) (1995). *Social Movements: Critiques, Concepts, Case Studies*. Houndmills, Basingstoke: Macmillan.

MacLeod, F. (1994). *An Analysis of Continuous Improvement Process Teams and their Impact on Knowledge and Acceptance of TQM Concepts at a Manufacturing Service Organization.* Saint Mary's University, Canada.

Madsen, M. (1997). "The 'Classroom' Hypothesis and Individualization" *Economic and Industrial Democracy*, 18 (3), pp. 359-391.

Malcolmson, R.W. (1988). "Ways of Getting a Living in Eighteen-Century England" in R.E. Pahl (ed.) *On Work*, pp. 48-60. Oxford: Blackwell.

Malloch, H. (1997). "Strategic and HRM Aspects of Kaizen: A Case Study" *New Technology, Work and Employment,* Vol. 12 (2), pp. 108-122.

Mantsios, G. (ed.) (1998). *A New Labor Movement for the New Century.* New York: Monthly Review Press.

Manz, C. and Newstrom, J. (1990). "Self-managing Teams in a Paper Mill: Success factors, Problems and Lessons Learned" in A. Nedd (ed.) *International Human Resource Management Review*, Vol. 1. Singapore: McGraw-Hill.

Manz, C. and Sims, H. (1980). "Self-management as a Substitute for Leadership: A Social Learning Theory Perspective" *Academy of Management Review,* Vol. 5, No. 3, pp. 361-367.

—— (1989). *Superleadership: Leading Others to Lead Themselves.* Englewood Cliffs, NJ: Prentice-Hall.

Marglin, S.A. (1974). "What Do Bosses Do? The Origins and Functions of Hierarchy in Capitalist Production", *Review of Radical Political Economy*, 6 (2), pp. 60-102.

Marino, D. (1997). *Wild Garden.* Toronto: Between the Lines.

Marshall, J. (1999). "Living Life as Inquiry", *Systemic Practice and Action Research*, 12 (6).

Martin, D. (1995). *Thinking Union*. Toronto: Between the Lines.

—— (1998). "A Decade on the Training Rollercoaster: A Unionist's View" in S. Scott, B. Spencer & A. Thomas (eds.) *Learning for Life: Canadian Readings in Adult Education,* pp. 153-163. Toronto: Thompson Educational.

Marsick, V.J. and Watkins, K.E. (1990). *Informal and Incidental Learning in the Workplace.* London: Routledge.

Maslow, A. (1954). *Motivation and Personality*, New York: Harper & Row.

Matthews, P. (1999). "Workplace Learning: Developing an Holistic Model." *The Learning Organization*, 6, pp. 18-29.

Max-Neef, M. (1991). *Human Scale Development.* New York: Apex.

McGregor, D. (1960). *The Human Side of Enterprise*, New York: McGraw-Hill.

McKinlay, A. (2002). "The Limits of Knowledge Management" *New Technology, Work and Employment*, 17 (2), pp. 76-88.

McKinlay, A. and Starkey, K. (eds.) (1998). *Foucault, Management and Organizational Theory,* London: Sage.

McShane, S. (2004). *Organizational Behaviour* (5th ed.). Toronto: McGraw-Hill Ryerson.

Merriam, S. (ed.) (1993). *An Update on Adult Learning Theory.* San Francisco: Jossey-Bass.

Mikkelsen, F. (1998). "Unions and New Shopfloor Strike Strategies and Learning Processes Among Public Employees" *Economic and Industrial Democracy*, 19 (3), pp. 505-538.

Mills, A.J. (1998). "Toward an Agenda of Radical Organizing" *Canadian Review of Sociology and Anthropology*, 35, pp. 281-299.

Mills, A.J. and Murgatroyd, S.J. (1991). *Organizational Rules: A Framework for Understanding Organizations*. Milton Keynes: Open University Press.

Mills, A. and Simmons, T. (1998). *Reading Organizational Theory*. Toronto: Garamond.

Mills, C.W. (1959/2000). *The Sociological Imagination*. New York: Oxford University Press.

Mishel, L. and Voos, P. (eds.) (1992). *Unions and Economic Competitiveness*. Boston: M.E. Sharpe Inc.

Mocker, D. and Spear, G. (1982). "Lifelong Learning: Formal, Nonformal, Informal and Self-directed" *Information Series No. 241, ERIC Clearing House on Adult Career and Vocational Education,* Columbus, Ohio: The National Center for research in Vocational Education, Ohio State University.

Monks, J. (1999). *Learning with the Unions: A Showcase of Successful Projects Sponsored by the Union Learning Fund.* London: Congress House.

Munby, H. (2003). What Does it Mean to Learn in the Workplace? Differing Research Perspectives. *Journal of Workplace Learning.* 15 (3), pp. 92-93.

Munro, A. (2001). "A Feminist Trade Union Agenda? The Continued Significance of Class, Gender and Race" *Gender, Work and Organization,* 8 (4), pp. 454-471

Munro, A. and Rainbird, H. (2000). "The New Unionism and the New Bargaining Agenda: UNISON-employer Partnerships on Workplace Learning in Britain" *British Journal of Industrial Relations.* 38 (2), pp. 223-240.

Nanda, A. (1996). "Resources, Capabilities and Competencies" in B. Moingeon and A. Edmondson (eds.), *Organisational Learning and Competitive Advantage,* London: Sage.

Newman, M. (1999). *Maeler's Regard: Images of Adult Learning.* Sydney: Stewart Victor.

Nichols, T. and Beynon, H. (1977). *Living with Capitalism: Class Relations and the Modern Factory,* London: Routledge and Kegan Paul.

O'Connor, F.V. (ed.) (1973). *Art for the Millions: Essays from the 1930s by Artists and Administrators of the WPA Federal Art Project.* Greenwich, NJ: New York Graphic Society.

O'Connor, J. and Brown, L. (1978). *Free, Adult Uncensored: The Living History of the Federal Theater Project.* Washington, D.C.: New Republic.

Oliver, J. (1993). "Shocking to the Core" *Management Today,* August 1993, pp. 18-21.

Ortiz, L. (1999). "Unions' Responses to Teamwork: Differences at National and Workplace Levels" *European Journal of Industrial Relations,* 5 (1), pp. 49-69.

Osterman, P. (1995). "How Common is Workplace Transformation and Who Adopts It?" *Industrial Labor Relations Review,* 47: pp. 173-87.

Pedler, M., Boydell, T. and Burgoyne, J. (1989). "Towards the Learning Company" *Management Education and Development,* 20, pp. 1-8.

Pedler, M., Burgoyne, J. and Boydell, T. (1994). *Towards the Learning Company : Concepts and Practices.* London; New York: McGraw-Hill.

Penrose. (1959). *The Theory of the Growth of the Firm,* Oxford: Blackwell.

Peters, K. (2001). "Individual Autonomy in New Forms of Work Organization" *Concepts and Transformation,* 6 (2), pp. 141-158.

Pfeffer, J. (1998). *The Human Equation: Putting People First.* Boston, Mass: Harvard Business School Press.

Phillips, P. and Phillips, E. (1993). *Women and Work: Inequality in the Canadian Labour Market,* Toronto: Lorimer.

Piore, M. and Sabel, C. (1984). *The Second Industrial Divide,* New York: Basic Books.

Platt, L. (1997), "Employee Work-life Balance: The Competitive Advantage" in F. Hesselbein *et al.* (eds.) *The Organization of the Future,* San Francisco: Jossey-Bass.

Posthuma, A. (1998). **"**Public Policies and Worker Training in Brazil: Innovating Through New Actors, Institutions and Course Design" *American Sociological Association* (ERIC), pp. 60-79.

Prahalad, C.K. and Hamel, G. (1990). "The Core Competencies of the Organization" *Harvard Business Review,* Vol.68, May-June, pp. 79-91

Prange, C. (1999). "Organizational Learning: Desperately Seeking Theory" in M. Easterby-Smith, J. Burgoyne, and L. Araujo (eds) *Organizational Learning and the Learning Organization,* pp. 23-44 . London: Sage.

Probert, B. (1999). "Gendered Workers and Gendered Work" in D. Boud and J. Garrick (eds.) *Understanding Learning at Work,* pp. 98-116. London: Routledge.

Proctor, S. and Mueller, F. (eds.) (2000). *Teamworking.* Basingstoke: Macmillan – now Palgrave Macmillan.

Purcell, J. (1995). "Corporate Strategy and its Link With Human Resource Management Strategy" in John Storey (ed) *Human Resource Management: A Critical Text,* London: Routledge.

Pyrch, T. (1983). *An Examination of the Concept of Community Development as Discerned Through Selected Literature in the Adult Education Movement in Canada and the United States, 1919-1960.* Doctoral dissertation, University of British Columbia.

Rainbird, H. (1988). "New Technology, Training and Union Strategies" in R. Hyman and W. Streek (eds.) *New Technology and Industrial Relations,* pp. 174-185. Oxford: Blackwell.

Ramsey, H., Scholarios, D. and Harley, B. (2000). "Employees and High-performance Work Systems: Testing Inside the Black Box" *British Journal of Industrial Relations,* 38 (4), pp. 501-531.

Reason, P. (1998). "Political, Epistemological, Ecological and Spiritual Dimensions of Participation" *Studies in Cultures, Organizations and Societies,* 4 (2), pp. 147-67.

Reason, P. and Bradbury, H. (eds.) (2001). *Handbook of Action Research.* London: Sage.

Reed, M.I. (1993). "Organizations and Modernity: Continuity and Discontinuity in Organization Theory" in J. Hassard and M. Parker (eds.) *Postmodernism and Organizations,* London: Sage.

Reich, R. (1991). "Who is Them?" *Harvard Business Review,* March-April: pp. 28-36.

Reinharz, S. (1988). "Feminist Distrust: Problems of Context and Content in Sociological Work" in D.N. Berg and K.K. Smith (ed.) *The Self in Social Inquiry.* Newbury Park, CA: Sage.

Resnick, L.B. (1987). "Learning in School and Out" *EducationalResearcher,* 16 (9): pp. 13-20.

Rifkin, J. (1996). *The End of Work.* New York: Tarcher/Putnam Press.

Ritchie, L. (1999). "Some Cautionary Notes on Prior Learning Assessment and Recognition" in M. Hynes (ed.) *Proceedings of the "Prior Learning Assessment and Recognition Centres: Who Needs Them?" Symposium.* Toronto: George Brown College.

Ritzer, G. (2000). *The McDonaldization of Society.* Thousand Oaks, CA: Pine Forge Press.

Roethlisberger, F.J. and Dickson, W.J. (1939). *Management and the Worker.* Cambridge, MA: Harvard University Press.

Rogoff, B. (1990). *Apprenticeship in Thinking: Cognitive Development in Social Context.* Oxford: OUP.

Roscigno, V.J. and Danaher, W.F. (2001). "Media and Mobilization: The Case of Radio and Southern Textile Worker Insurgency, 1929-1934" *American Sociological Review,* 66 (1), pp. 21-48.

Rousseau, D.M. (1995). *Psychological Contracts in Organizations: Understanding Written and Unwritten Agreements.* Thousand Oaks, CA: Sage.

Rylatt, A. (1994). *Learning Unlimited: Practical Strategies and Techniques for Transforming Learning in the Workplace.* Sydney: Business and Professional Publishing.

Sawchuk, P.H. (1998a). *The Final Report of the "Learning Capacities in the Community and Workplace Project": Unionized Industrial Workplace Site (Ontario). (*NALL Working Paper #45-2001) Toronto: NALL.

—— (1998b). "This Would Scare the Hell Out of Me if I Were a HR Manager: Workers Making Sense of PLAR" in *Proceedings of the 17th Annual Conference of Canadian Association for the Study of Adult Education.* Ottawa: University of Ottawa, May 1998.

—— (2000a). "Learning in the Union Local: Reflections on the Expansion of Union Education Practice" An unpublished paper. University of Calgary.

—— (2000b). "Building Traditions of Inquiry and Transforming Labour-Academic Collaboration at the Union Local: Case Studies of Workers' Research and Education" *Labour/Le Travail* 45, pp. 199-216.

—— (2001a). "Trade Union-based Workplace Learning: A Case Study in Workplace Reorganization and Worker Knowledge Production" *Journal of Workplace Learning* 13 (7/8), pp. 344-351.

—— (2001b). "The Pitfalls and Possibilities of Union-Based Telelearning: A Report of Preliminary Findings" *Proceedings of the Canadian Association for the Study of Adult Education Conference.* Quebec: University of Laval.

—— (2002). *Online Learning for Union Activists: Final Report of Findings of the "Informal Learning Practices Within Union-Based Telelearning Project."* Toronto: NALL Research Network.

—— (2003). *Adult Learning and Technology in Working-Class Life.* New York: Cambridge University Press.

Sayer, A. (1986). "New Developments in Manufacturing: The Just-in-time System" *Capital and Class,* 30 (Winter), pp. 43-72.

Schenk, C. and Anderson, J. (1999). *Reshaping Work 2: Labour, the Workplace and Technological Change.* Canadian Centre for Policy Alternatives. Ottawa: Garamond Press.

Schneider, F.H. (1941). *Patterns of Workers Education: The Story of the Bryn Mawr Summer School.* Washington, DC: American Council on Public Affairs.

Schön, D.A. (1987). *Educating the Reflective Practitioner.* San Francisco, CA: Jossey-Bass.

Schonberger, R. (1982). *Japanese Manufacturing Techniques: Nine Hidden Lessons in Simplicity,* London: Collier Macmillan.

Schultz, T.W. (1981). *Investing in People: The Economics of Population Quality.* Berkeley, CA: UC.

Scott, J. (1990). *Domination and the Arts of Resistance.* New Haven: Yale University Press.

Scott, S., Spencer, B. and Thomas, A. (eds.) (1998). *Learning for Life.* Toronto: Thompson.

Selznick, P. (1957). *Leadership and Administration,* New York: Harper & Row

Senge, P. (1990). *The Fifth Discipline.* New York: Doubleday.

—— (1994). *The Fifth Discipline: The Art and Practice of the Learning Organization.* New York: Doubleday.

Sennett, R. (1998). *The Corrosion of Character.* New York: Norton.

Sewell, G. (1998). "The Discipline of Teams: The Control of Team-based Industrial Work Through Electronic and Peer Surveillance" *Administrative Science Quarterly,* 43, 406-469.

Shostak, A. (1999). *CyberUnion: Empowering Labor through Computer Technology.* London: M.E. Sharpe.

Simon, B. (ed.) (1990). *The Search for Enlightenment: The Working Class and Adult Education in the Twentieth Century.* London: Lawrence and Wishart.

Sisson, K. (1986). "A Comparative Analysis of the Structures of Collective Bargaining" *Scottish Journal of Political Economy,* 21 (2), pp. 97-109.

Sisson, K. and Brown, W. (1983). "Industrial Relations in the Private Sector: Donovan Revisited" in G.S. Bain (ed) *Industrial Relations in Britain,* pp. 137-154. Oxford: Blackwell.

Sisson, K. and Storey, J. (2000). *The Realities of Human Resource Management Managing the Employment Relationship.* Buckingham, OUP.

Slepian, J. (1993). "Learning, Belief, and Action in Organizational Work Groups: A Conceptual Model of Work Group Learning" Paper presented at the *Academy of Management Meeting,* Atlanta, GA.

Smith, H. (1929). *Women Workers at the Bryn Mawr Summer School.* New York: AAAE.

Smith, S. (1991). *Report: Commission of Inquiry on Canadian University Education.* Ottawa: AUCC.

Solomon, N. (1999). "Culture and Differences in Workplace Learning" in D. Boud and John Garrick (eds.) *Understanding Learning at Work,* pp. 119-131. London: Routledge.

Spence, R. and Verner, C. (1954). "Adult Education and Desegregation" *Adult Education,* 5, pp. 41-44.

Spencer, B. (1989). *Remaking the Working Class?* Nottingham: Spokesman.

—— (1998). *The Purposes of Adult Education: A Guide for Students.* Toronto: Thompson.

—— (2001). "Changing Questions of Workplace Learning Researchers" in T. Fenwick (ed.) *Sociocultural Perspectives on Learning through Work,* pp. 31-40. San Francisco, CA: Jossey-Bass.

—— (ed.) (2002). *Unions and Learning: International and Comparative Perspectives.* Toronto: Thompson.

Spikes, W.F. (ed.) (1995). *Workplace Learning, New Directions for Adult and Continuing Education,* 68, (Winter), San Francisco: Jossey-Bass.

Starkey, K. (ed.) (1996). *How Organizations Learn.* London: International Thomson Business Press.

Steedman, H. (1998). "A Decade of Skill Formation in Britain and Germany" *Journal of Education and Work.* 11 (1), pp. 77-94.

Stephenson, C. and Stewart, P. (2001). "The Whispering Shadow: Collectivism and Individualism at Ikeda-Hoover and Nissan" *Sociological Research Online,* 6 (3).

Storey, J. (1992). *Developments in the Management of Human Resources,* Oxford: Blackwell.

—— (ed.) (1989). *New Perspectives on Human Resource Management.* London: Routledge.

—— (ed.) (1995). *Human Resource Management: A Critical Text,* London: Routledge

—— (ed.) (2001). *Human Resource Management: A Critical Text.* London: Thompson Learning.

Streek, W. and Hilbert, J. (1987). *The Role of Social Partners in Vocational Education and Training Including Continuing Education and Training.* Berlin, Germany: European Centre for the Development of Vocational Training. (CEDEFOP Publication No HX-58-90-207-EN-C, pp. 43-55.

Taylor, J. (1996a). "The Solidarity Network: Universities, Computer-mediated Communication, and Labour Studies in Canada" in T. Harrison and T. Stephen (eds.) *Computer Networking and Scholarly Communication in the Twenty-First-Century University.* Albany: State University of New York Press.

——— (1996b). "The Continental Classroom: Teaching Labour Studies Online" *Labor Studies Journal* 21 (1) (Spring).

——— (2001). *Union Learning: Canadian Labour Education in the Twentieth Century*. Toronto: Thompson.

Taylor, P. and Bain, P. (2001). "Trade Unions, Workers' Rights and the Frontier of Control in UK Call Centres" *Economic and Industrial Democracy*, 22 (1), pp. 39-66.

Taylor, W. (1988). "School to Work" in D. Corson (ed) *Education for Work: Background to Policy and Curriculum*, pp.195-213. Palmerston North, N.Z.: Dunmore Press.

Teece, D., Pisano, G. and Shuen, A. (1997). "Dynamic Capabilities and Strategic Management" *Journal of Strategic Management*, 18 (7), pp. 509-533.

Thompson, P. (1989). *The Nature of Work* (2nd. Ed.). London: Macmillan.

——— (1993). "Postmodernism: Fatal Distraction" in J. Hassard and M. Parker (eds.) *Postmodernism and Organizations*. London: Sage.

Thompson, P. and McHugh, D. (2002). *Work Organizations: A Critical Introduction*. London: Palgrave-Macmillan.

Thompson, P. and Warhurst, C. (eds.) (1998). *Workplaces of the Future*. London: Macmillan Business.

Thorn, I. (2001). "Literacy is a Labour Issue" in M. Taylor (ed.) *Adult Literacy Now*, pp.123-136. Toronto: Culture Concepts.

Thornley, C., Contrepois, S. and Jefferys, S. (1997). "Trade Unions, Restructuring and Individualization in French and British Banks" *European Journal of Industrial Relations*, 3 (1), pp. 83-105.

Tilly, L. and Tilly, C. (eds.) (1981). *Class Confict and Collective Action*. Berverly Hills, CA: Sage.

Tisdell, E. (1993). "Feminism and Adult Learning: Power, Pedagogy and Praxis" in S. Merriam (ed.) *An Update on Adult Learning Theory*, pp. 91-103. San Francisco: Jossey-Bass.

Tomaney, J. (1990). "The Reality of Workplace Flexibility", *Capital and Class*, 40, pp. 97-124.

Tough, A. (1971). *The Adult's Learning Projects*. Toronto: OISE.

Toulmin, S. (1996). "Introduction" in S. Toulmin and B. Gustavsen (eds.) *Beyond Theory: Changing Organizations through Participation* Amsterdam: John Benjamins.

Townley, B. (1994). *Reframing Human Resource Management: Power, Ethics and the Subject of Work*. Sage: London

Trades Union Congress (1996). *Partners for Lifelong Learning*. London: Congress House.

Trist, E.L. and Bamforth, V. (1951). "Some Social and Psychological Consequences of the Longwall Method of Coal-getting" *Human Relations*, 4, pp. 3-38.

Tuckman, B. and Jensen, M. (1977). "Stages of Small Group Development Revisited" *Group and Organizational Studies*, 2, pp. 419-427.

Turnbull, P. (1986). "The Japanisation of British Industrial Relations at Lucas" *Industrial Relations Journal*, Vol. 17, No. 3.

Turner, A.N. and Lawrence, P.R. (1965). *Industrial Jobs and the Worker*. Boston: Harvard University, Graduate School of Business Administration.

Tushman, M. and Nadler, D. (1996). "Organizaing for Innovation" in K. Starkey (ed.) *How Organizations Learn*, pp. 135-155. London: International Thomson Business Press.

Ulman, L. (1974). "Connective Bargaining and Competitive Bargaining" *Scottish Journal of Political Economy*, 21 (2), pp. 97-109.

Unwin, L. and Fuller, A. (2001). *From Skill Formation to Social Inclusion: The Changing Meaning of Apprenticeship and its Relationship to Communities and Workplace in England*. University of Nottingham, UK <*www.nottingham.ac.uk*>.

Usher, R., Bryant, I. and Johnston, R. (1997). *Adult Education and the Postmodern Challenge*. London: Routledge.

Verner, C. (1953). "Adult Education for Tomorrow's World" *Adult Education* 26 (1), pp. 32-41.

——— (1962). *A Conceptual Scheme for the Identification and Classification of Processes*. Washington: AEA of the USA.

Vygotsky, L.S. (1978). *Mind in Society*. Cambridge, MA: Harvard University Press.

Wallace, M. (1989). "Brave New Workplace: Technology and Work in the New Economy" *Work and Occupations*, 16 (4): pp. 363-392.

Wardell, M., Steiger, T. and Meiksins, P. (1999). *Rethinking the Labor Process*. Albany, USA: SUNY Press.

Waring, M. (1999), *Counting for Nothing: What Men Value and What Women are Worth*, 2nd ed., University of Toronto Press, Toronto.

Watkins, K. and Marsick, V. (1993). *Sculpting the Learning Organization.* San Francisco: Jossey Bass.

Watson, D. (1992). "Power, Conflict & Control at Work" in John Allen, Peter Braham & Paul Lewis (eds.) *Politic and Economic Forms of Modernity,* pp. 386-413. Cambridge, England: Polity Press.

Watson, T. (1986). *Management,Organization and Employment Strategy*, London: Routledge and Kegan Paul.

Weber, M. (1922/1968). *Economy and Society.* New York: Bedminster.

Weick, K. (1995). *Sensemaking in Organizations.* London: Sage.

Weick, K. and Westley, F. (1996). "Organizational Learning: Affirming an Oxymoron" in S. Clegg, C Hardy and W. Nord (eds.) *Handbook of Organization Studies,* pp. 440-458. Thousand Oaks, CA.: Sage.

Wells, D. (1993). "Are Strong Unions Compatible with the New Model of Human Resource Management?" *Relations Industrielles/Industrial Relations,* 48 (1), pp. 56-84

Welton, M. (1993). "Memories in the Time of Troubles: The Liberatory Moments History Project" *Convergence,* 26 (4), pp. 3-7.

—— (1995). "The Critical Turn in Adult Education Theory" in M. Welton (ed.) *In Defense of the Lifeworld.* Albany, NY: State University of New York Press.

—— (ed.) (1995). *In Defense of the Lifeworld: Critical Perspectives on Adult Learning.* Albany: SUNY Press.

—— (1997). "In Defence of Civil Society: Canadian Adult Education in Neo-conservative Times" in S. Walters (ed.) *Globalization, Adult Education & Training.* London: Zed Books.

—— (2001). *Little Mosie From the Margaree: A Biography of Moses Michael Coady.* Toronto: Thompson Educational.

Western, M. (1998). "Class Biography and Class Consciousness in Australia" *Research in Social Stratification and Mobility,* 16, pp.117-143.

Wets, J. (ed.) (2000) *Cultural Diversity in Trade Unions: A Challenge to Class Identity?* Aldershot: Ashgate.

Wharton, A. (2002). *Working in America: Continuity, Conflict, and Change.* Boston, IL: McGraw-Hill.

Willmott, H. (1995). "The Odd Couple?: Re-engineering Business Processes; Managing Human Relations" *New Technology, Work and Employment,* Vol. 10, No. 2, 89-97.

Wills, J. (2001). "Uneven Geographies of Capital and Labour: The Lessons of European Works Councils" *Antipode,* 33 (3), pp. 484-509.

Witz, A. (1986). "Patriarchy and the Labour Market: Occupational Control Strategies and the Medical Division of Labour" in D. Knights and H. Willmott (eds) *Gender and the Labour Process.* Aldershot: Gower.

Womack, J., Jones, D. and Roos, D. (1991). *The Machine That Changed The World,* New York: Rawson Associates.

Wong, K. (2002). "Labour Education for Immigrant Workers in the USA" in B. Spencer (ed.) *Unions and Learning in a Global Economy: International and Comparative Perspectives,* pp.70-78. Toronto: Thompson.

Woodcock, G. (1992). *The Monk and His Message: Undermining the Myth of History.* Vancouver: Douglas & McIntyre.

Wren, J. (2002). "Changing Conditions of Employment and the Implications for Apprenticeship Training" *UNEVOC 2002: International Technical Vocation Education and Training.* (October) Winnipeg, Manitoba (Canada).

Wright, C.D. (1908). "The Apprenticeship System in its Relation to Industrial Education" *Bulletin,* No 6. Washington: Government Printing Office.

Wright, P. (1996). *Managerial Leadership.* London: Routledge.

Yeatts, D.E. and C. Hyten (1998). *High-Performing Self-managed Work Teams.* Tousand Oaks, CA: Sage.

Index